TINY
ISLANDS

For my parents

Published by AA Publishing, a trading name of AA Media Limited,
Fanum House, Basing View, Basingstoke, Hampshire, RG21 4EA, UK.
Registered number 06112600.

First published in 2013.
Text © Dixe Wills 2013.
Island maps © Harriet Yeomans 2013.
Contains Ordnance Survey data
© Crown copyright and database right 2013.

A CIP catalogue record for this book is available from the
British Library.

ISBNs: 978-0-7495-7446-8 (HB) and 978-0-7495-7387-4 (PB)

A04847

Editor: Donna Wood
Design and layout: Nick Johnston and Tracey Butler
Picture Editor: James Tims
Regional locator maps: David Wardle
Image retouching and internal repro: Jacqueline Street

Printed and bound in Dubai by Oriental Press
www.theAA.com

TINY
ISLANDS

Dixe Wills

AA

Contents

England

Wales

Scotland

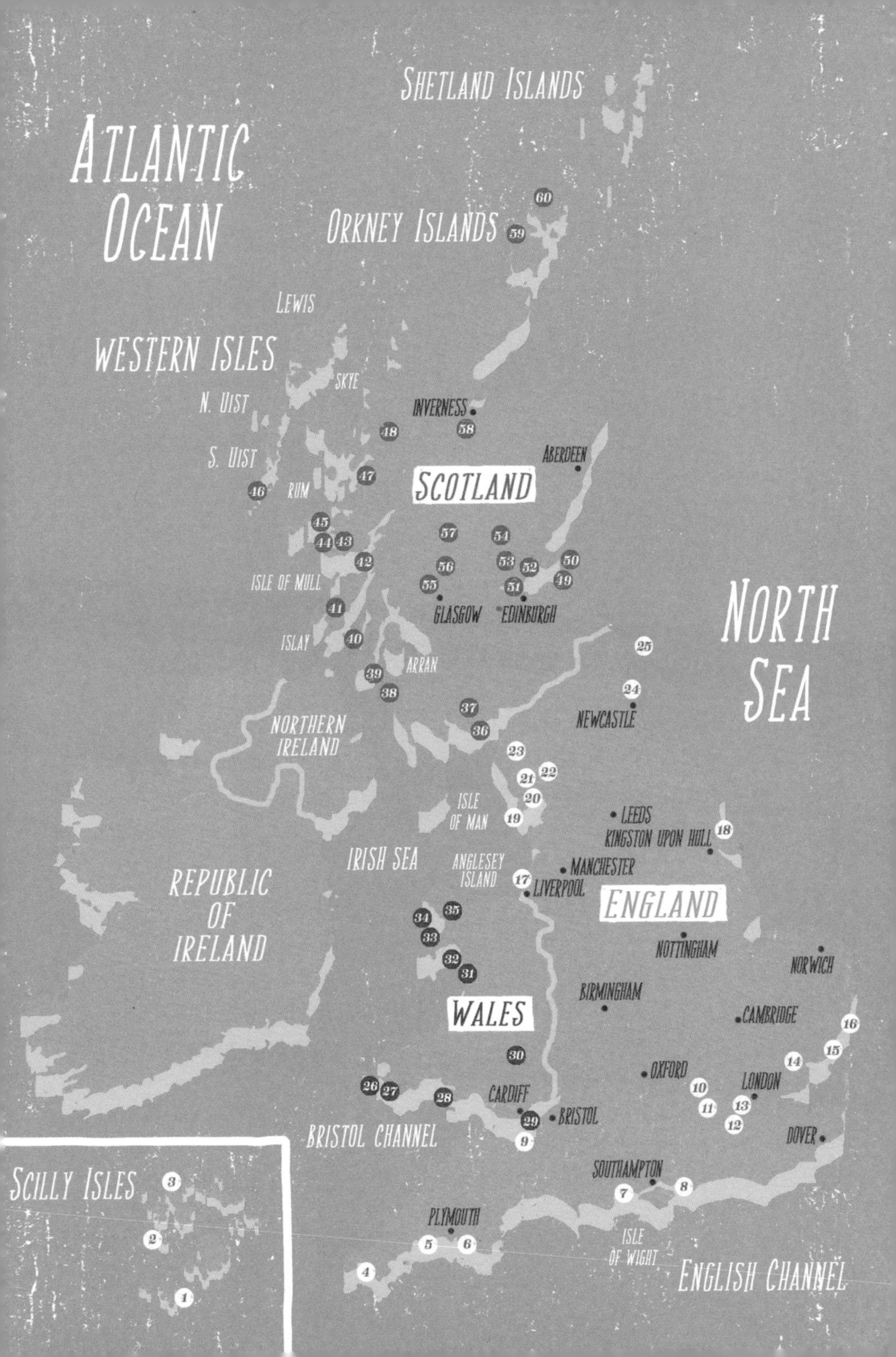

SHETLAND ISLANDS

ATLANTIC
OCEAN

ORKNEY ISLANDS

60
59

LEWIS

WESTERN ISLES

SKYE

N. UIST

INVERNESS
48
58

S. UIST

ABERDEEN

46 RUM
47

SCOTLAND

45
44 43
42

57
54

ISLE OF MULL

56
55
53 52 50
51 49

NORTH
SEA

41

GLASGOW EDINBURGH

ISLAY
40

39 ARRAN
38

25

37
36

24
NEWCASTLE

NORTHERN
IRELAND

23

21 22
20
19

ISLE
OF MAN

LEEDS
KINGSTON UPON HULL
18

IRISH SEA

ANGLESEY
ISLAND
17

MANCHESTER
LIVERPOOL

ENGLAND

REPUBLIC
OF
IRELAND

34 35
33
32 31

NOTTINGHAM

NORWICH

WALES

BIRMINGHAM

CAMBRIDGE

16

30

26 27
28

CARDIFF
29
9

BRISTOL

OXFORD

10
11

LONDON
13
12

14

15

DOVER

BRISTOL CHANNEL

SCILLY ISLES
3

2

1

5 6
PLYMOUTH

4

SOUTHAMPTON
7
8

ISLE
OF WIGHT

ENGLISH CHANNEL

Introduction

'It's over there,' John said as he pointed across the sea. I looked but all I could see was fog. 'There,' he persisted, 'you can just make out the outline of the castle.' I peered forward, straining my eyes, and, sure enough, a mighty stone keep materialised for a few seconds before vanishing again. Whatever land it was standing on was missing beneath the dense sea fret.

For all I knew, there might be a whole lost world out there full of knights and dragons, and downtrodden serfs gathering around the roaring fire of a venerable inn to warm their calloused hands and talk of insurrection.

'That's Piel Island,' John informed me, 'the scene of the last ever invasion of Britain.'

I nodded sagely as if I knew to its most intimate detail the incursion to which he was referring. 'What's on it?' I asked.

'Just the castle, and a handful of houses,' he replied, '...and an old pub.'

'A venerable inn – of course, there had to be,' I murmured.

And so began my love of tiny islands.

I'm not alone in that love. In the course of researching this book, I discovered that Britons have had a yen for tiny islands for thousands of years, and even have an honourable history of building their own. Inuits may have their 23 words for snow, but islands run so deep within our psyche that our various national languages overflow with words to describe them. There's ait, ayt, eilean, enys, eye, eyet, eyot, eyte, holm, holme, inch, innes, insh, insul, island, isle, islet, ynys and ynysig – and no doubt there are others I've yet to come across.

According to the Ordnance Survey, Britain rejoices in 6,289 islands, of which 803 are large enough for their cartographers to render a coastline on a map – the remainder are merely diminutive outcrops. So what were my criteria for choosing just 60? Well, for a start, I decided that for an island to qualify as 'tiny' it should be no larger than 300 acres. That might seem an arbitrary cut-off point (all right, it *is* an arbitrary cut-off point), but my experience has been that if you visit an island any larger than that it becomes possible at times to forget that it's an insular entity at all – in the same sense that those of us who wake each morning on mainland Britain don't immediately exclaim: 'How exciting! I'm on an island!' As it is, the vast majority of the islands in this book are much smaller than that – two-thirds are under 50 acres, of which over half are smaller than 10 (which is a quarter of the size of the gardens at Buckingham Palace).

At the other end of the scale, although rocks that happen to stick out of the water could technically be called islands, I prefer to call these 'rocks that happen to stick out of the water'. When my next book, the ground-breaking *Rocks That Happen To Stick Out Of The Water*, is published to huge critical acclaim, you can read all about them there.

And then there's the tortuous argument about what does and does not constitute an island. Is an island not an island if it's joined to the mainland at low tide? Does a bridge or causeway unisland an island? Frankly, who cares? Life is, after all, brief.

As it turns out, the vast majority of the entries in this book are islands in the classical sense, in that they are surrounded by water at all times and not connected to the mainland. Some others become islands as the tide comes in; a handful can be reached by bridge; while three have permanent causeways built out to them. Happily, whatever their circumstances, every single one of them feels like an island. You'll have to take my word for this, I know, but I wouldn't lie to you. Not about that, anyway.

I applied two other strictures for entry into this book: every island had to be accessible to members of the public, and each one had to have a story to tell and an allure of its own.

Visiting the islands – which I did almost exclusively by train and bicycle, the transport combination of the future – proved to be not only a joy (albeit a joy occasionally tempered by horizontal rain) but also an education. Who knew that Scotland was once briefly ruled from an obscure island on a river in Galloway; that the behaviour of eels down a well on a Welsh isle could foretell the faithfulness of one's lover; or that a pre-fame Jesus was said to have been dumped on a Cornish island while his great-uncle conducted some business with tin miners?

For such small and, as conventional wisdom would have it, insignificant parcels of land, it's astonishing just how much history they've managed to chalk up between them.

An account of Britain's past gleaned only from happenings on these 60 islands would, of course, have some holes in it, but would also give a visitor from Mars a fair idea of the framework of events that have shaped the nation as a whole. To this end, I have compiled a handy index (p9) so that everyone, whether Martian or not,

The author, with leaf

might be able to appreciate the breadth of experience gained on the islands featured.

I did get out to Piel Island, of course. While there I scraped acquaintance with its king, queen and princess (no, really – they're pukka royals and a lovely family to boot) and when night came I camped in the outer bailey of the castle. It proved, if anything, even more of an enchanted place than I had dared hope.

But then that is the wonder of tiny islands – more often than not they over-deliver. Whether reached by jumping off a little ferry onto a crumbling stone pier, by skimming up onto a deserted beach in a canoe, or by striding across a seaweed-spattered causeway built by the Romans, islands imbue their visitors with an immediate sense of escape, of getting away from it all, and the tempting if possibly fanciful notion that if you came to live here you could start your life all over again with a fresh slate.

Of course, some people have made such fantasies reality, and just over a quarter of the 60 islands featured in this book are populated for either a good part of each year or permanently. Now, there's a temptation to suppose that it takes a particular sort of person to reside on a miniature isle. However, we forget that to a great extent most of us contract our lives to the limits of our own tiny island, whether that be a town, village or borough, and spend the greater portion of our time within its boundaries. The only difference for those who live on actual islands is that they usually have to make more of an effort to get to the outside world and thus may need to inculcate a greater degree of resourcefulness and self-reliance. Going by the many islanders I spoke to during my research, this is a small price to pay and island life can indeed be very fulfilling.

Regardless of whether a tiny island is populated, each one is its own miniature kingdom, as often as not ruled over by wildlife, occasionally grazed by sheep or goats, and, if especially blessed, encircled by seals. By existing on a smaller scale, the tiny island affords visitors the pleasure of getting to know it completely. Spend a few hours on one of the particularly diminutive examples and you can familiarise yourself with every lump and crevice. Should you return some day, you come back to an old friend. And despite the profusion of tiny islands in Britain – around the coast, on rivers, on lochs and in lakes – each one has its own tales, its individual quirks, and its unique view of the world.

I hope that you derive as much enjoyment from visiting the islands in this book as I have done. Indeed, more so, because you won't even have to take notes.

Bestest,

Dixe

Dixe Wills
October 2012

The history of Britain in tiny islands

Settlers

Picts Brough of Birsay, Isle of May, Moncreiffe Island
Prehistoric Cara, Cramond Island, Eel Pie Island, Eilean Donan, Eilean Mòr, Flat Holm, Gateholm, Gugh, Holm of Papay, Inchbuie, Isle of May, Kisimul, St Helen's, St Michael's Mount, Sashes Island
Romans Cramond Island, Gateholm, Islands of Windermere, Moncreiffe Island, Northey Island, Sashes Island
Vikings Brough of Birsay, Eilean Mòr, Piel Island

Christians

Abbeys, convents and monasteries
Brough of Birsay, Chapel Island, Hilbre, Inchcailloch, Inchcolm, Inchmahome, Inner Farne, Isle of May, Looe Island, Piel Island, St Michael's Mount, Samson, Steep Holm, Ynys Llanddwyn
Churches, chapels and chantries Ailsa Craig, Bass Rock, Cara, Church Island, Cribinau, Derwent Isle, Eilean Mòr, Inch Kenneth, Inner Farne, Islands of Windermere, Looe Island, St Helen's, St Mary's Island, St Michael's Mount, Samson
Covenanters Bass Rock, Threave Island
Hermits Bass Rock, Inchcolm, Inner Farne, St Helen's, Steep Holm
Mystical murals of Christ crucified Davaar
Saints Bass Rock, Church Island, Cribinau, Eilean Donan, Eilean Mòr, Flat Holm, Inchcolm, Inchcailloch, Inch Kenneth, Inner Farne, Isle of May, Looe Island, St Helen's, St Mary's Island, St Michael's Mount, Steep Holm, Ynys Llanddwyn,
Seminaries Eilean Bàn

Monarchs

Albert, Prince Consort Samson, Staffa
Alexander I Inchcolm
Alexander II Eilean Donan, Inner Farne
Alexander III Cara, Eilean Donan
Alexandra Monkey Island
Alfred the Great Sashes Island
Anne Ynys Gifftan
Charles II Bass Rock
David I Inchcolm, Isle of May
David II Lochleven Castle Island, Hestan Island, Threave Island
Edward I Inchmahome, Lochleven Castle Island
Edward III Hestan Island, Inner Farne
Edward IV Eilean Mòr, St Michael's Mount
Edward VII Bass Rock, Monkey Island, St Michael's Mount, Samson
Edward VIII Burgh Island, Monkey Island
Edward the Confessor St Michael's Mount
Elizabeth I Bass Rock, Derwent Isle, Looe Island
George V Monkey Island
George VI Monkey Island
Henry III Inner Farne
Henry VI Threave Island

Henry VII Piel Island
James I (of Scotland) Bass Rock
James II (of Scotland) Threave Island
James III Eilean Mòr
James IV Eilean Mòr, Inchkeith (see Cramond Island)
James VI Bass Rock, Moncreiffe Island
Malcolm III Bass Rock, Inchcolm
Malcolm IV Eilean Mòr
Manuel II of Portugal Tagg's Island
Mary, Queen of Scots Bass Rock, Inchmahome, Lochleven Castle Island
Robert I (the Bruce) Inchcailloch, Inchmahome, Lochleven Castle Island, Threave Island
Robert II Lochleven Castle Island
Robert III Ailsa Craig
Stephen Piel Island
Victoria Inner Farne, St Michael's Mount, Staffa

Wars

American War of Independence Kisimul
Anglo-Dutch Wars Burrow Island
Anglo-Spanish War Looe Island, St Michael's Mount
Jacobite Rebellions Bass Rock, Derwent Isle, Eilean Bàn, Eilean Donan, Kisimul
The Lambert Simnel Rebellion Piel Island
Napoleonic Wars Inchcolm, Steep Holm, Threave Island
Prayer Book Rebellion St Michael's Mount
Scottish Wars of Independence Inchcolm, Isle of May, Lochleven Castle Island, Threave Island
War of the Three Kingdoms (the artist previously known as the English

Civil War) Bass Rock, Gugh, Islands of Windermere, St Michael's Mount
World War I Cramond Island, Eilean Donan, Inchcolm, Isle of May, Piel Island, Steep Holm
World War II Cara, Cramond Island, Davaar, Flat Holm, Havergate Island, Hilbre Island, Inch Kenneth, Inchcailloch, Inchcolm, Isle of May, Looe Island, Moncreiffe Island, Northey Island, Round Island, St Helen's, Steep Holm, Tagg's Island

Defences

Castles Bass Rock, Lochleven Castle Island, Piel Island, St Michael's Mount, Threave Island
Forts Ailsa Craig, Burrow Island, Derwent Isle, Eilean Donan, Hestan Island, Kisimul, Worm's Head
Guns Cramond Island, Flat Holm, Inchcolm, Steep Holm

Literary figures

Anderson, Edward Swan Island
ap Gwilym, Dafydd Ynys Llanddwyn
Atkins, Evelyn Looe Island
Banks, Sir Joseph Staffa
Barrie, J M Islands of Thorpeness Meare, Tagg's Island
Bartholomew Inner Farne
Beecham, Sir Thomas Round Island
Besant, Sir Walter Samson
Blake, William Looe Island
Boulton, Sir Harold Inch Kenneth
Bower, Walter and John of Fordun Inch

Kenneth, Inchcolm, Lochleven Castle Island
Camden, William Worm's Head
Carruthers, Robert Ness Islands
Christie, Agatha Burgh Island
Collingwood W G Peel Island
Collins, Wilkie Looe Island
Crockett, S R Hestan Island
Cunninghame Graham, R B Inchmahome
Defoe, Daniel Havergate Island, Islands of
Thorpeness Meare, Islands of Windermere
Dickens, Charles Eel Pie Island, Islands of
Thorpeness Meare
Firth, Tim Rampsholme (see Derwent Isle)
Giraldus Cambrensis Llangors Crannog
Gildas, St Steep Holm
Grahame, Kenneth Sashes Island
Johnson, Samuel and Boswell, James Inch
Kenneth, Staffa
Keats, John Staffa
Leland, John Worm's Head
Monro, Archdeacon Donald Inch Kenneth

Morpurgo, Michael Samson
Ogilvie, G Stuart Islands of Thorpeness
Meare
Palgrave, Francis Samson
Potter, Beatrix Islands of Windermere,
St Herbert's Island (see Derwent Isle)
Quiller-Couch, Sir Arthur Samson
Radcliffe, Ann Chapel Island
Ransome, Arthur Islands of Windermere,
Peel Island
Scott, Sir Walter Inch Kenneth,
Inchcailloch, Isle of May, Staffa
Shakespeare, William Inchcolm
Stevenson, Robert Louis Bass Rock, Staffa
Tennyson, Alfred Lord Samson
Thomas, Dylan Worm's Head
Verne, Jules Staffa
Wells, H G Monkey Island
West, Rebecca Monkey Island
Wordsworth, William Chapel Island,
Islands of Windermere, Piel Island, Staffa

Travel information

Here are some handy contact details for ferry and train companies that can whisk you towards the islands of your choice. I visited the vast majority of the islands in this book by bicycle, taking it on a train or a ferry or both (if you have no bike for onward travel, bus services are given in each island's info section wherever possible). The train/ferry option is not only the most relaxing way to get there, it's often the cheapest way too, especially if you book ahead. It's also less damaging (usually) to the environment than using cars and planes, which is good because tiny islands and rising sea levels are not a match made in heaven.

Ferry companies

Caledonian MacBrayne Ferries

Routes: If you want to go from the mainland to the Inner Hebrides or the Western Isles, it's a CalMac ferry you'll be stepping onto. If you're embarking on several different voyages in the same trip, check out the money-saving Island Hopper and Island Rover tickets.
Web: calmac.co.uk
Tel: 0800 066 5000

NorthLink Ferries

Routes: Serving the Shetlands Isles and Orkney with services from Aberdeen or Scrabster (next door to Thurso) on the mainland.
Web: northlinkferries.co.uk
Tel: 0845 600 0449

Orkney Ferries

Routes: Linking the Orkney mainland with 13 Orkney islands from Hoy in the south right up to North Ronaldsay.
Web: orkneyferries.co.uk
Tel: 01856 87 2044

Isles of Scilly Steamship Company

Route: From Penzance to Hugh Town on St Mary's in the Isles of Scilly (by a normal ferry, not a steamship).
Web: islesofscilly-travel.co.uk
Tel: 0845 710 5555

Train companies

Arriva Trains Wales

Network: ATW covers the whole of Wales and has lines reaching out from the principality to Manchester, Birmingham New Street and Cheltenham. The Explore Wales Pass allows passengers to travel over the entire ATW network, the Ffestiniog and Welsh Highland railways, and most scheduled bus services.
Web: arrivatrainswales.co.uk
Tel: 0870 900 0773 (Welsh language service: 0845 604 0500)

East Coast

Network: Stretching up the spine of Britain from London King's Cross to the East Midlands, Yorkshire and Humberside, North East England and Scotland, all the way north to Aberdeen and Inverness.

Web: eastcoast.co.uk
Tel: 0845 722 5225

First Great Western

Network: Includes South Wales, the West
Country to the far end of Cornwall, the
Cotswolds, and large parts of Southern
England, with frequent services to and
from London Paddington.
Web: firstgreatwestern.co.uk
Tel: 0845 700 0125

Greater Anglia

Network: Covers Cambridgeshire, Norfolk,
Suffolk, much of Essex and some of
Hertfordshire, with trains leaving London
from Liverpool Street.
Web: greateranglia.co.uk
Tel: 0845 600 7245

Northern Rail

Network: Spreads over the whole of
Northern England from Crewe, Stoke,
Buxton and Nottingham in the south to
Carlisle and Newcastle in the north.
Web: northernrail.org
Tel: 0845 000 0125

ScotRail

Network: ScotRail runs trains on all Scottish
routes and boasts a sleeper service linking
London with Northern Scotland.
Web: scotrail.co.uk
Tel: 0845 755 0033

South West Trains

Network: From London to Portsmouth,
Weymouth, Exeter, Reading and the
Isle of Wight.
Web: southwesttrains.co.uk
Tel: 0845 600 0650

Transpennine Express

Network: As the name suggests, TE covers
routes across the Pennines from Liverpool,
Blackpool and Barrow across to Hull,
Cleethorpes and Scarborough. They also
run services up the east coast to Newcastle
and the west coast to Glasgow and
Edinburgh.
Web: tpexpress.co.uk
Tel: 0845 700 0125

Virgin Trains

Network: The west coast line from London
to the West Midlands, North Wales,
Manchester, Liverpool, the Lake District,
Glasgow and Edinburgh.
Web: virgintrains.co.uk
Tel: 01709 849200

Further useful contacts

National Rail Enquiries

Web: nationalrail.co.uk
Tel: 08457 484950 (24 hours)

A to B Magazine

The Bike/Rail page is full of excellent
information on when and where you can
travel on trains, coaches, trams and ferries
with a bicycle.
Web: atob.org.uk/bike-rail

Rules

Since you're a pleasant, well brought-up person, this goes as read really, but don't do any damage to the islands. Please don't start fires or leave litter or pick flowers or disturb the peace or annoy the local population or harass the wildlife in any way (particularly birds in the nesting season, who can be frightened off their nests for good after just one slight disturbance). Many of the islands have additional rules ('no dogs' is a popular one – sorry, dogs): these are included in the info section for each island – please note these before you go and adhere to them scrupulously, along with any additional additional rules that may have popped up since the time of going to press.

To be honest, the vast majority of the islands in this book don't have huge long lists of rules and regs so it's nice if we, their guests, do our part to keep it that way.

Usual caveats

Islands are great places but they can sometimes be dangerous ones too, so don't mess with them or the water around them. Always check the weather forecast before setting off, even if you're not heading out to sea – lakes and lochs can get choppy and rivers flood if the conditions turn nasty – and if it's not looking great, or there's any other reason why you might not get to the island and back in safety, find something else to do.

If walking out to a tidal island, always (yes, always) check the tide timetable and make sure you know what time you will have to head back. Don't try to take on the sea – it has an unerring knack of winning. Make sure you go prepared in case, for whatever reason, you find yourself stranded until the next low tide, possibly without shelter. Don't rely on being able to summon help with your mobile phone since there are many islands with no coverage at all and you'll be talking to the wind.

Tide timetables are available at tidetimes.org.uk and often at Tourist Information Centres as well.

The author will not be around to help you out (he's enormously busy – he's probably doing something really important right now) and accepts no responsibility for whatever scrapes you might get yourself into.

So, don't risk becoming the star of your own 30-second slot on some regional news programme in which the newscaster puts on his or her sombre voice.

Nobody wants that.

Samson (p24), once home to unusually devout sheep

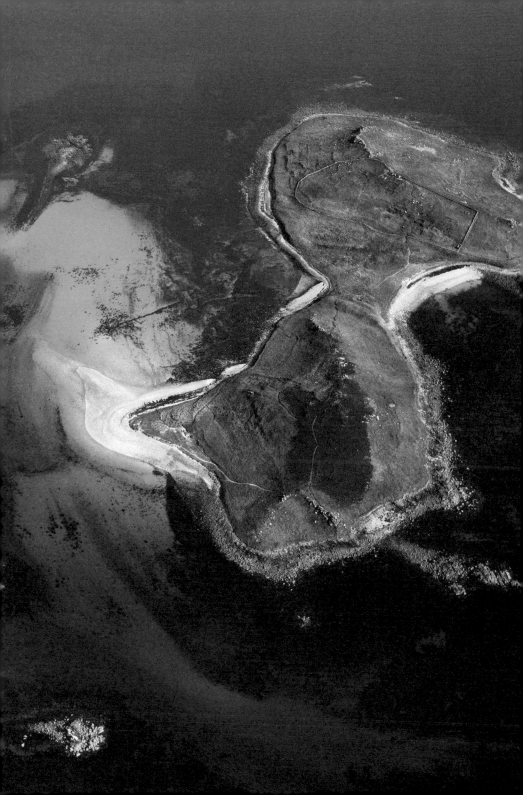

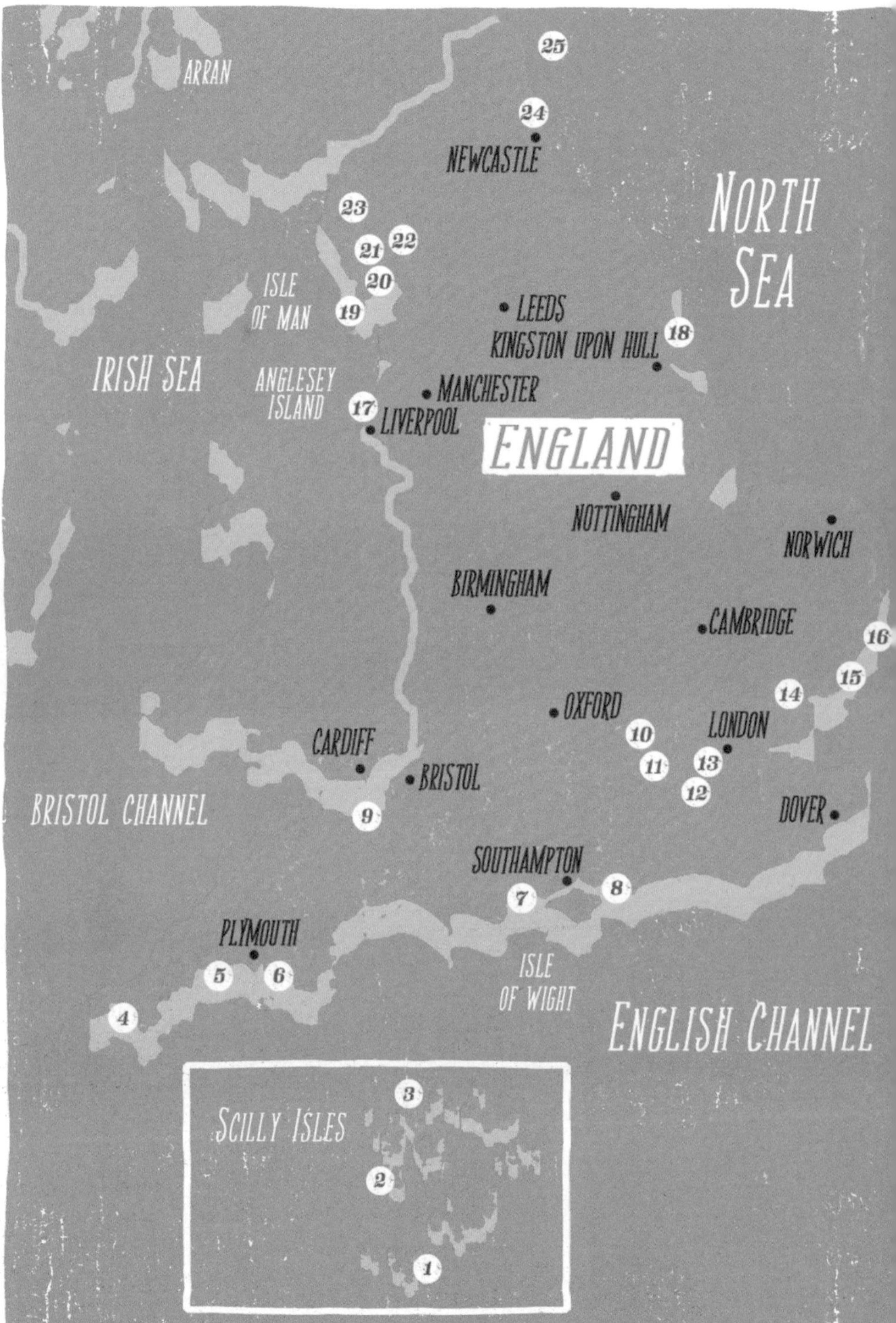

ARRAN

NORTH SEA

25

24
NEWCASTLE

23

21 22

20

ISLE
OF MAN   19

LEEDS
KINGSTON UPON HULL   18

IRISH SEA

ANGLESEY
ISLAND

17 MANCHESTER
LIVERPOOL

ENGLAND

NOTTINGHAM

NORWICH

BIRMINGHAM

CAMBRIDGE

16

15

OXFORD   14

CARDIFF   10   LONDON

11   13

BRISTOL   12

BRISTOL CHANNEL

9   DOVER

SOUTHAMPTON

7   8

PLYMOUTH

5   6   ISLE
OF WIGHT   ENGLISH CHANNEL

4

SCILLY ISLES

3

2

1

ENGLAND

1. Gugh

Isles of Scilly
Cornwall
OS Landranger map 203
Grid reference: SV 890 082
Size: 90 acres
Population: 2 (seasonal)

Gugh is not a place that has adapted itself to tourism. It is wild and untamed. If it were a poet, it would be Byron, perhaps with a bit of Seamus Heaney cragginess around the edges.

The island has always had an independent nature. Or at least a semi-independent nature. When Scilly drifted off from mainland Cornwall at the end of the last Ice Age, all the islands except Gugh and St Agnes were joined to each other in one land mass. While that main clump has broken apart somewhat, its constituent islands still form a cosy circle. Gugh and her mother, however, have kept themselves at one remove, yet still tentatively attached to each other by the slenderest of umbilical cords.

A short walk up from the pier on St Agnes, past the tempting front door of the Turk's Head – Britain's most southwesterly pub, as anyone and everyone on Scilly will inform you whether you have solicited the information or no – along a narrow lane and a sandy track and, if the tide is out, the cord swings into view. It's actually one of Britain's very few tombolos: naturally formed bars of shingle or sand that join an island to a mainland or another island. In Gugh's case, the tombolo – called simply The Bar – is of sand the colour of vanilla

The Bar leads across to Gugh's two solitary houses

ice cream. It looks friendly enough but, when the tide is in, strong and dangerous currents whip over it.

Two fantastical constructions stare down upon The Bar. They are Gugh's only houses and appear to be failed attempts to mimic Amish barns. They were built in the 1920s by a Mr Cooper, a retired surveyor from London, who designed their extraordinary curving roofs to withstand gales. Their continued existence nearly 100 years later suggests he was onto something.

A walk around the island is like a trip in a broken time machine, hurtling its occupants backwards and forwards apparently at random. Head towards the heather-strewn hillock at the southern end of Gugh and you'll come upon the Carn of Works Civil War battery. Built by Cavalier troops to hold two guns that would defend the southern approaches to the Isles of Scilly, the battery's designers appear to have pressed an ancient entrance grave within its walls into use as a magazine, which one would have thought was an act of sacrilege. Perhaps such matters matter less in times of war.

In spring and summer, any attempt to get near the battery is met with plangent howls of protest from lesser black-backed gulls. 'Get off! Get off!' they cry, as if in a former life they had all been farmers. They are backed up by the squeaky gate that is the herring gull's call and angry expletives uttered by oystercatchers, so let retreat be the better part of valour. It's as well that you know that the birds also reign supreme over the curious volcanic rock formations along the southern coast that look like miniature castles and they don't take kindly to an approach there either.

Turn north and you can strike up an altogether less frenzied acquaintance with the Old Man of Gugh, a 9ft-high leaning *menhir* (or standing stone). Etched with long grooves and placed here sometime during the Bronze Age, he may have served as a memorial or merely as a territorial marker. Apparently, there are over a dozen ley lines radiating from the Old Man, but when the ground around the stone was excavated no further clues were found.

There's less uncertainty about the goings on over the years on Kittern Hill. The tally of archaeological remains is remarkable for what is only a very humble knoll: 17 cairns; Bronze Age round houses; two stone-lined kelp pits; the remains of an ancient field system; Carn Valla, an entrance grave with (what may well be) capstones; and Obadiah's Barrow, another entrance grave but a hugely impressive one and rather splendidly named after the St Agnes man with whom George Bonsor, the archaeologist who excavated it in 1901, was lodging. From the summit of the hill there's also a great view of the Cow and Calf islets, on the first of which someone has planted a Jolly Roger.

It's the kelp pits that are the odd men out. They're practically modern, dating from somewhere between 1684 and 1835 when kelping was an important money-

Clockwise from top left: The Old Man of Gugh; sea holly; a makeshift shelter on the beach

maker on Scilly. Seaweed was burnt to produce sodium carbonate, which was exported for use in the making of glass, soap and bleach. Gugh's other major industry was bulb growing and in the springtime at the foot of Kittern Hill you can still see narcissi growing in neat rows. Even more noticeable are the island's remarkable lichens. At the southern end of Gugh there barely seems to be a rock face that isn't garlanded with some bright orange or silvery green growth.

We can't leave Gugh without a quick word about its name, with which outsiders perennially struggle. It's not 'guff' or 'goo' but rhymes with Hugh, with the hard g adding an extra half syllable. It's derived from the Cornish *keow*, meaning 'hedge banks' (walls are known as 'hedges' on Scilly). It's sometimes also known as The Gugh, although this makes it sound like a terrifyingly poor indie band, so it's probably best to step away from the definite article and we'll say no more about it.

How to get there

Take the train to Penzance (firstgreatwestern.co.uk; 08457 000 125), then sail to St Mary's (the main island of the Isles of Scilly) on the *Scillonian III* (islesofscilly-travel.co.uk; 0845 710 5555), which operates from near the end of March to early November. From the pier at Hugh Town a small ferry (stagnesboating.co.uk; 01720 422704) crosses St Mary's Sound to St Agnes, from where you can walk over to Gugh at low tide (hours of accessibility variable – ask locally for guidance).

Admission price/landing fee

Free. Gugh is looked after by the Isles of Scilly Wildlife Trust (ios-wildlifetrust.org. uk), so do think about giving them a little something to thank them.

View

From the top of Kittern Hill you can see Samson (p24), the Garrison walls on St Mary's, the Western Rocks (scene of many a tragic shipwreck) and Bishop Rock lighthouse, as well as St Agnes, just next door.

Facilities

None, but there are public toilets by the quay on St Agnes, 200yd from The Bar.

Accommodation

The **Troytown campsite** on St Agnes (0.75 miles; troytown.co.uk; 01720 422360) is one of the most glorious in all of Christendom. There are four guesthouses on St Agnes, the largest being **Covean Cottage** (coveancottage.com; 01720 422620), and 10 self-catering cottages. For information on St Agnes' accommodation, see st-agnes-scilly.org.

Nearest decent pub/café/tea room

The Turk's Head (200yd; 01720 422434) on St Agnes has real ales on tap, serves local produce in season whenever possible, and has views of Gugh from its picnic tables. The pub shares the island with a couple of cafés, a tea garden and a seafood restaurant.

Nearest shop

The **St Agnes Post Office Stores** (0.3 miles; 01720 422364) stocks a variety of groceries including organic, fair trade and local goods. The **Troytown Farm Shop** (0.75 miles; troytown.co.uk; 01720 423713) sells produce grown on the farm.

Rules

None.

Things to do

St Agnes, on the other side of The Bar, is a small and peaceful island ripe for an exploration followed by a good linger over a pot of tea.

The **St Agnes ferry** (stagnesboating.co.uk; 01720 422704) sails to the islands of Bryher, St Martin's and Tresco, as well as St Mary's.

Cow Rock with its Jolly Roger stiff in the breeze

2. Samson

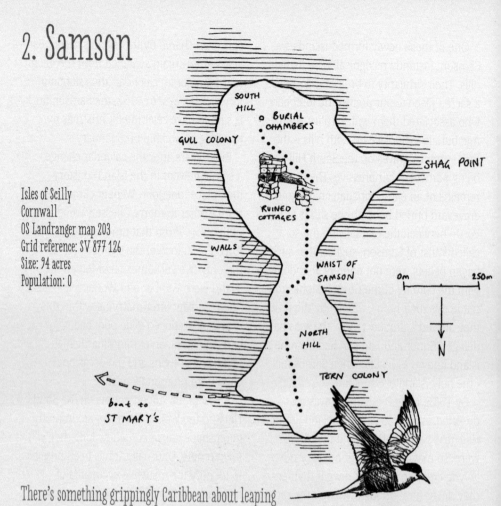

Isles of Scilly
Cornwall
OS Landranger map 203
Grid reference: SV 877 126
Size: 74 acres
Population: 0

SOUTH HILL

BURIAL CHAMBERS

GULL COLONY

SHAG POINT

RUINED COTTAGES

WALLS

WAIST OF SAMSON

NORTH HILL

TERN COLONY

0m   250m

N

boat to ST MARY'S

There's something grippingly Caribbean about leaping off the front of a boat into bright sparkly water and splashing up onto a crisp white beach to be greeted by the purple heads of pyramidal orchids and the octopus tentacles of sea spurge.

Uninhabited since 1855, Samson has taken on the look of an island uniquely blessed, with its sinuous profile and lush undergrowth. Even its generous scattering of ruined houses looks romantic rather than sinister. It's remarkable then to think that this is an island apparently labouring under a curse that goes back over 200 years. Samson has not long been a separate island. It was once part of Ennor, a much larger land mass that broke off from Cornwall, and is now some 28 miles from Land's End. In the early Middle Ages, rising sea levels submerged the valleys of Ennor and turned the island into the archipelago we know today as the Isles of Scilly (joined by St Agnes and Gugh (p18) which weren't part of Ennor).

24

One of these newly formed islands was Samson, instantly recognisable by its twin hills. Their similarity to breasts made this a sacred place to our prehistoric forebears who associated them with fertility. Bronze Age burials took place on both hills – the four entrance graves on the South Hill being particularly impressive. The bare remains of an early Christian chapel and graveyard buried beneath the sands at East Porth, between the two hills on the so-called Waist of Samson, suggest that such pagan beliefs were not entirely abandoned with the coming of the Gospel. Monks too made this their home, though by the time they arrived – around 1150 – the seas had deluged Ennor and Samson had become an island known as Insula Sancti Sampsonis ('the holy island of Samson').

By 1535, however, Samson was as deserted as it is today. John Leland, in his *Itinerary*, wrote of the island that there were 'so may rattes that yf horse or other lyvyng creature best be browght thyther they devor him', though whether the rats drove off the humans or merely swept in to fill a vacuum after the inhabitants left isn't known. One brave family had recolonised the island by the time Cosimo III, the Grand Duke of Tuscany, visited in 1669. We know because this wealthy member of the Medici family (his palace is now the renowned Uffizi art gallery) was so moved by the island and its solitary dwellers that he recorded his impressions in his journal.

The population grew very gradually and built a reputation for being profoundly religious. Legend has it that this outlook was even shared by the island's sheep. For years after Britain switched from the Julian to the Gregorian calendar (thus skipping forward 11 days) in 1752, the Samson flock is said to have celebrated Christmas by kneeling in worship on 5 January.

Eight years after the calendar change, a seminal event in the island's history took place: one John Webber came over from Bryher to marry Chessen Woodcock of Samson. From that time until the forced clearance of the island in 1855, the only two surnames recorded on the island were Webber and Woodcock. The incessant inter-marrying within this drastically reduced gene pool had its consequences: an extraordinarily high incidence of twins and the occasional child born profoundly deaf.

A few of the ruined houses on the South Hill and the Waist of Samson are in pretty good shape considering how long they've been empty. Unusually, it has been possible to identify the erstwhile occupants of as many as nine of the 12 dwellings, so you can wander from, say, the very well preserved remains of Richard Webber's two-room cottage to Honor Webber's former abode, before climbing South Hill to take in the place where Ann Woodcock lived. Here they eked out a living by fishing, burning kelp (see Gugh, p18) and tending a few crops, some Soay sheep and a herd of black Dexter cattle. It was an ancient way of life, for Samson had been farmed for thousands of years previously – at low tide the prehistoric field walls can still be seen stretching out into the water on

Samson Flats. Close by those walls, at East Porth, a woman who played a significant if pathetic role in Samson's history had her apportioned lot of fame. But before we come to Ann Webber, we must reluctantly allow two men onto the stage – Sir William Hamilton and Augustus Smith.

Sir William arrived unwittingly. The warship he was travelling on, HMS *Colossus*, drifted onto a reef just south of Samson on 10 December 1798. Aside from carrying wounded sailors home from Lisbon after the Battle of the Nile, the ship's hold contained part of Hamilton's extensive collection of vases, paintings and booty from Etruscan tombs. The next day, the crew and passengers had to be rescued by the men of Samson, who rowed out into the stormy seas in their gigs. They continued to risk their lives by rowing back and forth to the *Colossus* to retrieve cargo until it became too dark to do so. That night the ship rolled over and disappeared beneath the inky black waves.

Hamilton, desperately seeking his prized antiquities, found a salvaged crate and had it opened. Rather than the treasures he expected to find inside, it contained only the embalmed corpse of an admiral called Lord Shuldham (his coffin having been placed inside a crate to keep it a secret – sailors deemed it bad luck to have a cadaver aboard ship, and they clearly had a point in this case). Incandescent with rage that the men of Samson had inadvertently saved a dead man rather than his collection, the Scottish diplomat turned on them in the midst of the storm and cursed them with as much invective and hatred as he could summon up. It says much about the character of the islanders that not one of them picked the ingrate up and threw him back into the sea. If this was typical of Hamilton's behaviour, it's also easy to see why his wife Emma found consolation in the arms (or rather arm) of Lord Nelson.

That serial fraud, legend, would have us believe that Hamilton's curses found some traction. It is fabled that 19 men of Samson were drowned in a captured French brig in 1801. Such a loss would have wiped out the male population of the island and there is no record in Samson's burial registers of such a catastrophic blow. However, the isle did go through a series of disasters including the salting up of its well, the wrecking at sea of two cutters, the failures of several harvests and the consequent near starvation of its burgeoning population. In his report of 1818, unpromisingly headed 'Extreme Miseries of the Off-Islands of Scilly', the Rev G.C. Smith wrote:

The number of the inhabitants here is small, & their necessities extremely limited; they ask only for the means of obtaining just sufficient bread & potatoes to keep them alive. Two or three families are very poor, and have suffered much distress; their chief support has been limpets...

Samson also had the misfortune of suffering the attentions of Augustus Smith. The *soi-disant* philanthropist paid £20,000 for the lease of the Scillies in 1834, five years after a census had recorded 36 people living on Samson. Twenty years later, when he announced on the beach at East Porth that the inhabitants had a year in which to leave, there were only 10 islanders left. So incensed was one of them, Ann Webber, that she instantly spat out a curse on him. Eyewitnesses claim that Smith crumpled up on the spot and that a boatman had to beseech her to lift the curse so that the self-proclaimed Lord Proprietor could get up again. A year later, Ann Webber was the very last resident of Samson to leave the island. At least that's what some sources say. Others claim the woman who cursed Smith was the elderly Rachel Webber.

There are grounds for arguing that this new curse was itself partly successful. The island's lengthy dry-stone wall bears witness today to the failed deer farm that Smith attempted to establish once he had ridded the island of people. The deer escaped almost immediately and drowned in their attempt to swim back to Tresco. The black rabbits he replaced them with were wiped out by myxomatosis.

But Samson is not all curses and woe. It has inspired several novels including *Armorel of Lyonesse* by Sir Walter Besant and *Major Vigoureux* by Sir Arthur Quiller-Couch, and two Michael Morpurgo books: *Why the Whales Came* and *The Wreck of the Zanzibar*. Alfred, Lord Tennyson and Francis Palgrave visited Samson in 1860, following in the footsteps of Prince Albert and a five-year-old Prince of Wales, later Edward VII. They were given a tour by Augustus Smith, and it was reported that Albert caught a bird on the island 'to his great amusement'.

However, arguably the most unlikely event ever to take place on Samson occurred in 1965 when prime minister Harold Wilson refused to cut short his annual summer holiday in his beloved Scillies (he's buried on St Mary's) to attend to potential crises brewing in Westminster. His solution was to conduct a press conference on the beach at East Porth. Photos of the event show Wilson in sandals, a short-sleeved shirt, and really quite short shorts, while the gentlemen of the press (and they are all men) cluster around in ill-fitting suits and, bizarrely, overcoats. The prime minister talked about foreign policy and the possibility of a Lib-Lab pact, then got back to his holiday.

The island is barely ever that busy nowadays, aside from the hustle and bustle of the 2,000 seabirds who nest here. They include a common tern colony on North Hill and an internationally important lesser black-backed gull colony on South Hill.

The birds and the Scilly shrew are Samson's only nocturnal guests. An unsettling atmosphere is said to pervade the island as the crepuscular light fades, dissuading visitors from staying overnight. This would be difficult in any case, since there's no accommodation and camping is prohibited. It means, though, that there's no opportunity to discover if, when darkness falls, the curse of Samson lingers on.

Clockwise from top left: Wall pennywort; view north from South Hill; info board with North Hill behind

Welcome to the
Island of Samson

How to get there

Take the train to Penzance (firstgreatwestern.co.uk; 08457 000 125), then sail to St Mary's (the main island of the Isles of Scilly) on the *Scillonian III* (islesofscilly-travel.co.uk; 0845 710 5555), which operates from near the end of March to early November.

Admission price/landing fee

Free. The Isles of Scilly Wildlife Trust (ios-wildlifetrust.org.uk) manage Samson and would welcome donations to the cause.

View

Bryher, Tresco, St Mary's and across to St Agnes and Gugh (p18).

Facilities

None.

Accommodation

The usual route to Samson is via St Mary's, on which you'll find the friendly owners of **Sylina Guesthouse** (3.2 miles; sylina. co.uk; 01720 422129). There's a campsite on the neighbouring island of Bryher (bryhercampsite.co.uk; 01720 422559) and others on St Mary's, St Agnes and St Martin's.

Nearest decent pub/café/tea room

The **Fraggle Rock Bar** on Bryher is a treat not to be missed (1.2 miles; bryher. co/fraggle-rock-bar; 01720 422222) – specialising in Cornish food and drink and beloved of Jamie Oliver.

Nearest shop

The **Bryher Shop** (1.2 miles; bryhershop. co.uk; 01720 423601) opened in 2011 and has a good range of food and drink, including produce from Scilly.

Rules

Keep away from bird nesting areas (the tern colony is clearly marked during the breeding season). No climbing on buildings or burial sites. Dogs must be kept under control at all times. No camping.

Things to do

The sub-tropical **Abbey Garden** (tresco. co.uk; 01720 422849) on Tresco makes excellent use of the archipelago's warm microclimate. Also on display is a collection of ship's figureheads and other maritime memorabilia.

Watch some highly competitive gig racing. Female crews power these traditional Scillonian 30ft rowing boats on Wednesday evenings in the summer, while on Friday evenings the men turn out.

3. St Helen's

Isles of Scilly
Cornwall
OS Landranger map 203
Grid reference: SV 900 170
Size: c. 50 acres
Population: 0

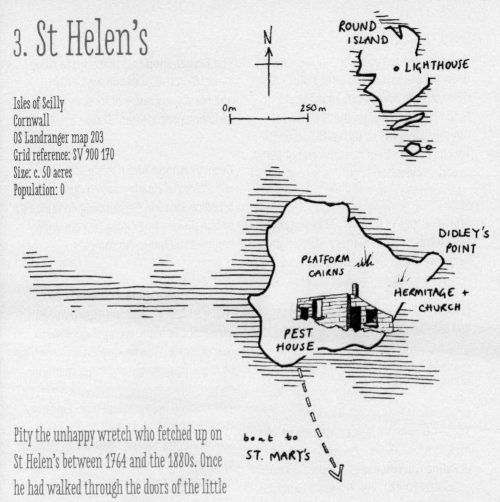

Pity the unhappy wretch who fetched up on St Helen's between 1764 and the 1880s. Once he had walked through the doors of the little granite Pest House, the chances of a sailor leaving this hump of an island were not significant, especially if he arrived with a fever and with his lymph nodes a little swollen.

The Pest House (the name coming from an abbreviation of Pestilence) was a slightly tardy response to an Act of Parliament passed 10 years earlier that had decreed that any plague-ridden ships passing north of Cape Finisterre en route to England must be quarantined at Scilly until they were declared free of the disease. Sailors dumped here were therefore given an indeterminate sentence. Even those not affected by the plague must have been all but bored to death. The island – a single low hill – can be explored from top to bottom in under two hours, even if taken at a leisurely pace. After that it would be endless games of cards, or perhaps chess or draughts if they could fashion themselves a set.

At least there was the consolation that St Helen's, if not exactly in the Samson (p24) league when it comes to good looks, is a handsome enough isle which, from the top of its 130ft hill, commands a wonderful panorama of the Scilly archipelago. It's rather apt that, in the absence of a harbour or jetty, landing here is a difficult proposition – it's as if the island knows that it's better for people never to set foot on it.

The dreaded Pest House is the first thing visitors encounter once they have been carefully dropped off among the maze of submerged rocks in the southeastern corner of the island. In its day, the quarantine station consisted of the Pest House (or isolation hospital, as we might refer to it today), a slipway and quay, a well, and a field system. The Pest House itself consists of a two-room main building with a lean-to. The pyramidal slate roof has long since disappeared but enough of the building survives – including a defiantly tall chimney stack – to give a very good impression of what life must have been like in one of those three tiny rooms, none of which were interconnected.

Patients do appear to have had some sort of medical attention – a young surgeon named Lt. James Allen Corsse, who died of cholera a week after he started work here, is buried in the nave in the Old Town Church on St Mary's. One hopes he was replaced.

Leaving the sad little hospital behind, a walk around the eastern edge of the island brings the visitor to a half-acre enclosure inside which lie the ruins of a small 8th-century chapel and cell and an 11th-century church. The fact that there is barely anything left to see here is probably down to Barbary pirates – the most romantic set of rogues ever to sail the Seven Seas, though doubtless their romanticism lost its sheen when one was a victim of it. The cell is believed to have been built by St Elidius, which gave rise to the isle's earlier Cornish name of Enys Elidius ('island of Elidius'). The label St Helen's is an error made by 16th-century cartographers, who inadvertently changed not only the saint's name but his sex too.

A saga written by Snorri Sturluson has the King of Norway, Olaf Tryggvason, bumping into St Elidius in his hermitage and promptly becoming a Christian. However, if this was so, his apparent conversion did nothing to turn his sword into a ploughshare, for 11 years later he turned up at the head of a rampaging army on Northey Island (p86) in Essex, where he broke any number of commandments.

Continue around the foot of the hill, steering clear of any kittiwake nests, and you'll notice two rocks on the sandy beach that resemble a baby elephant sad beyond all human knowing. Amble past woody nightshade far from any wood, cross the start of Didley's Point and at last you gain the northeastern shore, a place a world apart. With its back turned on the rest of Scilly, the island here appears to be engaged in an illicit liaison with Round Island, a scrap of a thing with a white finger of lighthouse protruding from it.

Here, above St Helen's attempted cliffs, grow shoulder-high pittosporum trees, glossy-leaved affairs with fruits resembling walnuts. They were incomers from New Zealand used as windbreaks but now self-seed wherever they will. Above them, heather and brambles strew themselves about the hill. The former apparently stepped in to fill a vacuum after a bombing incident in 1940 in which incendiaries set the island burning for days.

Climb the hill here to see four Bronze Age ring cairns – one of the reasons why St Helen's has been designated a Site of Special Scientific Interest. Drop back down to the Pest House and you'll find an extraordinary ground-covering succulent taking over large parts of the shore. These Hottentot figs produce a sea of thick green fleshy spikes splattered with huge yellow and pinkish flowers across which bumble bees stride with workmanlike intent. The plant may be an invasive species that is fast becoming problematic but it's nice to know that at least one visitor to the island has thrived.

How to get there

Take the train to Penzance (firstgreatwestern. co.uk; 08457 000 125), then sail to Hugh Town on St Mary's (the main island of the Isles of Scilly) on the *Scillonian III* (islesofscilly-travel.co.uk; 0845 710 5555), which operates from near the end of March to early November. There are only very occasional scheduled services from St Mary's to St Helen's (and then only in the summer) so your first port of call should be the über-helpful Tourist Information Centre in Hugh Town (01720 422536) to ask about boat taxi services or kayak hire from Tresco (see 'Things to do').

Admission price/landing fee

Free. The Isles of Scilly Wildlife Trust (ios-wildlifetrust.org.uk) manages the island, so if you've enjoyed it, you might want to consider sending them a donation.

View

The rocks of Men-a-vaur, and various other islands in the archipelago, most notably Tresco, St Martin's, Teän and Round Island.

Facilities

None.

Accommodation

As with Samson, since you're most likely to arrive here from St Mary's you could try that island's friendly **Sylina Guesthouse** (sylina.co.uk; 01720 422129). Perched up on Telegraph Hill, there are excellent views of St Helen's from just a short walk away. Campers, meanwhile, can either head for the **Garrison campsite** (garrisonholidays. co.uk; 01720 422670) on St Mary's or those on Bryher, St Agnes or nearby St Martin's.

Nearest decent pub/café/tea room

As the crow flies, your closest watering holes are on Tresco (1 mile) and St Martin's (1.25 miles). The former has the smart **New Inn** (tresco.co.uk; 01720 422844) and sundry cafés, while the latter pitches in with the **Sevenstones Inn** (01720 423560) and the **Little Arthur café and bistro** (01720 422457). Hugh Town on St Mary's also has a good sprinkling of pubs, cafés and tearooms.

Clockwise from top left: The Pest House; Hottentot figs; elephant sad beyond all human knowing

Nearest shop

Tresco (with an r) **Stores** (1.3 miles; tresco.co.uk; 01720 422806) and **St Martin's Post Office and Stores** (01720 422801) are just across the water. There's a good concentration of small shops in Hugh Town on St Mary's.

Rules

None.

Things to do

Hire a **kayak**, **dinghy** or **windsurfing board** on Tresco or St Mary's and explore the archipelago by paddle or wind power (sailingscilly.com; 01720 422060) – lessons also available from Tresco.

Take a wander around **The Garrison** (free; open all the time), the military defences on St Mary's that were built (then strengthened) between the 16th and 18th centuries and have been preserved as in aspic since then.

4. St Michael's Mount

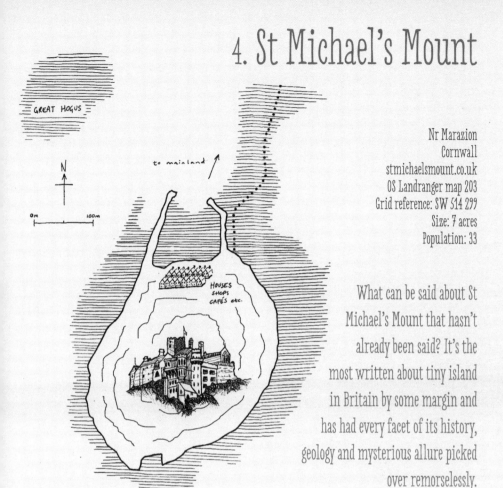

GREAT HOGUS

N

0m   100m

to mainland →

HOUSES
SHOPS
CAFÉS etc.

Nr Marazion
Cornwall
stmichaelsmount.co.uk
OS Landranger map 203
Grid reference: SW 514 299
Size: 7 acres
Population: 33

What can be said about St Michael's Mount that hasn't already been said? It's the most written about tiny island in Britain by some margin and has had every facet of its history, geology and mysterious allure picked over remorselessly.

Even if one were to fabricate details about the place, there's a good chance they still wouldn't be original, such is the volume of myths and inaccuracies that have attached themselves to this towering rock off the southwest coast of Cornwall. Indeed, there's a sense in which the legends and falsehoods say more about St Michael's Mount than does the truth, since they reveal what people have longed for the isle to represent. It's not enough for it merely to be a chunk of granite transformed into an island with each incoming tide, it must also fulfil the role of an entranceway into the presence of a higher power or a portal into some other world more magical than our own. So, before Dr Freud bursts in and reminds us that sometimes a cigar is just a cigar, let's stand at the start of the causeway, drink in the view worn into comfortable cliché by innumerable holiday snaps, and let the myths begin.

The island's colony of lesser black-backed gulls patrols the shore near the Pest House (far left)

Inevitably, one of the plethora of Cornish giants claimed the mount as his own some once-upon-a-time ago. Like a lot of his county's fellow behemoths, Cormoran came to a sticky end. He was quite harmlessly playing pitch and toss with a giant on the neighbouring hill of Trencrom when he was murdered by the apparently heroic Jack – he of the beanstalk – proving once again that it's the winners who get to write history.

The fact that the island was now a notorious crime scene didn't dissuade St Cadoc from dropping by some time in the 5th century, only to discover that his aunt, St Keyne, had already taken up residence. It's surprising to find that Cadoc was supposedly hale enough to build a cell on Flat Holm (p163) in the late 6th century.

The cult of St Michael, the archangel who 'fought against the dragon' according to the book of Revelation, had a good many adherents in the early Middle Ages. Visions of the saint were so numerous that in time there was a serious shortage of hilltops on which he hadn't been seen. Given these circumstances, it would have been an oversight if he hadn't put in an appearance on the tidal island otherwise known as Karrek Loes yn Koes ('grey rock in the woods' in Cornish). One night in AD495, the crew of a fishing boat duly witnessed him standing at the top of the isle (or hovering above it, depending on your choice of source). Michael's predilection for the summits of hills seems to spring from his cult's links with earlier hilltop pagan worship, so it's no surprise to find Victorian writers fancifully sprinkling the early history of St Michael's Mount with Celtic druids practising their rituals and generally being mystical.

Unusually, there's even a legend pinpointing the exact year St Michael's Mount became an island. Fable has it that Land's End was joined to the Isles of Scilly by a land called Lyonesse until 1099. In this year a great flood inundated the area – killing all the inhabitants bar one man who saved himself by riding the waves on a white charger – and created the coastline we have today. The flood waters also burst inland around St Michael's Mount, leaving it stranded a quarter of a mile from the newly formed Mount's Bay. In reality, the tidal island is likely to have held that status for about 5,000 years, though one can see why it would be more fun to ascribe its creation to a single cataclysmic event.

Historical facts about the island attempt to make up for their lack of mystique through sheer weight of numbers. An account of all the notable events that have occurred here would fill a book, which is no doubt why several have been written. This, then, is merely a lightning tour of the highlights.

From about 350BC, the mount was used as a port for trading Cornish tin. In the 11th century, Edward the Confessor granted the island to the Benedictine monks of Mont St-Michel, its counterpart off the coast of Normandy. The monastery became a place of pilgrimage, with Pope Gregory

VII announcing a special offer of a third off all penances to anyone who made it. The mount was seized five times – first by Henry de la Pomeray in 1193, who had his soldiers cunningly disguised as pilgrims; next by John de Vere, 13th Earl of Oxford in 1473, who was only dislodged after a five-month siege laid by troops loyal to Edward IV; then just 24 years later by Perkin Warbeck, pretender to the throne and, so it has been claimed, 'the greatest subject to fail to become king'. The oppressed Cornish masses took control here in 1549 (a year after the monastery was dissolved) during the Prayer Book Rebellion; and finally, after holding out for the King between 1642 and 1646, the Royalists lost the mount to Parliamentary forces. The next year, Colonel John St Aubyn was named Captain of the Mount. He later bought the island and it has been in the St Aubyn family ever since, though they donated most of it to the National Trust in 1954. In all the hurly-burly, the island also managed to be the first place to light a beacon alerting the nation to the coming of the Spanish Armada in 1588.

Amble across the well maintained causeway today and you'll find more of interest on its meagre 7acres than in many a large town on the mainland. There's a landward-facing harbour and terraces of neat houses behind it in which the majority of the population live; a 14th-century priory church; a cemetery; a castle, complete with mummified cat, Samurai warrior and a magnificent Bronze Age hoard discovered on the island in 2009; sub-tropical gardens featuring plants from the Canary Islands, Mexico and South Africa, among others; three pillboxes left over from World War II; a curious collection of bronze casts of the footprints of royal visitors, including Queen Victoria, Edward VII, Prince Charles and the Duchess of Cornwall; and an underground tram that ferries freight up to the castle from the harbour. This unlikely miniature railway, built over 100 years ago, still serves the St Aubyn family today, although sadly the public aren't allowed to interact with it.

However, this is an island that is so much more than the collection of things that have accumulated on it over the centuries. To visit St Michael's Mount is to view something of the quiddity of Albion: the singular and often bizarre beliefs, events and people that have helped make England what it is. What's all the more remarkable is that St Michael's Mount isn't even in England. As anyone born in Cornwall will be quick to tell you, this is a country unto itself – if you want to see England, you'll have to go east of the Tamar river.

How to get there

From Penzance railway station (firstgreatwestern.co.uk; 08457 000 125) there's a 2.5-mile cycle/footpath around Mount's Bay that takes you practically all the way to the head of the causeway. Alternatively, take the 2/2A bus (firstgroup.com; 0845 600 1420) to Marazion. The island is accessible for roughly four hours at each low tide. When the tide is in, you can catch one of the little ferries that

serve the island from 9am to 5pm when the causeway is closed. For tide and ferry information, call 01736 710265.

Admission price/landing fee
Free to land on the island. Entrance to castle and garden: adult £9.25, child £4.50, family £23 (National Trust members free). Cheaper entry for castle only or garden only.

View
The Cornish coastline from Penzance in the west to Cudden Point in the east.

Facilities
Two sets of public toilets, two shops, a restaurant and a café.

Accommodation
Blue Horizon (1 mile; holidaybreaks marazion.co.uk; 01736 711199) is a B&B in Marazion whose seaward rooms enjoy views of St Michael's Mount.

Nearest decent pub/café/tea room
The island has two places to eat: the National Trust's **Sail Loft Restaurant & Tearoom** and the **Island Café**.

Nearest shop
There are two shops on the island – one run by the National Trust and another offering locally produced gifts and artwork. For basic food supplies, there's **Cobble Corner** in Marazion (0.75 mile; 01736 710373).

Rules
None.

Things to do
Though small, it's worth setting aside the best part of a day to see the island properly. The castle, gardens and church would all merit a visit on their own account (open Sunday to Friday, castle from mid-March to early November, gardens mid-April to mid-September; stmichaelsmount.co.uk; 01736 710265).

A sneaky free way to see the gorgeous **priory church** is by going to a service there (they last about 45 minutes). These are mostly held in the summer from the end of May to the end of September at 11.15am.

5. Looe Island

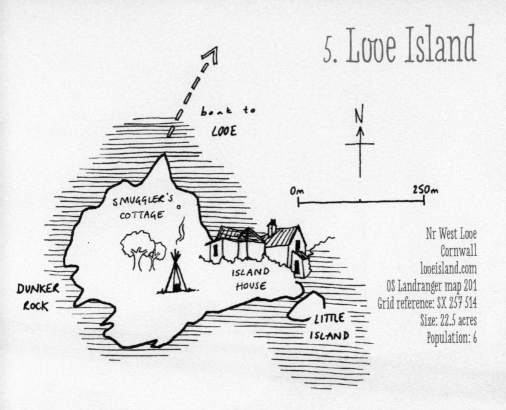

boat to
LOOE

N

SMUGGLER'S
COTTAGE

DUNKER
ROCK

ISLAND
HOUSE

LITTLE
ISLAND

0m   250m

Nr West Looe
Cornwall
looeisland.com
OS Landranger map 201
Grid reference: SX 257 514
Size: 22.5 acres
Population: 6

It's extraordinary that, although Jesus definitely and without a trace of a doubt visited Looe Island as a boy back in the early first century, if you've heard of the place at all it's almost certainly down to two elderly sisters from Epsom.

In 1964, Evelyn and Roselyn Alice Atkins (forever known as Attie and Babs respectively), purchased the island almost without meaning to. They had moved down to Looe in Cornwall and were offered the isle by the then owner who, because of illness, was having to relocate to the mainland. So keen was he for the sisters to have the island (he feared that otherwise it might be turned into a holiday camp) that he himself granted them the £22,000 mortgage in order that they could buy it from him. For the rest of their lives the sisters worked hard to make something of the island, which had rather gone to seed. Attie wrote about their adventures in a couple of books, the first of which was the bestselling *We Bought an Island*.

While a previous owner would dissuade people from landing by firing a shotgun above their heads, the sisters opened up the island, charging a 2s 6d landing fee. They were so overwhelmed with visitors that to keep the numbers sustainable, they restricted the landing licence to a single boatman, a practice that is still

in place today. Attie died aged 87 in 1997, with Babs – who is buried on the island – following seven years later. They bequeathed the isle to the Cornwall Wildlife Trust, thus ensuring that it continued in safe hands.

A visit to Looe Island begins at the main beach, which thrusts itself out of the northern end like an arrowhead. Up until the 12th century it was possible to walk the half mile over at low tide via a causeway but that's now impossible except at the very lowest ebb of the biggest spring tide. Even then, only those who know where to cross have been brave enough to attempt it, since the sea never drops below ankle height. Not that getting over by boat is always the easy option as landings are in the gift of Neptune and often cancelled.

The first port of call for visitors is the Tractor Shed where Jon or Claire, the island's wardens, give a short introduction and hand out laminated notes for those who fancy guiding themselves. Sweetly, there's homemade produce for sale here too – raspberry jam and apple juice and elderflower champagne (a favourite of the Atkins sisters). You can even buy a book or two from the collection that kept Attie and Babs going through the long winter evenings.

Looe Island's main street is a narrow grassy track along its northeastern edge between the sea and a small wood. Tucked in alongside it, behind a high hedge of roses and ivy, is the tiny Smuggler's Cottage, which is still occupied today. The placement of the apostrophe would have you believe that only the one smuggler ever lived here, but history suggests this is rather under-egging the pudding. The island was an ideal place for the clandestine landing of contraband, and the seaward side is said to be full of long caves and prehistoric chambers where spirits, tea, silk stockings and the like were stashed until they could be run onto the mainland on a conveniently moonless night.

Tales of these 'free-trading' enterprises on the island during the 18th and 19th centuries are numerous, with the most notorious Smuggler's Cottage inhabitants being a brother and sister with the unlikely names of Amram and Jochabed – or Fyn and Black Joan to give them their outlaw nicknames. Unusually, the law doesn't seem to have caught up with either of them and they eventually ended up marrying locals and living respectable lives on the mainland.

Cheekily, their nefarious activities took place just 200yd along the track from Coastguard Watch House (now called Island House), built in the early 19th century to put a stop to such goings-on. Unfortunately for the authorities, the excise men stationed there would often throw their lot in with the smugglers, who were, after all, usually their friends and neighbours.

Sadly, the island does not appear to be awash with hidden or forgotten booty. The Atkins sisters did once receive what appeared to be a genuine treasure map sent to them by a clergyman in Cumbria who claimed his family had owned it for generations. Attie's and Babs' excitement increased when their dousing rods crossed over the spot indicated on the map. However, all hopes of a chest containing rubies, emeralds and doubloons were dashed when the site was dug up and nothing but earth was found there.

Next door to the newly renovated Island House is Jetty Cottage, home to the wardens during the visitors' season. It has a marriage licence but can only seat up to 36 people, which seems an excellent excuse for keeping one's nuptials intimate.

Beyond the cottage, the tiny breakaway rock that is Trelawny's Island bears witness to the proud Cornish family who owned Looe Island for several generations after Sir John Trelawny bought it from a cash-strapped Elizabeth I in 1600. Around the corner, a small green bird hide stares out to sea. Greater black-backed gulls are the big attraction, though cormorants and shags and about 450 pairs of herring gulls also nest here. The rocks down below are the haunt of a small number of grey seals. Another laminated sheet is charmingly filled with colour photos of each of the island's resident herd so that you can have a go at identifying them by name.

In Mike Dunn's painstakingly researched *Looe Island Story*, he mentions the fact that one of the major engagements between the Spanish Armada and the English fleet took place just south of the island on 30 July 1588 and would have been clearly visible to anyone looking out from here. The English,

by sneaking ships behind the Spanish fleet at night and then coming upon them in the morning with a following wind, came out victorious but one can't help feeling it would have been unsettling to see so many enemy ships at such close quarters.

The only other known brush with an armed conflict happened in World War II when an aerial mine struck near the summit of the hill, leaving a crater 30ft wide and 12ft deep. It's supposed that the crew of the plane, struggling to see through the fog, believed the island to be a ship.

Climbing the hill that occupies most of the island, we rise above the wood and come to the more open half of the island, kept in trim by a flock of 20 Hebridean sheep. At the summit, 150ft above the waves, lie a few stones of what was once a Norman chapel. The island belonged to the Benedictines of Glastonbury from 1144 to 1289 and they installed a couple of monks here. The island was then known as Lamene or Lamane but began to be referred to as St Michael of Lamanna after the saint to whom the chapel was dedicated. Mike Dunn charts the island's extraordinary nomenclatural odyssey from that point to 1851, when Wilkie Collins mentions 'Looe Island' in a tale inspired by the apparently true story of a resident family who rid the isle of its rats by eating them. In between the monks and the novelist, the island notches up 15 different names, some of which die off, only to be resurrected centuries later. So, you can take your pick from Lamanna, St Nicholas Isle,

the Isle of Lemayne, Island of St Michael's, St George's Island, St Michael's Insul, Loos Island, Loo Island, Love Island and several other variations on these themes. The confusion continues to this day. If you turn up at the pier on East Looe to put your name down for a boat trip over to Looe Island, you'll find the advertising hoarding refers only to St George's Island.

But what of Jesus, the island's most renowned visitor? Was the Holy Lamb of God on England's pleasant pastures seen? As anyone who has been to Glastonbury Abbey will know, Joseph of Arimathea brought his great-nephew to Cornwall and southwest England – possibly while on a trip to trade with Cornish tin miners. The

Countenance Divine was then left on Looe Island for a spell while his great uncle went off to do some business. This story was put about by the same Benedictine monks who posited that Jesus and Joseph had also dropped in on Glastonbury to build a wattle-and-daub church there. This made both Looe Island and Glastonbury enormously popular with pilgrims, whose offerings swelled the coffers of those same Benedictine monks, which, on reflection, does perhaps cast a shadow of doubt over the claims, and is possibly why William Blake couched so much of his poem *Jerusalem* in interrogatives. However, if it's any consolation to modern-day pilgrims, excavations here have uncovered some

Romano-British wooden chapels, which would at least make the island one of the earliest outposts of Christianity in the whole of Britain. Not bad for a place that can't even make up its mind what its name is.

How to get there

Take the train down the lovely branch line to Looe (firstgreatwestern.co.uk; 08457 000 125) from where the aptly named *Islander* (adult £6 return; under 10 £4; Dave Butters 07814 264514) leaves from the RNLI slipway at East Looe. The trip takes about 15 minutes each way, with about two hours on the island. The boat does not sail every day and you need to book in advance by adding your name to a sheet attached to the information board (advertising trips to 'St George's Island') at the harbour. Several other boats sail around the island but this is the only one that lands there.

Admission price/landing fee

Adult £2.50, under 10 £1.

View

The village of Hannafore on the mainland, and Eddystone lighthouse out to sea.

Facilities

A compost loo.

Accommodation

A single solitary **tipi** in its own little clearing now gives outsiders the opportunity to stay for a three-night break on Looe Island and help fund the worthy causes of the Cornwall Wildlife Trust at the same time (tinyurl.com/ cyznpqt; 01872 273939). On the mainland, there are a few **B&Bs in Hannafore** (1.25 miles from RNLI slipway) with views of Looe Island, including **Hillingdon Guest House** (hillingdonguesthouse.co.uk; 01503 262906).

Nearest decent pub/café/tea room

It would be invidious to pick one of the many little cafés in **Looe**'s narrow streets – wander around and see which one takes your fancy.

Nearest shop

There are some cracking little shops in both **West** and (even more so) **East Looe**, from where the boat for Looe Island leaves.

Rules

Keep to marked paths; no dogs allowed; some nesting areas out of bounds; and please respect the privacy of the island's small population.

Things to do

The 15th-century **Old Guildhall Museum and Gaol** (150yd from slipway; eastlooetowntrust.co.uk; 01503 263709) takes visitors through Looe's long history of fishing, boat building and, naturally, smuggling.

6. Burgh Island

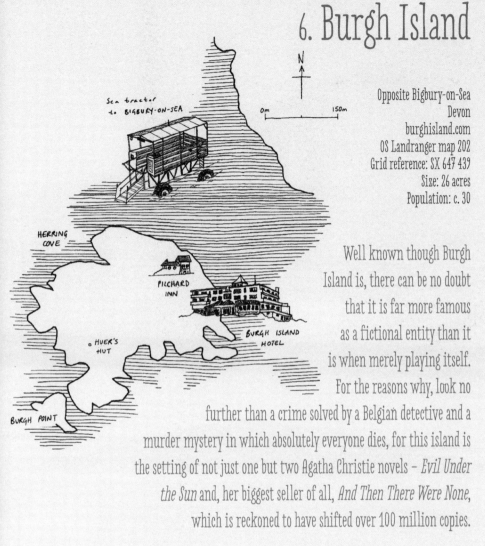

Sea tractor to BIGBURY-ON-SEA

0m 150m

HERRING COVE

PILCHARD INN

HUER'S HUT

BURGH ISLAND HOTEL

BURGH POINT

Opposite Bigbury-on-Sea
Devon
burghisland.com
OS Landranger map 202
Grid reference: SX 647 439
Size: 26 acres
Population: c. 30

Well known though Burgh Island is, there can be no doubt that it is far more famous as a fictional entity than it is when merely playing itself. For the reasons why, look no further than a crime solved by a Belgian detective and a murder mystery in which absolutely everyone dies, for this island is the setting of not just one but two Agatha Christie novels – *Evil Under the Sun* and, her biggest seller of all, *And Then There Were None*, which is reckoned to have shifted over 100 million copies.

Christie was one of many celebrities who visited Burgh Island's hotel in the 1930s and she wrote both stories while staying in the Garden Suite, an annexe with its own private garden.

Fans of the hotel in those troubled times were an eclectic bunch that included Noël Coward, songstress Josephine Baker, speedster Malcolm Campbell and George Formby, among many others. Lord Louis Mountbatten also came to Burgh Island, in the company of the Prince of Wales, who was later to become King Edward VIII, albeit for less than a year.

To discover the particular attraction that this little green hump off the south Devon coast had for the rich and famous, we have to go back to a music hall entertainer

named George Chirgwin, a.k.a. 'The White-Eyed Kaffir' (not a name, one suspects, he would have used today). He made a mint singing falsetto while blacked up with his trademark diamond of white make-up over his right eye, and bought Burgh Island in 1895 for £100, erecting the island's first ever hotel, a small wooden affair.

However, it was left to a later owner, Archie Nettlefold, to build the establishment that drew the stars down to Devon. Nettlefold's family was the N in GKN, an engineering firm that profited greatly from its production of munitions during World War I (it's always heart-warming to hear that at least some folk reap the rewards of mass slaughter), though Archie styled himself as a financial backer of plays and films. Having bought the island, he commissioned an architect to build him a concrete house with the air of a castle about it. The result was an elegant, bright white Art Deco pile that was completed in 1929. After a few years of having friends come down to share his 'Great White Palace', he apparently tired of offering hospitality for free and converted the place into a hotel.

Today, many of its rooms are named after the stars who stayed in them. You can even book the very suite in which Christie spun the webs of her devious plots, although fans of Churchill and Eisenhower will be disappointed to learn that there are no rooms named after them, for the oft-told tales that they held meetings together here during World War II are, to put it mildly, contentious.

One thing we do know is that Burgh Island was requisitioned for service during the war – two bunkers from this period still adorn the place. In 1942, the hotel suffered the misfortune of being hit by a bomb dropped by a German plane. As in the case of Northey Island (p86), it's likely that there was little intent behind the action other than a desire by the pilot to get rid of unused bombs before returning home.

After the war, the island experienced rather mixed fortunes. Two separate owners attempted to make a go of things but met with only mild success. By the time husband and wife Tony and Bojena Porter bought Burgh Island in 1986, the hotel was in a very sorry state, having been defaced by the imposition of the tackiest elements of 1960s and 70s decor and ham-fisted attempts to turn the rooms into self-catering apartments. The couple's battle to return the hotel to the splendour of its 1930s heyday – complete with natural swimming pool – is retold in Tony Porter's book *The Great White Palace*. The current owners, Tony Orchard and Deborah Clark, took over in 2001 and have lavished further funds on the hotel, rendering it even more luxurious (it even offers Botox injections, which perhaps says something about the hotel's target market).

The island is eminently roamable, with only the eastern part (the grounds of the hotel) off limits. Reached by crossing a beach from the small resort of Bigbury-on-Sea, its grassy slopes rise abruptly about 200ft to the summit of its one hill, with cliffs around the western shores and, to the south, a tiny headland misleadingly called Little Island. Once known as St Michael's Island (probably for the same reasons St Michael's Mount (p37) came by its name), its current moniker is a corruption of Borough Island. The earliest known inhabitants were, as on so many other tiny islands, monks. However, there's little trace of their presence now though the remains of their 14th-century monastery may well be found buried beneath the hotel. It's also been conjectured that the island's Pilchard Inn – which proudly bears a plate displaying the date 1336 – may originally have been one of the monastery buildings.

In the 18th century, the island became a haunt of smugglers, so it is perhaps appropriate that the ghost of one of them is said to haunt the Pilchard. In life he was one Tom Crocker who was shot dead by a customs official in the doorway of the pub in 1759 at the tender age of 19. By all accounts his passing was little mourned. A tradition has established itself that whoever locks up the pub of an evening makes sure to bid Tom goodnight. It certainly appears advisable to keep him sweet. Gary McGuire, who has worked on the island for 20 years, tells of people seeing objects levitating in the pub, and pint pots mysteriously smashing at night.

There's also said to be an old smugglers' tunnel running from the pub cellar to Herring Cove, at the far side of the island, where contraband could be offloaded away from the prying eyes of excise men on the mainland. Unpleasantness has tainted this (real or imagined) place since the night that Tom was shot; his friend Matthew Horseley is said to have attempted to escape down the tunnel only to be walled in and left to die. If the tale is true, he's presumably still down there. At low tide, a tunnel-like opening can still be seen at Herring Cove, though it has been blocked off, possibly during the last war.

Happily, you can leave all the skulduggery behind by climbing the island's hill and gulping in the breezes sweeping up the Channel from the Atlantic. At the top there stand the four stone walls of a small 17th-century building known as the Huer's Hut. From here a lookout would be kept for the silver shoals of pilchards off the coast. When seen, the observer would raise a hue and cry, alerting the fishermen below. The hut was raised on the site of an earlier chapel dedicated to St Michael and is often mistaken for it, though a less chapel-like ruin it would be harder to imagine.

From here one can watch the incoming tide as it engulfs the 250yd strip of beach back to the mainland. However, unlike with most tidal islands, there's rather less of an imperative to keep an eye on the waves, for down below sits Burgh Island's most photographed attraction – the sea tractor.

Built in 1969 to carry visitors back and forth safely above the brine, whether foaming or not, this unique beast cost £9,000 to construct – around £125,000 in today's money – and runs on demand from about eight in the morning to as late as midnight, if needs be. The monstrous roar of the engine and the Tonka Toy look of its Brobdingnagian wheels have men and boys dancing from foot to foot with glee while their womenfolk and girlfolk exchange knowing glances and roll their eyes as if they themselves have never once become overexcited about a pair of shoes.

It is an extraordinary thing to ride upon and, at £2 each way, is an admirable way of partaking in the life of Burgh Island without breaking the bank.

How to get there

This is a tricksy one. From Plymouth station (firstgreatwestern.co.uk; 08457 000 125), walk down to the Barbican (0.75 miles) where you can pick up the 93 bus (firstgroup.com) to Modbury. Then it's a breezy 5.5-mile hike or taxi ride (modburytaxis.co.uk; 01752 696969) to Bigbury-on-Sea, from where you can stroll across to Burgh Island at low tide. When the tide is in, you can pick up the famous Burgh Island sea tractor (8am until late evening).

Admission price/landing fee
Free.

View
Bigbury-on-Sea, Eddystone lighthouse, the glow of Plymouth at night.

Facilities
A hotel (no access for non-residents) and a pub. There are public toilets and an outdoor shower in the car park on the mainland opposite the island.

Accommodation
The **Burgh Hotel** (burghisland.com; 01548 810514) is an exclusive and luxurious place with a price tag to match (the cheapest room is over £300, with the most expensive more than twice that – though at least breakfast and dinner are included). If you haven't the wherewithal to stay there, try Bigbury-on-Sea's more modest **Summer Winds B&B** (01548 810669), some of whose rooms look over to Burgh.

Nearest decent pub/café/tea room
Burgh's very own **Pilchard Inn** (01548 810514) puts on live music on Wednesday and Saturday nights, has an open fire and serves food.

Nearest shop
There's a small seasonal **beach shop** (0.3 miles) on the corner of the car park opposite the island, and **Bigbury-on-Sea Post Office and Stores** (0.4 miles; 01548 810274) with a wider selection of goods.

Rules
Keep to the permissive footpaths.

Things to do
The 630-mile **South West Coast Path** (southwestcoastpath.com) passes the island on its way west towards Plymouth and east to Salcombe around some largely unregarded yet sumptuous coastline.

7. Round Island

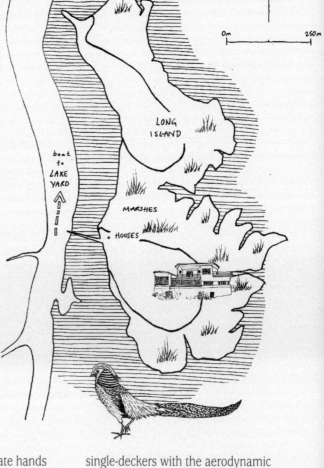

Poole Harbour
Dorset
roundisland.co.uk
OS Landranger map 195
Grid reference: SY 988 874
Size: 35 acres
Population: 2

There are eight islands in Poole Harbour but only one that anyone can ever name: Brownsea, the 500-acre plot that witnessed the birth of the scout and guide movements and which is now owned by the National Trust.

All the other seven are in private hands and, of those, the only one with the happy distinction of allowing non-island-owning mortals to stay on it is Round Island. It's not an island that deals in enigmas but it does have one oddity to its name, and that is the oddity of its name.

However you try to squint at it, the island is simply not round. Turn the map upside down and the isle looks more bus-shaped than anything – one of those modern single-deckers with the aerodynamic fronts. The reason the island was saddled with this misnomer has become a subject for idle conjecture, and in the taverns of Poole on a Saturday night they speak of little else. Perhaps it is the proximity of Long Island (literally a single stride away except at high tides) that is to blame. Compared with the sausage shape of its neighbour, Round Island conforms to the very nature of a circle.

Just don't go looking there for ancient history. While nearby Brownsea Island was pillaged by the Vikings, there's no evidence that they came to Round Island (possibly on the grounds that it was uninhabited, the Vikings' dictum being 'What's the point of robbery when nothing is worth taking?'). It did at least achieve footnote status in World War II when it was requisitioned by the Royal Navy and became part of HMS *Turtle*, a Combined Operations assault gunnery school that trained troops for the D-Day landings. It was evidently a popular place to be posted. Coxswain Jack Gaster recalled it being 'A wonderful location…the main house had a magnificent view of Poole and Sandbanks from the principal bedroom; this had mirrors set in the walls at a level so that if you were seated or lying down, a panoramic view of the harbour was there to be seen.'

Aerial photographs taken during the war show the isle virtually treeless. Conversely, when seen from a distance today, the first thing you notice is the island's pine trees, no doubt planted for their love of acidic soil. There are some silver birch here too, with the odd rowan and oak thrown in. However, fully 23 of the island's 35 acres are accounted for by a low scrubby fringe called The Saltings, which, at the very highest tides, completely disappears beneath the waters. The second thing you notice is the 110ft pier thrusting out of the northwestern tip like a sabre. This is where four of the island's half-dozen houses cluster, forming a brick-built hamlet.

From there, the ground rises moderately towards the east before dipping down to the main house (called Main House, to avoid confusion). Still used frequently by the Palmer family who have owned the island since 1968, it's a sumptuous Art Deco construction. Commissioned around 1935 by Kathleen Laurence, daughter of newspaper baron Edward Iliffe (who was also an actual baron), it was skilfully designed by architect Sir Edward Maufe, who three years previously had knocked up Guildford Cathedral. The house resembles an ocean liner, and at night, with its lights blazing through the windows, it must have fooled many a sleepy sailor. The conductor Sir Thomas Beecham visited the island several times in the 1950s and found the atmosphere at Main House so inspirational that he wrote his biography of the composer Frederick Delius there.

The island holds a couple of surprises outdoors too: its own little miniature colonies of peacocks and golden pheasants. By their mere existence, the latter must heap whole mountains of self-doubt upon the heads of the vain peacocks. With their bright yellow heads and backs, tiger-skin necks, scarlet bellies, satin blue and black wings, and long pebble-dash tails, they look as if they've just rolled around in a child's painting set. The island also lays claim to some free-range chickens, the occasional deer that swims over at particularly low tides, and a solitary grey squirrel who has lived the life of a hermit on Round Island for several years. Meanwhile, one or two common seals can be seen lurking about on the island's outer environs.

For those interested in befriending the seals and the squirrel, there's good news. David and Dawn, who have seen long service as caretakers of the island, are soon to retire. This opens up a vacancy for what David describes, now rather wistfully, as 'the best job in the world'.

How to get there

Hop on the train to Poole (southwesttrains. co.uk; 0845 6000 650), and from the bus station take the 152 (Damory Coaches; 01722 336855) to Lake. The island's caretaker will ferry you over to the island from the Lake Yard (lakeyard.com), assuming you've booked a stay on the island. Alternatively, sightseeing cruises from Poole Quay to Sandbanks that take in all the islands in Poole Harbour are run by Brownsea Island Ferries (adult £9, child £5.50; brownseaislandferries.com; 01929 462383).

Admission price/landing fee

Included in price of holiday let on the island.

View

Poole Harbour, including Poole, Long Island, Brownsea Island, Green Island and the oil derrick on Furzey Island.

Facilities

See Accommodation.

Accommodation

The island has **three cottages** and a **wooden chalet** (sleeping between 4 and 8; roundisland.co.uk; 01202 882885) to let. The cottages have their own wet rooms into which you can stagger from whatever waterborne pursuit has taken your fancy.

Nearest decent pub/café/tea room

The Club at the Lake Yard marina (lakeyard.com; 01202 676953) is open to non-members. They serve food and their bar and patio have views across Poole Harbour.

Nearest shop

There's a little parade of shops including a **Happy Shopper** at the southern end of Coles Avenue in Hamworthy (0.3 miles from the Lake Yard marina).

Rules

You have to book yourself into the accommodation here in order to visit.

Things to do

There are copious ways of interacting with the surface of Poole Harbour – windsurfing, wakeboarding, kitesurfing, waterskiing, kayaking, paddleboarding or plain old sailing. They're all possible at the **Watersports Academy** in Sandbanks (6 miles; thewatersportsacademy.com; 01202 708283).
Brownsea Island (nationaltrust.org.uk/brownsea-island; 01202 707744) is a natural wonderland and a rare southern hideout for red squirrels. Brownsea Island Ferries (brownseaislandferries.com; 01929 462383) sail there from Poole Quay (2 miles) and Sandbanks (6.5 miles).

Top: Golden pheasant – not a natural chameleon; Bottom: Round Island proving itself anything but

8. Burrow Island

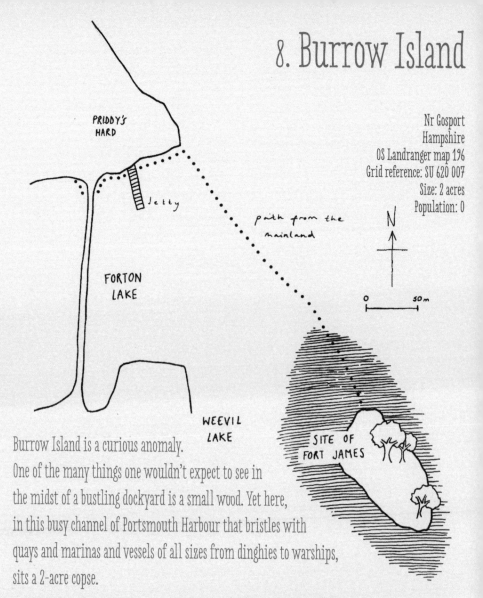

PRIDDY'S HARD

Jetty

FORTON LAKE

WEEVIL LAKE

path from the mainland

N

0   50m

SITE OF FORT JAMES

Nr Gosport
Hampshire
OS Landranger map 196
Grid reference: SU 620 007
Size: 2 acres
Population: 0

Burrow Island is a curious anomaly.
One of the many things one wouldn't expect to see in
the midst of a bustling dockyard is a small wood. Yet here,
in this busy channel of Portsmouth Harbour that bristles with
quays and marinas and vessels of all sizes from dinghies to warships,
sits a 2-acre copse.

One would imagine that such an oddity would have gained some sort of celebrity by now but it seems that for those who live or work around the harbour, the miniature forest has become such a part of the furniture that it goes unregarded. The walk out to the island is spectacularly unheralded too.

From Priddy's Hard on the edge of Gosport, visitors must work their way down to the harbour bed by the new Millennium Bridge, pass underneath it, skirt the harbour wall, attempting to avoid the worst of the glutinous grey mud around the edges of Forton Lake, and trudge across a shingle causeway.

Burrow Island at low tide with warning sign

The sludge at the water's edge is the domain of the ragworm and it's a common sight to see fishermen floundering about in waders digging for bait. Meanwhile, on the stony crest of the causeway beneath a gelatinous skin of seaweed, hide the remains of a narrow-gauge railway that used to run towards Burrow Island, stopping at a place called Burning Point. It's the first indication that this little tidal isle hasn't always enjoyed a peaceful existence.

For 200 years, Priddy's Hard was a major explosives depot for the navy and Burning Point is the spot where any that were no longer fit for purpose were destroyed. They would be soaked in diesel (this tempered the rate at which they burnt), then set alight. When the next tide came in, it would wash any detritus away. The effect of those tides has also caused the rails to slalom eccentrically about and no doubt someday they too will be washed away.

It was fear of the Dutch that brought Burrow Island to prominence. The first three of the four Anglo-Dutch Wars had occurred in quick succession between 1652 and 1674 and Charles II feared for the safety of his ports. He called on Sir Bernard de Gomme to design defences for Portsmouth and Gosport. For the latter, he proposed three strong fortifications – a battery on Blockhouse Point, and a stone-built tower on each of Gosport Quay and Burrow Island. The towers were completed in 1679 and became known as Charles Fort and James Fort respectively.

James Fort was the baby of the three, just 20ft high, surrounded by an earthwork parapet. It contained rooms for its small garrison and had around 20 cannons at its disposal, mounted on its roof and outer wall. Its main purpose was to ensure that the Dutch could not take the island and then use it as a base from which to bombard Gosport and the dockyard at Portsmouth. As it turned out, the Dutch made no attempt to do so and James Fort never fired a gun in anger.

Less than 40 years later it was reported as being in very poor shape and, as other defences around Portsmouth were strengthened, it became surplus to requirements and was left to moulder amongst the rodents who give the isle its alternative name, Rat Island. The ruins of James Fort were largely demolished in 1827 and sadly there's nothing left of it today of any significance, though if you're desperate to see something, there's a tiny bit of wall beneath the undergrowth on the eastern side of the island.

Nowadays, a few interlocking rough paths snake their way across the island through brambles and deciduous trees, predominantly hawthorns, with the odd periwinkle growing beneath. The brambles get in touch with their inner architect at one point, forming a dome-like tent. Meanwhile, in roughly the middle of the island stands a forlorn-looking gatepost without its partner. Nearby is a large metal box, a dump of discarded cables and a telegraph pole with a collection of inexplicable metal attachments at one end. It's hardly a treasure trove.

The joy of Burrow Island (the name, by the way, has nothing to do with rabbits but is probably a corruption of 'borough') comes from the novelty of being in the middle of a harbour, especially if you venture out along the exposed hooked spit at the southern end, although even amidst the island's dense thickets it's not possible to forget where you are. The wash from the smallest of tugs creates what seems an exaggerated noise on the eastern beach, as if the isle's sound effects department has left a fader up by mistake. When visibility is poor, a foghorn groans repeatedly like a beached whale cursing the world and all its doings. The tinny sound of broadcast voices drifts over from the naval base opposite, snatches of sentences suggesting nautical busyness: '...in the next one-zero minutes...', '...officers should report to the...' It's a reminder that Nelson's HMS *Victory* and Henry VIII's pride and joy, the *Mary Rose*, sit in dry dock right next door, the former enjoying a long retirement, the latter still dazed at having been hauled from her long sleep on the seabed.

Though the fort has disappeared, Burrow Island still boasts two structures of interest, though both are relatively modern. Rising above the canopy of the trees are a pair of huge warning signs declaring 'DANGER HIGH TENSION SUBMARINE CABLES' in large red letters. The cables they refer to can apparently be raised to prevent enemy submarines from penetrating the harbour

Clockwise from top left: Digging for bait; Burrow behind a forest of yacht masts; flotsam on the island's hooked spit

– for Burrow Island, for all its overgrown dereliction, still belongs to the Ministry of Defence. It may look like it's whistling a tune and innocently proclaiming 'I'm just an island with a scrubby wood on it', but in reality it's still preparing to resist an invasion. Just not so much from the Dutch these days.

How to get there

Take the train to Fareham station (southernrailway.com; 020 8185 0778, southwesttrains.co.uk, 023 8021 3605) then hail the E1 bus (firstgroup.com) to Hardway, from where it's a half-mile amble to the Millennium Bridge on the far side of Priddy's Hard. Alternatively, take the train to Portsmouth Harbour, then the ferry to Gosport (gosportferry.co.uk; 023 9252 4551) and stroll 1.2 miles to Priddy's Hard. The walk across to Burrow Island can be rather muddy, so come prepared. In summer, access may be possible for up to seven hours at low tide, in winter this drops to up to five hours.

Admission price/landing fee

Free.

View

The narrow entrance to Portsmouth harbour, including the Royal Clarence Marina, Shell Pier, various Royal Navy vessels and the Spinnaker Tower.

Facilities

None.

Accommodation

Make tracks for nearby Lee-on-the-Solent and the Art Deco **Milvil Corner** (4.5 miles; milvilcorner.co.uk; 023 9255 3489), a beautifully turned out B&B.

Nearest decent pub/café/tea room

Head for the dainty and much lauded **Pump House** coffee shop on Cooperage Green (which sadly is merely a large car park). There's also the warehouse-like **G's Wine Bar and Restaurant** (gsgosport. com; 023 9251 3202) in the Royal Clarence Marina opposite the island.

Nearest shop

Without being the most prosperous of places, **Gosport** (1 mile over the pedestrian Millennium Bridge) has many shops.

Rules

None.

Things to do

Explosion! (0.2 miles; open daily April to October and weekends November to March; explosion.org.uk; 023 9250 5600) is an award-winning museum of naval warfare housed in the Royal Navy's former armaments depot on Priddy's Hard. It also has a coffee shop.

9. Steep Holm

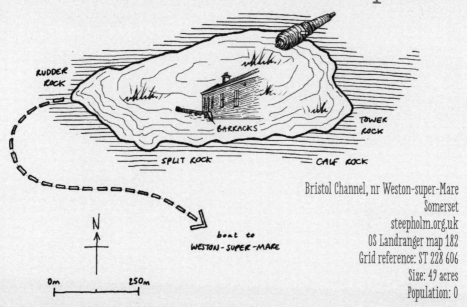

RUDDER ROCK

BARRACKS

TOWER ROCK

SPLIT ROCK

CALF ROCK

boat to WESTON-SUPER-MARE

N

0m   250m

Bristol Channel, nr Weston-super-Mare
Somerset
steepholm.org.uk
OS Landranger map 182
Grid reference: ST 228 606
Size: 49 acres
Population: 0

The notion that Steep Holm may play by different rules first enters the mind of the visitor before she or he has even set foot on the island. Viewed from the pier at Weston-super-Mare, neighbouring Flat Holm appears cheery and welcoming, if a little exposed. Steep Holm, in contrast, presents a bluff and forbidding demeanour, its sheer and scrubby cliffs bidding the seafarer, 'Move on – there's nothing to see here.'

Very often the island gets its way too – the 20 or so scheduled sailings each year across the 5 miles of salty brine from Weston are extremely susceptible to cancellation. The tides here are some of the most extreme on the planet – the difference between high and low water can be a staggering 47ft – and landings can only be made when the sea calms down sufficiently to allow them. Further complicating matters is the fact that boats can only dock here when the water is at its highest, so it requires consecutive tranquil high tides in daylight for day-trippers to get on and off the island. Back in 1985, a dozen tourists found themselves stranded on Steep Holm for four days when the sea turned rough unexpectedly, so unless the weather forecast is very good for the journey both out and back, the boat remains resolutely in its harbour.

It's a wonder that, way back in the 6th century, St Gildas managed to get here at all when he probably had only a coracle at his disposal. What is even more extraordinary is that he would sometimes leave the cell and oratory he built here in honour of the Blessed Trinity to paddle the two nautical miles over to his friend Cadoc on Flat Holm (p163). The currents between these islands are notoriously strong and one can't help wondering whether it was these perilous journeys that gave Gildas the idea for the Lorica, a prayer for deliverance from evil that he's credited with writing.

In the end it was not the vagaries of the sea or even the unrelenting toil involved in keeping body and soul together on Steep Holm that drove Gildas off after seven years, but the unwanted attentions of pirates from far-off Orkney. He packed up his few possessions and headed for Glastonbury, where he became the abbot and wrote *De Excidio et Conquestu Britanniae* ('On the Ruin and Conquest of Britain'), an excoriating attack on contemporary society (and now a significant source for historians researching 5th- and 6th-century Britain).

Back then, Steep Holm was known to Anglo-Saxons as Steópanreolice ('island of the bereaved' or possibly 'churchyard of the bereaved'), a name that strongly suggests the existence of a burial ground here once (and indeed some evidence of this has been uncovered). However, it wasn't until the 12th century that Augustinian monks founded a small priory on the island.

Sadly, a few low walls at the eastern end of Steep Holm are all that remain of their building work. Their legacy lives on in the rare plants they brought over with them for their 'physick garden'. The descendants of those first wild leek, henbane and caper spurge still flourish here among the golden Alexanders and the matted brambles, while the wild peony can be found nowhere else in Britain in the wild. Look in the vertical cracks in the cliffs and you might also spot a variety of buck's-horn plantain called *Plantago coronopus* that is unique to the island. Add colonies of gulls and cormorants, and the fact that some of Europe's largest slow-worms wriggle about here – having evolved differently from their cousins on the mainland – and it's no surprise that Steep Holm was designated a Site of Special Scientific Interest in 1952.

As you climb the 250ft up the steep zigzagging path to reach the island's overgrown summit plateau there's also a chance of a brief encounter with Steep Holm's largest wild mammal – the Reeve's muntjac. These labradors of the deer world are a relatively recent addition, having been introduced by an island warden in 1977. The path itself was created during World War II, when a railway line – much of which is still in situ – was laid to haul up materials for the construction of fortifications on the summit.

This constituted the second attempt to get the steel, concrete and military hardware up the hill. Improbably, the first time round the authorities had imported mules and their handlers from India. The precipitous inclines – between 1-in-3 and 1-in-2 – defeated the poor animals and so a narrow-gauge railway and diesel-powered winches were brought in. Ironically, the track and rolling stock were German, having been captured during World War I and held in storage in Salisbury.

These were by no means the only batteries ever stationed on Ynys Ronech (as Steep Holm is known in Welsh). The first half dozen were built as a result of the Napoleonic invasion scare of the 1860s (see Flat Holm, p163). Since the Victorian military planners had chosen their locations wisely, the same sites were employed during World War I and then again in World War II. Searchlight posts and even rocket launcher pads from the latter conflict are still in evidence today, as are subterranean munitions stores and nine of the cannons dating from the Napoleonic crisis, mercifully spared from the scrapyard by the inconvenience and expense of hauling them off to the mainland.

However, the most obvious manifestation of Steep Holm's military past is the former barracks which now houses an exhibition room that tells the island's story, and a café that ministers to any home-baked cake-based needs visitors may have. The wind-powered centre is run by the Kenneth Allsop Memorial Trust, which purchased the island in 1976. In keeping with the ideas of the late author, broadcaster and naturalist, the Trust has ensured that, despite lying so close to several large centres of population, the island has retained its distinct character.

With a little help from the Bristol Channel, that is.

How to get there

Take the train to Weston-super-Mare (firstgreatwestern.co.uk; 08457 000 125) from where it's a 15-minute walk to Knightstone Island (despite its name, it's firmly attached to the mainland) whence the boat leaves for Steep Holm (steepholm.org.uk; 01934 522125). There are usually about 20 sailings a year between the end of March and mid-September. It takes about an hour each way and most trips allow around 10 hours on the island. Sailings are at the mercy of often unfavourable sea conditions so ring after 7pm on the evening before you're due to visit to check that the trip has not been cancelled. The boat from Weston-super-Mare costs £25 for adults and £15 for children (5–16). Tickets must be booked in advance. NB: Do remember to take a torch in order to explore the underground munitions stores.

Admission price/landing fee

Free.

View

The summit commands a panorama of the Somerset coastline (including Brean Down and Weston-super-Mare), the Mendip and Quantock Hills, Flat Holm (p163), the two Severn bridges and the South Wales coast.

Facilities

Loos, exhibition room and a visitor centre (cash only) selling drinks, snacks, souvenirs and Steep Holm stamps.

One of the island's many elegantly wasted buildings

Accommodation

Weston-super-Mare is a holiday resort whose goblet of accommodation o'erfloweth. For B&Bs and hotels, swing by visitsomerset.co.uk. For a bit of camping with a difference, there's the **Uphill Boat Centre** (2 miles; uphillboatservices.co.uk; 01934 418617), where you can pitch up on the shores of a marine lake with a chandlery on tap.

Nearest decent pub/café/tea room

The island's **Victorian Barracks Visitor Centre** provides not only hot and cold drinks, but 'irresistible' home-made cakes, soup and snacks. It's also licensed.

Nearest shop

Weston-super-Mare is a large town with shops to fulfil your every need, while always leaving you feeling unfulfilled, but that's the retail experience for you.

Rules

No animals, metal detecting or barbecues. On the boat there's just one medium-sized bag allowed per passenger.

Things to do

Weston-super-Mare's **Grand Pier** (grandpier.co.uk; 01934 620238), built in 2010 after the previous one was destroyed by fire, is filled with all the usual amusements, only these are shinier, gaudier and with the volume turned up. **Weston Walks** (westonwalks.co.uk; 07903 278496) offer entertaining guided walking tours around the town featuring 'Weston Tales' during the day and 'Murder and Ghosts' in the evening. Both walks start on Royal Parade (the seafront road).

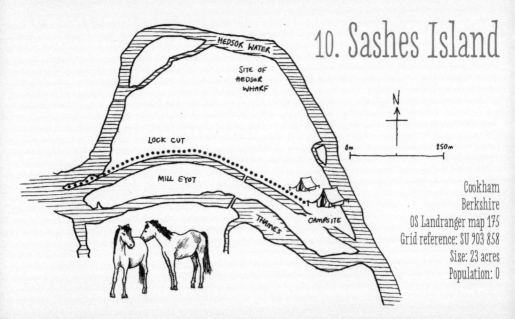

10. Sashes Island

HEDSOR WATER

SITE OF HEDSOR WHARF

LOCK CUT

MILL EYOT

THAMES

CAMPSITE

N

0m   250m

Cookham
Berkshire
OS Landranger map 175
Grid reference: SU 903 858
Size: 23 acres
Population: 0

For an isle that only took its current form as recently as 1829, the history of Sashes Island goes back a mighty long way. You'd never think it today. The flat triangle of land caught in a bend of a river chiefly comprises an unspectacular open field on which horses are kept.

A footpath runs down one side, sheltered by a row of mature trees that stretches down almost as far as the eastern tip of the island, where one of Britain's loveliest tiny campsites resides. A stream is said to run across the island but its course is only visible in aerial photographs, meaning that the island's most obviously noteworthy feature is that it holds up one side of Cookham Lock, but even this shows no great signs of antiquity. Come here out of season and your visit is likely to be a solitary one, unless you bump into Adam, the friendly lock-keeper. It's surprising to consider, therefore, that this was once an important place for both Romans and Saxons and the scene of a thriving trading

post from the 14th century until the coronation of Victoria.

To reach it requires some satisfying island hopping. First you must wander down a rustic lane out of the village of Cookham and cross a bridge spanning the gentle Lulle Brook to Formosa Island, so named by previous owner Admiral Sir George Young after the island (now called Taiwan) off which he served. A walk over Formosa's Odney Common brings you to the Thames, though it is so narrow that it's difficult to believe that this is truly the Old Father himself. A short hop across the river over the top of a weir lands you on the eel-like Mill Eyot, from where a graceful iron bridge takes you at last to Sashes Island.

The Lock Cut with Sashes Island on the left

Turn right here and the footpath leads to the lock and campsite. Turn left, however, and you are plunged into a mystery. At the narrow tip of the island closest to Cookham, the footpath, finding it has nowhere to go and no bridge to cross, comes to a peremptory end. [Those who wish to visit the island to solve the puzzle à la Sherlock Holmes should read no further.]

There are two clues to solving The Mystery of the Apparently Pointless Public Footpath. The first can be found at the end of the path near a crab apple tree: a stub of rusting metal post. The second can be seen on the opposite bank of the river: a pub. The latter is called the Ferry Inn, while the former is part of a winch post – the last remnant of the ferry that once carried bargemen and their horses from this towpath across the water to continue their journey up river. A ferry once operated at the other end of the island, where the campsite is today, but it ceased in 1956.

Neolithic and Bronze Age items have been found on or around Sashes Island, and during Roman times it became part of a major thoroughfare. A bridge across to the northern side of the isle carried the Camlet Way, the Roman road linking St Albans to Silchester, and there was possibly a port where part of the island has been sliced off by a narrow cut. Under Alfred the Great, the then Sceaftessige (the acrobatics this name had to go through over the centuries to become 'Sashes' would impress the harshest of Olympic judges)

became a fortified site, known as a *burh*, to ward against possible Danish attack. The Burghal Hiladge records the defences as being 4,125ft long (roughly 0.75 miles), so they were not insubstantial. The Danes certainly appear to have found their way here – the *Anglo-Saxon Chronicle* relates that after they were defeated at the battle of Farnham in AD894 by Alfred the Great's son Edward, they 'fled across the Thames where there is no ford, and up on the Colne onto an islet' called Thorney where they were besieged. Thorney means 'island of the stake' while Sceaftessige means 'island of the pole', so it's possible that this is the island referred to. Danish weaponry, including a winged axe and a spearhead, has been recovered here, adding credence to the claim.

Hedsor Water, which flows around two of the three sides of the island, was once the main route for Thames traffic. There was a busy wharf here for over 500 years that serviced Cookham, a community that possessed a paper mill of some significance. However, in 1829 a cut incorporating Cookham Lock (which opened the following year) was dug, scything off the bend in the river to improve navigation. Lord Boston, the owner of the Hedsor Wharf, sued for loss of trade, and sued again in 1837 when a weir was built that all but denied shipping access to Hedsor Water, effectively bringing activities at Hedsor Wharf to an end. He got his own back by building a fish weir at the lower end of Hedsor Water and claiming the newly blockaded river as his own property. Today, it's the only section of river that was once the main Thames channel to be in private hands.

Though unexceptional in appearance since the disappearance of the Saxon fortifications, the isle has still managed a couple of brushes with the arts. In *The Wind in the Willows*, Kenneth Grahame has Otter teaching his son Portly to swim at the ford near the old fort of Sashes Island; and Gilbert Spencer, Stanley's less celebrated brother, painted a more than passable landscape of the island.

Though just a few hundred yards from Cliveden – the magnificent, if somewhat notorious, stately home hidden behind the wooded Cliveden Cliffs – Sashes Island inhabits a tranquil world of its own. Beyond the leisurely phut-phutting of pleasure cruisers passing in and out of the lock, the occasional neighing of a horse, or the chatter of campers as evening falls, nothing much happens here, and it is a state with which it appears to be profoundly content.

How to get there

From the railway station at Cookham (firstgreatwestern.co.uk; 08457 000 125) it's a 0.75-mile walk to Cookham village. Once there, stroll down Odney Lane and over a weir to Cookham Lock Island and across a bridge to Sashes Island. The gate over the weir opens at 9am from April to October (9.15am all other months) and closes at 5pm (April and October), 6pm (May to June and September), 7pm (July to August) or 4pm (all other months).

Admission price/landing fee

Free.

View

Cliveden Cliffs, Cookham Lock Island, the far banks of the Thames.

Facilities

On Cookham Lock Island there is a loo for lock users and campers that you can ask to use.

Accommodation

Sashes Island has its own campsite (tinyurl.com/99d6s6u; 01628 520752) run by the Environment Agency. To find such a winsome one so close to London is a rare and wondrous thing, so you really should take advantage of it. However, if camping isn't your thing, then there's **Wylie Cottage** B&B in Cookham (0.8 miles; 01628 520106).

Nearest decent pub/café/tea room

Cookham's **Bel and the Dragon** (0.5 miles; belandthedragon.co.uk; 01628 521263) is one of the few gastropubs in England to be named after a book of the Bible accepted as canonical by Catholic and Orthodox believers but not by Protestants. Meanwhile, 2 miles west along the Thames Path, there's **The Bounty** (open daily except October to Easter when only open at weekends; 01628 520056) – a maverick drinking hole with no access by road.

Nearest shop

Barnside Motors (0.75 miles; 01628 525555) in Cookham is a very small news-tob-con. **Countrystore**, opposite Cookham station (2 miles; 01628 522161), is a better stocked mini-supermarket.

Rules

Dogs must be kept under control. Children to be kept away from the lock side.

Things to do

The wonderful **Stanley Spencer Gallery** (0.5 miles; stanleyspencer.org.uk; 01628 471885) in Cookham is a showcase for the much-loved local artist.
The 375-acre estate at **Cliveden** (3 miles; nationaltrust.org.uk/cliveden; 01628 605069), the magnificent Italianate stately home once owned by Nancy Astor, includes a yew maze, woodland and a colourfully planted parterre.
You can explore the Thames from nearby Maidenhead in a **Canadian canoe** (2.5 miles; thamescanoehire.co.uk; 0787 484 9120).

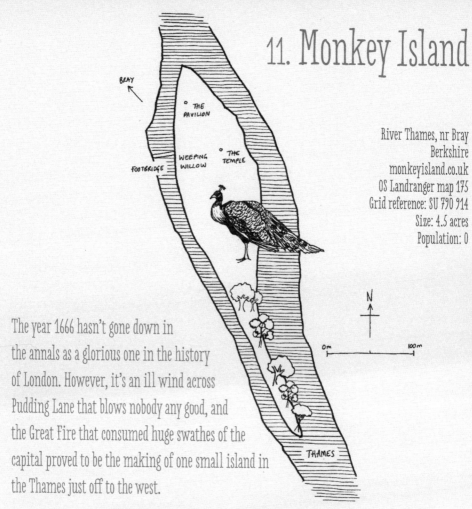

11. Monkey Island

BRAY

THE PAVILION

WEEPING WILLOW

THE TEMPLE

FOOTBRIDGE

THAMES

N

0m   100m

River Thames, nr Bray
Berkshire
monkeyisland.co.uk
OS Landranger map 175
Grid reference: SU 790 914
Size: 4.5 acres
Population: 0

The year 1666 hasn't gone down in the annals as a glorious one in the history of London. However, it's an ill wind across Pudding Lane that blows nobody any good, and the Great Fire that consumed huge swathes of the capital proved to be the making of one small island in the Thames just off to the west.

In the aftermath of the conflagration, Berkshire stone was transported to London to help in the great rebuilding project. It was taken down from the quarries on barges past Monkey Island to the city. When the boats returned they were filled with rubble and spoil that had to be dumped somewhere.

One of the many Thames islands to receive this little bit of scorched and broken London was Monkey Island, which, at a single stroke, was raised comfortably above the river and supplied with the foundations on which building could commence.

That's not to say that the island was immediately snapped up by property developers. It was to be another 57 years before Charles Spencer, the Third Duke of Marlborough, bought the island after chancing upon it while attending nearby meetings of the shady Kit-Cat Club, and began dreaming up the follies he would place on it.

Crossing via the graceful arc of the narrow footbridge – built in 1949 so that the then owner's pregnant wife could reach the island safely – today's visitor is met by a prospect of calm, rather formalised serenity. Beyond the effusive welcome of the enormous weeping willow, beyond the well-tended lawns grazed by peacocks and Canada geese, beyond the gardeners patiently watering the ornamental shrubberies, stand two equally effulgent but very different Palladian buildings, each in their own separate space and each exuding a sense of timeless solidity. If Spencer were to return today he would doubtless recognise the scene, though he might be somewhat surprised that his small private buildings have grown into a sizeable hotel.

Back in the 1740s he employed a pair of architects to create two decadent fantasies – a fishing lodge and a fishing temple. The lodge – now known as the Pavilion – was a structure that cleverly used wooden blocks cut to resemble stone. It's still fooling the eye today. The building had just two rooms: a kitchen and a parlour. The latter became known as the Monkey Room after Spencer commissioned French artist Andien de Clermont to paint the walls and ceiling with depictions of our primate friends clothed as humans and fishing, shooting, hunting, smoking, optimistically hurling tiny harpoons at vast whales, and generally living the life of the country gentleman in the reign of George III. The room can still be viewed today but is now part of a much larger edifice housing the Monkey Island Hotel's conference facilities, bar and restaurant.

De Clermont's murals are often mistakenly believed by visitors to have lent the island its name. However, that distinction goes back a long way before he brought his Gallic brushes to Berkshire. Back in the late 12th century, monks from Merton Priory at Bray Lock used to fish from the island, and at low tides it's still just about possible to make out the edge of their fishing ponds. The island was thus called Monks' Eyot – 'eyot' being one of several names used to denote islands in the Thames – from which it's a short step to 'Monkey'. Not that it was quite as simple as that. In between times the isle became known as Bournhames Eyte and Burnham Ayt (two further designations for 'island') after the Burnham Abbey, whose canonesses came into possession of the island in the 14th century.

The Monkey Room has, however, spawned an unhealthy amount of monkey-based activity on the island – or at least rumours of same. George III was sent here during his more extreme episodes of insanity and is said to have brought his pet monkey along with him. Much more recently, a monkey called Jacko was chained to a walnut tree on the island as a stunt to publicise the hotel. He escaped and, quite rightly, took out his vengeance on the people of Bray.

The Temple – the other of Spencer's little angling follies – had less of an influence on the island's future. Originally open to the elements on the ground floor, it had a billiard room above with a ceiling adorned with plasterwork on a sky-blue background

in the Wedgwood style depicting King Neptune and various mermaids. Today it is the jewel among the hotel's 26 rooms and suites, and comes complete with a super-king-size four-poster bed.

The hotel, while never achieving quite the splash of The Karsino on Tagg's Island (p77) further downstream – doubtless the owners would have viewed the upstart as somewhat vulgar – has snared its fair share of famous admirers. Edward VII and Queen Alexandra took tea on the lawns with their children and grandchildren (including the future George V, Edward VIII and George VI). Edward Elgar visited many times while composing his Violin Concerto in B Minor across the river at a house called The Hut. Dames Nellie Melba and Clara Butt both sang to guests here, while H.G. Wells would row up from his uncle's pub in Windsor to meet Rebecca West, with whom he later had a son. West found the atmosphere magical, and Monkey Island forms the setting for a great deal of her first novel *The Return of the Soldier*.

The island that stole her heart is a quarter of a mile long and indisputably tadpole-shaped. South of the hotel, the lawns give way to pleasant greenswards dotted with lamp posts and ever-thickening copses that eventually taper to a point at the tip of the tail. The tranquillity of the setting is only tarnished at the northern end of the isle where the sight and sound of the M4 crossing the Thames 300-odd yards away reminds one of the wearisome world outside.

According to Miranda Vickers in her book *Eyots and Aits*, in 1991 the wrongly jailed IRA pub bomb suspects, the Birmingham Six, were whisked away from the cameras to spend the first night of their newly found freedom here. No doubt the authorities believed that having made monkeys of them for 16 long years, the ex-prisoners would feel at home in a hotel with a similarly simian past.

How to get there

Take the train to Maidenhead station (firstgreatwestern.co.uk; 08457 000 125), followed by bus 6 (courtneybuses.com; 0118 973 3486) to the village of Bray (alighting at the village hall), from where it's a mile to Monkey Island, with access via a footbridge.

Admission price/landing fee

Free.

View

Exclusive houses with big gardens on both banks of the Thames, and the bridge carrying the M4 over the river.

Facilities

A bar and restaurant open to non-residents.

Accommodation

You can stay on the island by checking in at the **Monkey Island Hotel** (monkeyisland.co.uk; 01628 623400). Though the Wedgwood Suite, which was once part of the Duke of Marlborough's fishing temple, will set you back a pretty penny, the standard rooms are more reasonably priced.

The narrow bridge across to the island

Nearest decent pub/café/tea room

Bray, of course, is the foodie capital of Britain, but if you don't have the dosh for a slap-up meal at **The Fat Duck** or **The Waterside Inn**, the **Monkey Island Hotel** (see 'Accommodation') has a restaurant with patio that is open to non-residents.

Nearest shop

Depending on your definition of reasonable, there's a reasonably sized **Londis** (1.5 miles; 01628 780302) on the Bray Road up towards Maidenhead.

Rules

None.

Things to do

Canoe and Kayak Tours (4 miles; canoeandkayaktours.co.uk; 07585 907734) will lead you on a paddling tour of the local Thames landmarks, including Windsor Castle. If hip, hop and happening contemporary arts and culture are more your thing, or you like to pretend that they are, breeze by Windsor's **The Firestation** (4 miles; firestationartscentre.com; 01753 866865).

12. Tagg's Island

River Thames, nr Hampton
Middlesex
taggs-island.com
OS Landranger map 176
Grid reference: TQ 146 690
Size: 5 acres
Population: Just over 100

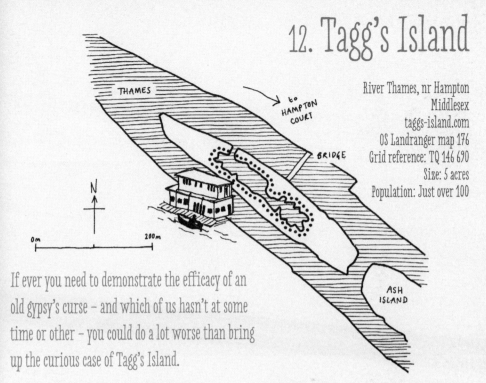

THAMES

to HAMPTON COURT

BRIDGE

ASH ISLAND

N

0m   200m

If ever you need to demonstrate the efficacy of an old gypsy's curse – and which of us hasn't at some time or other – you could do a lot worse than bring up the curious case of Tagg's Island.

A teardrop in the Thames between the East Molesey Cricket Club on the Surrey side and Bushy Park on the Middlesex side, Tagg's Island lived through an extraordinary 125-year period. It began in 1850, when Francis Kent bought the island and evicted a group of basket makers who were squatting it. According to local tradition, some of those he turfed off were gypsies. They are said to have laid a curse on both him and the island, declaring that no one who had anything to do with either of them would prosper.

The curse (we'll assume for the moment that there was one, and that it had some sort of inexplicable supernatural power to undermine human endeavour) claimed a good many scalps, but the most celebrated of all was that of Frederick Westcott, better known by his stage name, Fred Karno.

Karno was a successful entertainer and producer of music hall shows – his Fred Karno's Circus included artistes such as Charlie Chaplin, Stan Laurel, Max Miller, and Flanagan and Allen. He bought the lease to Tagg's Island in 1911 and two years later created The Karsino, feted as 'the finest and most luxurious River Hotel in Europe'. A massive building combining continental chic and clumsy kitsch in equal measure, it boasted a huge ballroom and no-expense-spared interiors that hoovered in the well-heeled and the celebrities of the day – frequent visitors included King Manuel II of Portugal and the Duchess of Albany. Karno became exceedingly rich, although he paid his musicians and entertainers so poorly that at one point they went on strike.

The huge early success of The Karsino was blunted abruptly by the outbreak of World War I, which deprived it of a huge swathe of its clientele. Though losing money, Karno kept the hotel open until successive inclement summers forced him into bankruptcy in 1925. The Karsino was finally pulled down in March 1971 (there's an affecting video of the event on the Tagg's Island website).

Karno's legacy has not been entirely lost, however. *Astoria*, the ludicrously luxurious houseboat he built himself, is moored close by. Charlie Chaplin is said to have had his first audition on the boat, which was bought by Pink Floyd's Dave Gilmour in 1986 and converted into a recording studio.

Fred Karno was by no means the only man to be brought low by Tagg's Island.

The litany of disasters begins with Joseph Harvey, who rented part of the island from Francis Kent in 1852. Ten years later, his pub, the Island Hotel, went bust. In 1868, a young man called Thomas Tagg – after whom the island is named – spent long years constructing and renting out houseboats, one of which was lived in by *Peter Pan* author J.M. Barrie. With the eventual building of a swish hotel, he turned the island into a resort that, like The Karsino that was to follow, attracted the cream of society. Tagg was the only man in the island's history to die while still on top – the curse causing his sudden death from a mere cold at the age of 57. His son George took over but was soon undone by three harsh blows: a devastating flood, the outbreak of the Boer War and the death

Houseboats on Tagg's Island

of Queen Victoria, the latter two events casting the nation into a mournful attitude that made engaging in frivolous revelries not the done thing.

Karno was the next lamb to the slaughter, succeeded by Beaumont Alexander in 1926. He tweaked the name of the hotel to The Casino, dotted the island with palm trees and found himself penniless within two years. Herbert Cyril immediately took the reins, made the island even more popular than in the early days of Karno, and was bankrupt inside six months. In 1930 the curse, now running riot, brought the island's next entrepreneur, A.E. Bundy, to his knees a mere six weeks after he had re-opened The Casino as the Thames Riviera (now with its own skating rink and indoor tennis courts).

World War II saw the arrival of AC Cars. They built the first known bridge to the island and converted part of the complex into a munitions factory. After the war, the plant turned out the famous sky-blue three-wheeler invalid cars that scooted around the nation's roads into the 1980s. Clearly the curse was not effective against enterprises with an altruistic slant.

A Mr J Rennie was the next owner in 1956. He was a man with big plans for the island, all of which were rejected by the local council. Amid legal wrangling with a man to whom he tried to sell the isle nine years later, the bridge collapsed. Leon Bronesky, the next man to put his head above the parapet, obtained permission to throw up a luxury hotel in place of Karno's

now dilapidated Karsino/Casino/Thames Riviera. Although he pulled down the old hotel, that was as far as his plans got and in 1975 he became yet another attendee at the bankruptcy courts.

Tagg's Island became a wilderness until Gerry and Gillian Braban came along in 1980. They bought the freehold, cleared the island of the vast accumulated debris, dug the picturesque lagoon that still surprises visitors today, and built a new bridge wide enough to admit motor vehicles.

There are now 62 houseboats (some of them two storeys high) on Tagg's Island, 20 of which sit in the lagoon. Two photographers live here but the likelihood of a Bohemian community of struggling artists forming about them is slim: such is

Rowers gliding around the island's somnolent back channel

the desirability of the locale that, in 2012, the asking price for one particular single-decker houseboat was £725,000.

Tagg's Island (shamefully, the apostrophe is often left out nowadays) – previously known as Garrick's Lower Eyot and Walnut Tree Island – is not the first isle to fall under a curse. Samson (p24), for instance, has been similarly jinxed. However, as long as there are no plans to build a huge hotel here in a bid to pull in supermodels, Premiership footballers and Russian oligarchs, the residents of Tagg's Island can sleep soundly in the knowledge that the curse has been laid to rest.

How to get there

Take the train to either Hampton Court station (0.75 miles) or Hampton station (1 mile – both southwesttrains.co.uk; 0870 906 6649). Tagg's Island is accessible across a bridge from Hampton Court Road.

Admission price/landing fee

Free.

View

Bushy Park, East Molesey Cricket Club and the banks of the Thames.

Facilities

None. Non-patrons are allowed to use the loos in The Bell Inn (0.5 miles) on Thames Street, Hampton.

Accommodation

You can stay on the island at the two-storey **Houseboat Riverine** (feedtheducks.com; 020 8979 2266), which has three rooms overlooking the Thames, one with its own balcony.

Nearest decent pub/café/tea room

There's not a surfeit of great places to eat and drink in the area, but there's a handful of pubs in Hampton including **The Bell Inn** (0.5 miles; thebellinnhampton.co.uk; 020 8941 9799). There are also a couple of cafés in **Hampton Court Palace** (see 'Things to do').

Nearest shop

St John's Superstore (0.8 miles; 020 8979 5887) in Hampton has an adequate selection of food and drink, even if it's not quite as super as the name suggests.

Rules

It's a privately owned island, so be especially nice to everyone on it.

Things to do

Hampton Court Palace (0.7 miles; hrp.org.uk/HamptonCourtPalace; 0844 482 7777) is deservedly considered to be one of Britain's great historical treasures. Henry VIII's former residence has some wonderful gardens and a maze too.

If you fancy chugging around Tagg's Island or some of the other aits and eyots along the Thames, there are little motorboats and covered day boats for hire at **Hampton Ferry Boathouse** (0.25 miles; hamptonferryboathouse.co.uk; 020 8979 7471).

13. Eel Pie Island

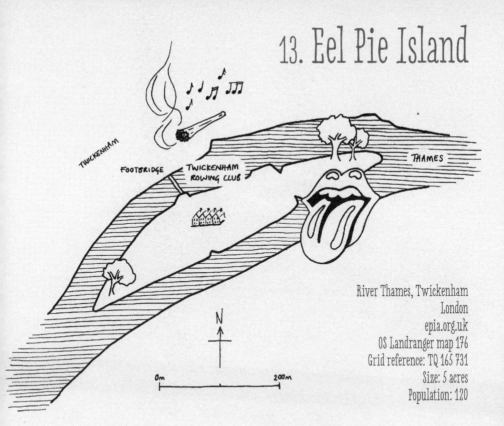

TWICKENHAM
FOOTBRIDGE
TWICKENHAM ROWING CLUB
THAMES
N
0m   200m

River Thames, Twickenham
London
epia.org.uk
OS Landranger map 176
Grid reference: TQ 165 731
Size: 5 acres
Population: 120

What Mick Jagger sang is true: you can't always get what you want. However, for two whole decades, Eel Pie Island got so much of what it wanted it would be startlingly greedy if it ever asked for anything else ever again.

When local antiques dealer Michael Snapper bought the Eel Pie Hotel in 1951, it's unlikely he could have dreamt what a seminal impact it would have on the British music scene. The roster of musicians who performed on the 5-acre Eel Pie Island includes a vast array of luminaries, many of whom were unknowns when they played their early tentative gigs here.

Teaming up with Arthur Chisnall to form Eel Pie Entertainments, Snapper's hotel became a magnet for young fans of jazz and skiffle drawn to hear acts such as George Melly, Acker Bilk, The Temperance Seven, Lonnie Donegan and the late great Ivor Cutler. Chisnall established the Eelpiland Jazz Club in 1956, issuing its members with cards that resembled passports – a declaration, if one were needed, that Eel Pie was truly a place apart. Indeed, up until the following year, when the island's first-ever bridge linked it with the Twickenham bank of the Thames, the only way musicians and devotees could get

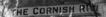

over to the island was by a punt hauled on a chain, for which the fare was 2d.

As the 1950s gave way to the 60s, so jazz and skiffle made way for music with a slightly harder edge and a more rebellious message. The island provided early audiences for Pink Floyd, Long John Baldry and his Hoochie Coochie Men (featuring Rod Stewart, whom Baldry had famously spotted playing harmonica outside Twickenham station), The Tridents (featuring Jeff Beck), ska and reggae star Jimmy Cliff, The Moody Blues, The Yardbirds and John Mayall's Bluesbreakers (featuring Eric Clapton). It also saw the first-ever performance by a band called Davie Jones and the Manish Boys. The then teenage Jones was to find fame after changing his surname to Bowie. However, the band most associated with the island is the Rolling Stones. In 1963, they had a residency at Eelpiland that often saw them playing to crowds so large they poured off the island and across the bridge.

Unlike the establishments further up the Thames on Tagg's Island (p77) and Monkey Island (p72), the Eel Pie Hotel was not a luxurious set-up aimed at the wealthy. On the contrary, it revelled in its advanced state of decay and was a place where there were apparently no rules – a state of affairs that naturally attracted the youth of the day. It also fostered a culture of drug taking, under-age drinking and a less buttoned-up attitude to sexual mores than existed among 'the squares'. Eventually, the police demanded the closure of the

hotel – citing safety grounds – unless substantial repairs were made. Unable to meet the astronomical costs involved, on 4 September 1967 Snapper was forced to shut up shop.

In 1969 the music venue was reborn as Colonel Barefoot's Rock Garden. Yet another slew of bands with household names graced the stage, including The Who, Black Sabbath, Led Zeppelin, Deep Purple, Hawkwind and, for good or ill, Genesis. However, by this time, the hotel had been thoroughly taken over by squatters and in the winter of 1970/71 the residents began pulling the hotel building apart for use as firewood. Four weeks after Snapper had made a planning application to replace the hotel with housing, it burnt down in circumstances that it is perhaps best not to delve into too deeply.

Today, some of the island's 57 varied properties occupy the site of the hotel. Non-islanders are lucky to see much of them though, since the island is screened by tall mature trees and its only thoroughfare is a relatively short alleyway between high walls and hedges that leads to the Twickenham Rowing Club and ends at a boat repair yard.

Thus by far the best time to visit the island is on one of its occasional open days, when the 26 artists who now reside here open the doors of their studios to all comers. If you're lucky you might also bump into island resident Trevor Baylis, who invented his famous wind-up radio here.

Eel Pie has been inhabited – mostly by lesser luminaries – for thousands of years. A prehistoric causeway once linked what was then a group of three islands to the northern bank of the river. The three had become two by the mid-18th century, by which time they were treated as one and known as Eel Pie Island after the delicacy that was served here. Before then the islands were known as Twickenham Ait, then Parish Ait and later Osier Ait – 'ait' being one of the words used to denote an island on the Thames ('eyot' and 'ayte'

being two other common variations). 'Osier' is a reference to the reeds that used to grow here and which were used for basket making. Fittingly, although the reeds are no more, the island retains two nature reserves, one at each end.

The Eel Pie Hotel made its entrance in 1830, replacing an earlier inn called The White Cross. It seems it was always destined to play a significant part in the shaping of the nation's musical tastes since within its first decade it had already garnered a reputation as a place to seek

out the terpsichorean muse. In Charles Dickens' 1839 novel *Nicholas Nickleby*, Miss Morleena Kenwigs receives an invitation to 'Eel Pie Island at Twickenham...to dance in the open air to the music of a locomotive band conveyed thither for the purpose...'

The island's musical legacy is by no means over. It perpetuates just a few hundred yards away at Twickenham's Cabbage Patch pub whose Eel Pie Club hosts live rhythm and blues nights. There may not be so much in the way of sex and drugs, but the rock and roll lives on.

How to get there
From Twickenham railway station (southwesttrains.co.uk, 023 8021 3605) it's less than half a mile through the town to the footbridge over to Eel Pie Island. For the full Eel Pie experience, go on one of the biannual open weekends (usually June and December) when you can visit the island's 26 artists' studios (eelpieislandartists. co.uk).

Admission price/landing fee
Free.

View
The posh houses and trees of the Twickenham river front.

Facilities
None.

Accommodation
Tucked away in a quiet cul-de-sac is the **Wright Residence** (0.8 miles; thewrightresidence.co.uk; 020 8894 1055) whose one room opens onto a rather nice patio.

Nearest decent pub/café/tea room
The Barmy Arms (0.1 miles; tinyurl.com/ bmnwlf9; 020 8892 0863) has a beer garden that looks onto Eel Pie Island. There are myriad other pubs (including one called The Eel Pie), bars, restaurants and cafés in Twickenham.

Nearest shop
The all-too-numerous shops of **Twickenham** are a two-minute walk away.

Rules
No cycling.

Things to do
Learn to row at **Twickenham Rowing Club** (twickenhamrc.co.uk; 020 8892 5291), which is based on Eel Pie Island and offers coaching to children and adults, from absolute beginners upwards.

If that sounds rather too aerobic, you can instead brush up on your creative skills with one of the island's artists, **Lee Campbell** (leecampbell.co.uk; 07900 242997), who teaches drawing, oil painting and watercolour work from her studio.

Meanwhile, the **Twickenham Museum** (0.1 miles; free; twickenham-museum.org. uk; 020 8408 0070) is a veritable trove of local history.

14. Northey Island

River Blackwater,
Nr Maldon, Essex
northeyisland.co.uk
OS Landranger map 168
Grid reference: TL 880 061
Size: 300 acres
Population: 2

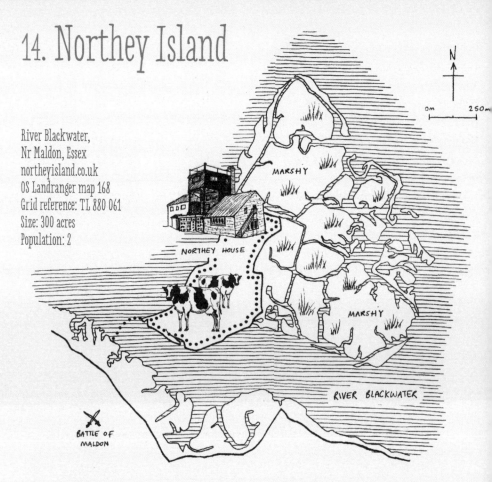

Walk across the short causeway to Northey Island and you're travelling over a strip of land that has arguably had a greater and longer lasting impact on the history of Britain than almost any other portion of the nation.

Furthermore, when it comes to the act of misguided chivalry that took place here, it would be difficult to find a rival that had given rise to such disastrous consequences. None of this, however, could be guessed at on arriving at the scene today. Less than 2 miles out from the fishermen's cottages and weatherboarded terraces of Maldon, Northey Island is a low, marshy,

unprepossessing place speckled with trees. Apparently protected by an encircling grassy embankment, closer inspection reveals that this is breached in numerous places. Stone Age flints have been found here but the ancient inhabitants who chipped them into being have left no discernable mark on the landscape. The narrow causeway – probably built by the

Romans – is just a few hundred yards long, threading itself out across marshland and then over the deep black mud of the riverbed, which, when the sun is out, shines like molten jet. As you cross over to Northey, take note of the slenderness of the causeway, for this detail plays a great part in the events that unravelled here.

It was in the year AD991 that a Viking fleet of 93 ships led by Olaf Tryggvason sailed up the Blackwater and landed on Northey Island, apparently having mistaken it for the mainland in the mist. Warned of the invasion, a small militia was hastily assembled by a local Saxon ealdor called Byrhtnoth (a man who presumably spent his entire life repeating, 'That's with an h-t, not a t-h. No, the one at the end is t-h, but the one before it is h-t. Look, it's all very simple, it's B-y-r-h-t- etc.'). Tryggvason shouted over to Byrhtnoth – a man in his sixties – that he and his horde would go away if they were given gold, an offer the ealdor rejected. Both sides then patiently waited for the tide to go out so that they could settle the matter by force of arms.

Not having read their *Horatio at the Bridge*, the Vikings were surprised to find that the extreme narrowness of the causeway meant that a mere three of Byrhtnoth's soldiers – Wulfstan, Aelfere and Maccus – were able to hold back their 3,000-strong army.

Knowing his adversary was English, Tryggvason whined to him that having his troops cooped up on the island was 'simply not cricket', or words to that effect.

Byrhtnoth, chivalrous to a fault, agreed. He fatally allowed the Vikings to come across the causeway unmolested so that the opposing forces might fight on equal terms on an adjacent field, somehow forgetting that his band of peasant warriors was rather seriously outnumbered. The Vikings thanked their hosts, before taking great care to butcher them almost to a man, no doubt all the while laughing pitilessly in a deeply foreign, not altogether decent sort of way. According to an epic poem about the battle written four years later by an anonymous hand, Byrhtnoth himself was killed (pierced by a poisoned Viking spear) before being hacked to pieces.

So began that inglorious chapter of Anglo-Saxon history that saw the country bled dry by the payment of Danegeld. Naturally enough, each time the hapless king – take a bow, Æthelred II (the Unready) – paid the Danes off with boatloads of money (the initial payment in 991 was an eye-watering 3,300kg of silver), he found that they returned not long afterwards to ask for more. Then the Swedes got in on the act and proved themselves even more adroit at it than the Danes. Indeed, such was the success of the extortion racket that archaeologists have excavated more English coinage from this period in Sweden than in England.

However, it needn't have been that way at all. Had Byrhtnoth instead kept Tryggvason's forces cooped up on Northey Island until an army large enough to defeat it had been assembled – thus avoiding

the need for England to attempt to buy its way out of trouble – the nation may not have found itself visited 75 years later by Harald Hardrada of Norway. Hardrada thought to go one better than his Nordic cousins: rather than extort money out of the English, he rather cheekily aspired to their throne.

Now, if he hadn't landed in 1066, King Harold would not have had to speed his soldiers from London to Yorkshire to defeat him at Stamford Bridge on 25 September. Consequently, the English king's army would not have been so exhausted and depleted in numbers when, just 19 days and a heroic 240-mile southward march later, it had to face the Duke of Normandy's invaders near Hastings. Since, even under these circumstances, Harold's forces came close to winning the battle, it's not stretching credibility to claim that at full strength they would have done so.

Nowadays, the island is in the hands of the National Trust, which took over its stewardship after the death of former owner and Nobel Peace Prize winner Sir Norman Angell. Aside from a bird hide, the house he constructed here to his own design is the only building on the island, an earlier farmhouse and barn having been destroyed in an air raid in World War II. Angell claimed that the Nazis were out to get him personally but it's more likely that the bombs were released by a plane heading for home and keen to empty itself of its payload before crossing the Channel.

The tidal creeks that feed the saltmarshes, and which reduce the island from 300 acres at low tide to a mere 80 at high spring tides, also provide habitats for overwintering birds. Northey is internationally important for its large numbers of Brent geese, shelduck and widgeon, making it an excellent spot for birdwatching, particularly in the colder months of the year.

While sitting in the island's hide waiting for the birds to show themselves, you might wish to fill your time speculating on the many ways Britain would have been a different country had Byrhtnoth decided not to be quite so accommodating to the Viking invaders.

Take the English language, for example. If Harold had not had to fight Hardrada and had thus beaten William (henceforth known as William the Vanquished), English would have far fewer of those sensuous Norman French words in it and would have continued to sound a lot more like German. That wouldn't have been a complete disaster, of course. However, any form of oral communication that can't come up with a better sound to convey the inherent bendiness of 'malleability' and 'pliable' (both derived from Old French) than 'schwank' is not one to imitate at will.

Moral? If you do the right thing, it pays off, albeit sometimes in a rather delayed fashion. This should comfort us all.

How to get there

From Witham railway station
(greateranglia.co.uk; 0845 600 7245)
take the 90 bus (stephensonsofessex.
com; 01702 541511) to Maldon and
walk just over a mile along the very
pleasant riverside footpath that begins in
Promenade Park. The island is accessible
across a causeway for between three and
eight hours at low tide, depending on the
size of the tide.

Admission price/landing fee

Free.

View

Across the mud to Maldon, Heybridge Basin
and the private holiday resort of Osea
Island.

Facilities

A loo on the outside of the warden's house;
a hide.

Accommodation

The island's **Northey House** (sleeps 10;
northeyisland.co.uk; 01279 722272),
former home of Sir Norman Angell, is now
a rather wonderful holiday cottage. It's
also possible to camp on Northey during
the annual Weekend Camping and Open
Day (last weekend of August; nationaltrust.
org.uk/northey-island; 0844 249 1895).
In Maldon, **The Hythe** (1.5 miles;
thehythemaldon.co.uk; 01621 859435)
has B&B rooms with views of the
Blackwater River.

Nearest decent pub/café/tea room

Maldon (1.5 miles) has a great many places
of refreshment including the **Oakhouse bar
and café** (oakhouse.co.uk; 01621 859965),
which is open from morn 'til night.

Nearest shop

There are a good many shops in **Maldon**
(1.5 miles) in which to fritter away your
hard-won cash.

Rules

To visit the island, a permit (which is free
of charge) is required from the resident
warden (ring 01621 853142 beforehand).

Things to do

Maldon's **Moot Hall** (1.5 miles;
themoothall.co.uk) is a 15th-century brick
building containing a venerable courtroom,
police cells and exercise yard. Guided
tours occur on Saturdays and occasional
other days.
New Hall Vineyards (3.5 miles;
newhallwines.co.uk) near Purleigh has
over 160 acres of vines and is one of the
oldest in the land (it was established in
the dark ages of 1969). It's open daily
for tastings and for walks along a
vineyard trail.

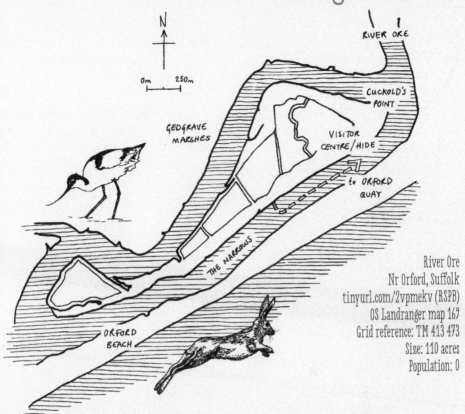

N

0m 250m

RIVER ORE

CUCKOLD'S POINT

GEDGRAVE MARSHES

VISITOR CENTRE/HIDE

to ORFORD QUAY

THE NARROWS

ORFORD BEACH

River Ore
Nr Orford, Suffolk
tinyurl.com/2vpmekv (RSPB)
OS Landranger map 169
Grid reference: TM 413 473
Size: 110 acres
Population: 0

In the year of 1947 a seminal event took place in the life of Havergate Island: eight avocet chicks were reared here. That may not seem such an extraordinary occurrence, but for the fact that avocets had abandoned Britain 100 years beforehand and had not been seen since.

The Royal Society for the Protection of Birds (RSPB) promptly snapped up the island the following year (brilliantly, the first warden was called Reg Partridge). Suffolk's only island (assuming you don't count the manmade ones on Thorpeness Meare (p96)) is a joy to visit, though its status as a bird sanctuary makes the joy a rare one, with boat trips strictly rationed. It's also in no danger of being mistaken for any other British island. For all that it's a river isle – squeezing itself into the narrow Ore – it feels distinctly as if it's off the coast, since it is separated from the sea only by Orford Ness's narrow strip of shingle, and is surrounded and often flooded by saltwater.

91

Furthermore, it only came into being some hundreds of years ago and has retained its sense of impermanence.

The quay from which the boat to Havergate sets sail provides a clue to the mystery of the island's relatively recent creation. This is the Orford Quay, once a substantial seaport, where ships were built that waged war for a succession of English monarchs and made Orford one of the most important towns in the land. Today it is a quiet and unassuming place on the River Ore. When Daniel Defoe visited in 1722, Orford was already so reduced in stature that he could describe it as 'once a good town but now decayed'. Orford Ness, the nemesis that brought about the town's downfall, is almost literally a stone's throw away. A bank of shingle that once made Orford a safe and valuable harbour stretched an arm 5 miles southwards, all but cutting the community off from the English Channel and, at the same time, moulding two marshy islands in the newly formed river. By the 16th century this pair had become one and Havergate Island – just under 2 miles long and half a mile in breadth at its very widest – came into being.

Landing at a long wooden jetty poking out into the river, visitors become aware immediately that much of the island is under water. A series of lagoons of varying brackishness takes up much of the northern half. These were partly created by the RSPB and are managed by a system of sluices to ensure the most favourable conditions for a variety of birds. Meanwhile, marshes and little artificial islets on the lagoons provide space for building nests.

As a result, Havergate Island has become *the* place to come to if you want to get your fill of avocets. The series of five hides – four in the east and a single lonely one in the west – allows visitors to watch not only avocets but a huge array of other feathered guests including curlew, terns, redshanks, gulls, turnstones, lapwings and plovers (including the beautiful golden plover). Spoonbills feed here, sweeping their extraordinary probosces from side to side in the shallows before flipping their heads skywards to swallow the stickleback or shrimp or whatever other doomed prey they've hoovered up from the mud.

It's not all waders and seabirds though. Barn owls are a common sight, plundering the grassland for voles and shrews, while wheatears arrive en masse in the spring and autumn.

Understandably, given its recent arrival on the planet, Havergate Island does not have much of a history prior to the coming of the RSPB. An embankment was built around it some 500 years ago to allow agriculture to take place, and there were farmers here eking out a living until the 1920s, when the island's cottage was finally abandoned. A short-lived experiment soon after to extract shingle proved a financial failure. Somewhat comically, the electric generator installed in the cottage (to power the buggies that took the shingle from the pits to the Thames barges) shook the

building to pieces. The foundations are all that remain, though nowadays there is a little cluster of wooden huts providing temporary accommodation for Kieren, the island's warden, and the volunteers who help keep the island in order.

Earlier visitors included smugglers, who found Havergate Island's isolation and proximity to the sea particularly advantageous, and made it a base for operations. In 1800, a local maidservant called Margaret Catchpole fell for one of these smugglers. Fell so badly indeed that she stole a horse and rode to London on his behalf, an offence for which she found herself on a ship bound for Australia. Inside the entrance to the Jolly Sailor pub in Orford you can see the poster offering a reward of £20 for her capture.

While there was much ado during World War II on Orford Ness – most of the radar that was used so effectively during the Battle of Britain and afterwards was developed there – Havergate Island has less of a distinguished military record. Although it was taken over by the War Office, it was neglected and became partially flooded.

Only when the RSPB stepped in were matters remedied. Through their work, Havergate Island has become a glorious place to watch birds. Perhaps more surprisingly, it has also become a glorious place to watch hares. With no natural predators (assuming they keep their newborn from the attentions of the barn owls) a thriving colony has developed among the gorse bushes towards the western end of the island. They show rather less fear of humans than their mainland cousins and allow visitors to come quite close. 'If the birds can find sanctuary here,' they seem to say, 'then so shall we.'

How to get there

The large village of Orford is surprisingly ill-served by buses. From Melton railway station (greateranglia.co.uk; 0845 600 7245), you could take the 165 bus to Rendlesham (angliancoaches.co.uk; 01502 711109) and then make your own way the last 7 miles, or jump straight in a taxi at Melton (10.5 miles). It's a lovely bike ride (and flat too) so the best option is to pop a bicycle on the train. Access to the island – an RSPB reserve – is strictly controlled. Boat trips run from Orford Quay on the first Saturday of most months of the year. Booking is essential (01728 648281). The boat fare is £15 per person (no discounts for children).

Admission price/landing fee
Free.

View
The low attempted hills of Suffolk, Orford's castle and church, and the myriad masts on Orford Ness.

Facilities
A compost loo, five bird hides and a small visitor centre.

Accommodation

Those with an interest in ornithology can stay for a week in one of the island's RSPB huts (first two weeks of every month from May to September; tinyurl.com/9x2zlsn; 01767 680551) acting as observers and doing other voluntary work around the island. Facilities are basic (there's no running water, for instance) but the rewards are plentiful.

Otherwise, in Orford there are swish rooms to be had at **The King's Head** (0.3 miles from Orford Quay; thekingsheadorford. co.uk; 01394 450271) and **The Crown & Castle** in the heart of the village (crownandcastle.co.uk; 01394 450205). Campers, meanwhile, should head for the tree-lined site at **High House Fruit Farm** (2 miles from Orford Quay; high-house. co.uk; 01394 450263).

Nearest decent pub/café/tea room

There's a little wooden chalet at Orford Quay called the **Riverside Tearoom** (01394 459797), while Orford (0.3 miles) offers a clutch of venerable pubs and the **Pump Street Bakery and Café** (pumpstreetbakery. com; 01394 459829), the 'Best Bakery in Suffolk' in 2011.

Nearest shop

Orford General Store (0.3 miles; orfordgeneralstore.com; 01394 450219) is a grocer's, deli and café all rolled into one.

Rules

No dogs allowed (except guide dogs).

Things to do

Orford Castle (0.4 miles; tinyurl. com/367aeoz; 01394 450472) is an impressive 12th-century polygonal tower built by Henry II, or at least by people working for him.

Orford Ness (0.1 miles) is an experimental weapons facility turned nature reserve, which, excitingly, is accessible only by ferry from Orford Quay (nationaltrust.org.uk/ orford-ness; 01728 648024).

Other river trips are available on *Regardless* (orfordrivertrips.co.uk; 07900 230579) and *Lady Florence* (lady-florence.co.uk; 07831 698298).

Looking across a lagoon to Orford Castle

16. Islands of Thorpeness Meare

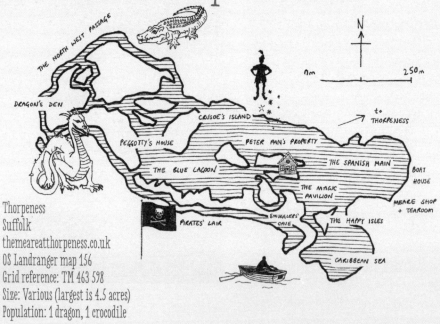

Thorpeness
Suffolk
themeareatthorpeness.co.uk
OS Landranger map 156
Grid reference: TM 463 598
Size: Various (largest is 4.5 acres)
Population: 1 dragon, 1 crocodile

While humans have been building their own islands – so-called crannogs (p168) – since prehistoric times, it's unusual, to say the least, for someone to go to the bother of creating an entirely new waterscape and then plop not just one but a whole host of brand new tiny islands upon it. Yet this is precisely what happened at a small fishing hamlet on the Suffolk coast just before the outbreak of World War I.

Graeme Kemp, in his book *Concerning Thorpeness*, published in 1924, recorded the revolution like this:

What was an expanse of dreary and sunburnt clay flats has been transformed, by the Imagination and Arts of Man, into a romantic Lake with wide stretches of open water, peculiarly adapted for sailing purposes, from which winding channels have been cut through acres of towering reeds, often taller than a man's full height, to secret backwaters and silent eyots overhung and hidden by the foliage of innumerable trees.

The man blessed with the Imagination and Arts was one Glencairn Stuart Ogilvie (understandably, he never used his first name). The fifth of six sons in a family of eight children, he quite reasonably never expected to inherit his parents' estate. However, due to various premature deaths and other catastrophes that visited themselves upon his older siblings, he found himself taking over the family fortune in 1908 on the death of his agéd mother. She and his father had bought just 2.5 acres of land and a little holiday home back in 1859, yet handed on to the 50-year-old Stuart a 6,000-acre demesne that included Sizewell Hall and a whole 7 miles of coastline.

The name G Stuart Ogilvie may be little known nowadays but by the time he came into the estate he was a hugely successful playwright, with one of his plays, a dramatisation of Charles Kingsley's *Hypatia*, breaking the record for the longest ever run on the London stage.

But Ogilvie had dreams far greater than those that could be fitted into a mere proscenium: he wanted to build an entire village. Calling it his 'model holiday village', it would be a place where those wanting to get away from city life but who also wished to avoid the tacky seaside resorts with their penny arcades and What the Butler Saw machines could buy themselves a little bolt hole. He wanted to build something for that most oppressed of people-groups in post-Edwardian England: the upper-middle classes.

In November 1910 he set up a company, Seaside Bungalows Ltd, and registered it in the Isle of Man, proving that the two certainties in life – death and the avoidance of taxes – have been with us for some time. The heart of Ogilvie's perfect holiday village was to be a mere. This was to be located on the 'dreary and sunburnt clay flats' just a few hundred yards from the sea. Sluice gates were built, banks were strengthened, the sporadically flooding River Hundred diverted, and the soggy mere (at that time written in lower case and without that peculiar extra 'a') was drained. The water took three whole weeks to leave – the summer's sunburnt clay clearly became a ghastly soggy mess come the winter. Now all that was needed was some manpower to dig the new Meare out.

Fifty unemployed Londoners were drafted in to shift the vast sea of muck, and a former children's convalescent home pressed into service to house them. They had a thoroughly unpleasant job to do, on top of which it was bitterly cold. Most were not suited to navvy work and soon begged to be allowed to go home. After just a week they were paid off and sent back whence they came, no doubt much relieved. After that, only local, less pressed men were employed – among them 16 fishermen whose oilskin sea-proof clothes were ideal for wading about in mud.

Ogilvie would direct operations from his roan horse, telling the men where the sludge should be moved to create islands, and making sure that the natural layer of blue-slipper clay was kept intact, for this would keep the water for his Meare from draining into the permeable sandy soil beneath. He also had thousands of willows

and alders planted on the islands, as well as oaks, holly and the odd poplar and conifer. When it was all done, the lake covered 62 acres of which around 20 acres were islands. Crucially, Ogilvie ensured that at no point was the Meare deeper than 2ft 6in. As Kemp observed: 'A child of six can safely walk across its length and breadth.'

Had that been the end of it, Ogilvie would have simply created an agreeable and safe boating lake. However, further inspiration was about to strike. One night in the winter of 1911 Thorpeness experienced a terrible sea storm that wreaked havoc on seafront houses and beach huts. In the morning, a friend of Ogilvie's called Alfred Alexander went in search of any booty that might have been washed ashore or unearthed on land by the seething waves and came across a hoard of 110 coins dating from the 17th century right back to Roman times.

Delighted by his friend's good fortune, Ogilvie suddenly formed the idea that children visiting his Meare, when it was finally filled, might enjoy the fun of a treasure hunt themselves. He began to place on the islands things that would thrill a child's heart when they found them – a Pirates' Lair here, a Smugglers' Cave there, a Dragon, a Crocodile – and all scaled down to a child's size. He asked his good friend J M Barrie if he could borrow some of the characters from *Peter Pan* (throwing in a sweetener by naming a Meare-side path 'Barrie's Walk') and so were born Wendy's House and Peter Pan's Property.

In 1912, with the Meare taking shape, Ogilvie sent Kemp (the master of works for the project as well as its biographer) to scour the country for secondhand rowing boats, sailing dinghies, canoes, punts and anything else that would float and could be hired out. Astonishingly, a century later, a lot of these early finds are still doing service, so when you launch yourself out on the Meare, you may well be in one of the very same craft that were used on the day it opened.

That day was 11 June 1913, when local dignitary Lord Huntingfield said a few words and cut the proverbial ribbon. Ogilvie's own speech ended with the hope that those present were 'assisting in the inauguration of what will, in a few brief years, have grown into one of the beauty spots in Suffolk and afford golden hours of happy, healthy recreation now and long after we and the words we speak today pass into the limbo of forgotten things'. The crowds then rushed for the boats. Back then, for a half crown you could even book an entire island for an afternoon for your exclusive use. Meanwhile, a popular old sea salt gave children their first sailing lessons. The Meare was an instant and overwhelming success. In 1925 Kemp wrote: '70 rowing and sailing boats, Thames punts, canoes and motor launches often proves all too small for the public request.'

The Meare was forced to close during World War II, when the estate was requisitioned by the army for training purposes. Fiona Gimson, a great-granddaughter of G. Stuart Ogilvie, remembers soldiers having to cross a monkey rope suspended over a section of the Meare. The challenge came at the end of an exhausting assault course and there were apparently a good many who ended up going for an unwitting dip.

A hundred years on from its opening, the Meare is not all that different from the one portrayed in early photographs and it's easy to imagine you have time-travelled to a distant, far more innocent age. Colourful wooden rowing boats with names such as *Sophie*, *Rose*, *Trixie*, *Pamela*, *Joyce* and (for some reason) *Alan* ply the Spanish Main, the Caribbean Sea and the North West Passage, their passengers calling out these names from the beautiful hand-drawn map given them by the boatman. The wonderful carefree mish-mash of fantasies means that Peggotty's boat-roofed house (after Clara

Peggotty, the gentle housekeeper in *David Copperfield*) is next to Crusoe's Island from where you cross the Blue Lagoon to the Magic Pavilion. Many of the score or so of islands have landing stages, so you can tie up and seek out the treasures that may be hidden upon them. Curiosity and adventure are what the Meare has always been about, so if you can't get in touch with your inner child here, it's very likely that you no longer have one.

In Kemp's book about Thorpeness, a passage that quickly degenerates into a gushing panegyric to the Meare ends in a flourish with '...this Pool of Peace – this Temple of Tranquillity, where the Soul of over-civilised Man may escape the thraldom of great cities and find its Self alone with Nature and at one with God'. Don't be too disappointed if a visit today doesn't quite achieve all of that. However, it does make for a very pleasant and strangely fulfilling day out.

How to get there

Although Saxmundham (6.75 miles) is the closest railway station to Thorpeness, your best hope of getting a bus is to alight at Melton (greateranglia.co.uk; 0845 600 7245) and snag a 165 (angliancoaches.co.uk; 01502 711109) which runs all the way to the village. The Meare is at the southwestern edge of Thorpeness. Rowing boats (adult- and child-size), kayaks, canoes, punts, dinghies and sailing boats can be hired at the Meare (themeareatthorpeness.co.uk; 01728 832523) from 8.30am to late afternoon daily between Easter and the October half-term holiday. Various rates apply – as a guide, the cost of a rowing boat for two adults and two children for two hours is £19.50.

Admission price/landing fee

Free.

View

Other islands, luxurious houses on the edge of Thorpeness, the House in the Clouds (see 'Accommodation').

Facilities

None, though there are some toilets near the boat hire kiosk.

Accommodation

If there's a whole gang of you and you're prepared to shell out, the dream-like House in the Clouds (houseintheclouds.co.uk; 020 7224 3615) is available for one-night stays as well as week-long lets. The former water tower is the landmark in the area, and enjoys bird's eye views of the Meare. Otherwise, the Dolphin Inn (0.25 miles; thorpenessdolphin.com; 01728 454994) has comfy rooms.

Nearest decent pub/café/tea room

A venerable weatherboarded café called **The Meare Shop and Tearoom** (meareshop.co.uk; 01728 452156) serves cream teas among other tasty refreshments and is just a scone's throw away.

Nearest shop

The **Thorpeness Village Store** (0.25 miles from boat hire kiosk; 01728 451930) offers a very few basic supplies, many from local producers, as well as fresh-baked savouries and drinks, both soft and alcoholic.

Rules

None.

Things to do

The justly famous **RSPB reserve** along the coast at Minsmere (7 miles; rspb.org.uk/minsmere; 01728 648281) throngs with bearded tits, bitterns, nightingales and avocets, as well as red deer. There's also a **Wild Zone** and **Wild Wood Adventure** for visitors with children.

Benjamin Britten turned the **Snape Maltings** (6.5 miles; aldeburgh.co.uk; 01728 688303) near his beloved Aldeburgh into a hothouse of classical music and his legacy blossoms in the form of a popular year-round programme of events.

17. Hilbre Island

Dee Estuary, The Wirral
Merseyside
deeestuary.co.uk/hilbre
OS Landranger map 108
Grid reference: SJ 185 879
Size: 11.5 acres
Population: 0

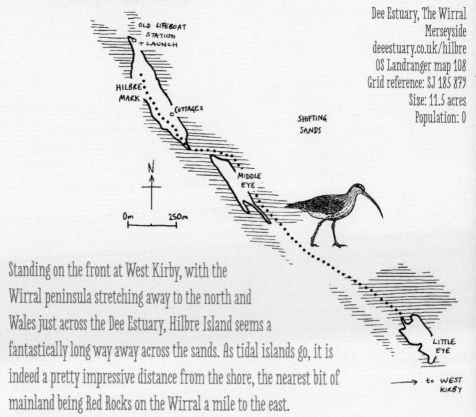

Standing on the front at West Kirby, with the Wirral peninsula stretching away to the north and Wales just across the Dee Estuary, Hilbre Island seems a fantastically long way away across the sands. As tidal islands go, it is indeed a pretty impressive distance from the shore, the nearest bit of mainland being Red Rocks on the Wirral a mile to the east.

To get to the island, visitors set off from West Kirby and must take in two even smaller isles along the way. That's not a must as in a must-see film but a must as in 'if you don't you may end up sinking beneath the sands never to be seen again'. The safe route out to Hilbre thus covers the best part of 2 miles, which feels like an adventure. In summer, families and guided groups stride purposefully off with day sacks filled with picnics and cameras and a sense of freedom.

Little Eye is the first island on the itinerary but is little more than a sand dune supported by the red Bunter sandstone of which all three isles are composed. The only feature of note is the stone base of a landmark that once stood here to help guide shipping safely through the dunes.

Turning sharp right, the next island, Middle Eye, is a far more substantial prospect, covering about 3 acres. Miniature bleached beaches of ground mussel shells are sheltered by beige wind-carved cliffs with an extraordinary Gaudí-esque look to them. The flat-topped island is an expanse of grass and bracken, the only human intrusions being a life belt, two rusted gateposts devoid of gate, and a metal post that may once have supported some official notice. Off to the west, grey seals haul out onto West Hoyle Bank, causing a flurry of rifling through bags for pairs of binoculars.

A hundred yards further on, over sea-flattened rocks, we come at last to Hilbre and again are confronted by mysterious sculptured shapes in the cliffs, now of a deep, almost unnatural orange. The worn stone track up onto the island becomes a narrow concrete road, at the top of which the greater part of Hilbre's buildings come into view. There seems to have been an unwritten law that no structure on this gaunt, pinched isle might resemble the style of any other in even the slightest detail.

In summer the swallows arrive, only to be so tossed about by the wind that it's difficult to tell what acrobatics are intentional and which ones are purely the work of the gusting air. Down below them at the tide line, waders and other seabirds patrol the beach seeking sustenance.

The Dee is one of the top 10 most important estuaries in Europe in terms of overwintering wildfowl and waders, and the Hilbre Islands – as the three isles are called – also provide a staging post for birds migrating up the west coast. Come the summer, the sands are a constant cree-cree-cree of calling beaks, as if the strand has been strewn with thousands of squeaking doors rocking ceaselessly on their hinges. Herring gulls, oystercatchers, common terns, Sandwich terns, dunlin,

whimbrel, curlew and many others come here to dine, to roost, or merely to rest.

This influx of avian life led to the creation in 1957 of the Hilbre Island Bird Observatory and it is its headquarters – once a private residence – that is the first building that visitors pass. It seems remarkably at home, seeing as it was brought here on a barge from the Manchester Ship Canal where it started off life as a navvy's hut. The two trim wooden bungalows next to it are both private dwellings used as holiday homes, much to the envy of day trippers. However, with no mains electricity or running water, life on the island is perhaps harder than is imagined. It's also the reason there's no permanent population any more: in 2011 the owners of Hilbre, Wirral Borough Council, announced that there would no longer be a resident warden on the island because they couldn't find anyone prepared to live here.

Following the isle's one track northward, a grassy mound looms up to the right. This was Hilbre's contribution to the war effort. Underneath there lies not only an air raid shelter but also a room in which a generator powered some lights installed on Middle Eye to fool enemy bombers into thinking they were over Liverpool. Beyond the mound the island gets positively busy. Here a hamlet's worth of oddly assorted, mainly Victorian buildings cluster together. These include the Telegraph House, where the telegraph keeper and his family used to live (succeeded by the island warden until recently); the Buoymaster's House,

for the family of the man responsible for maintaining all the local navigation buoys; and squeezed in between them a single-storey building that may be all that is left of the Seagull Inn, a pub that flourished between the 1790s and the 1830s when passengers for ships to Ireland would embark here. Tradition has it that the innkeeper, Joseph Hickson, grew rich on the spoils of wrecking and smuggling activities, but this may merely have been malicious gossip.

There are no ancient constructions left on the island, which is surprising since it has been occupied for thousands of years. If one were to dig beneath the buildings at the northern end of Hilbre, one might come across the foundations of the house and chapel kept going by Benedictine monks from Chester Abbey for nearly 400 years until the monastery's dissolution in 1538. Just a pair of monks and their servants lived here at any one time, so it was not a religious house on the grand scale of those that graced so many other tiny islands around Britain. However, it did at least lend the island its name (pronounced 'hill-bree'), which is derived from St Hildeburgh, the woman to whom the chapel was dedicated.

Prior to the arrival of the brothers, Hilbre appears to have been rather more densely populated. The head of a cross and a burial slab have been discovered from the late Saxon period, as well as pottery and jewellery from the 7th, 4th and 3rd centuries, and Roman coins and brooches from the time Hilbre served as a defensive outpost for the then new city at Chester. However, even these are relatively modern when compared with Bronze Age axe heads and flint arrowheads and scrapers left here by our Neolithic ancestors.

The final buildings on the island include the Mersey Canoe Club's century-old green-painted clubhouse and an early Victorian telegraph station with a wonderful half-moon of windows peering out into the Irish Sea. The men stationed here would inform passing ships of weather forecasts and any other information they required.

The most unexpected item on the island is located inside the disused lifeboat station on the far northern tip. Built in 1839, the station was kept going for exactly 100 years, the lifeboatmen from Hoylake (on the mainland) running or riding on horseback across the sands before rushing headlong into the sea in a boat powered by oars and a small sail. While their time has passed, there's a small antiquated piece of equipment inside the station that is still providing a vital service today. The Hilbre Island tide gauge dates from the 19th century and has a clockwork mechanism that needs winding once a week. Its tide height recordings, however, remain essential reading for the captain of every large ship that enters Liverpool. It's satisfying to know that an island so used to being useful is still proving its worth today.

How to get there

From West Kirby railway station (merseyrail.org; 0151 702 2071), it's a five-minute stroll down Dee Lane to the slipway from where you can walk to the island at low tide. Do follow the prescribed route (deeestuary.co.uk/hilbis.htm), which avoids areas of dangerously deep mud. Don't attempt to cross from Hoylake. The route (1.8 miles) and tide times are displayed on a noticeboard at the slipway. The island is usually accessible for around six hours at each low tide.

Admission price/landing fee
Free.

View
Hoylake to the north, the Welsh coast to the west, and a couple of inshore windfarms.

Facilities
Compost toilets on Hilbre Island. There are also some loos by the Dee Lane slipway.

Accommodation
Try West Kirby's stylish **Caldy Warren Cottage** (1.25 miles from Dee Lane slipway; warrencott.demon.co.uk; 0151 625 8740) with its brass bedsteads and views over the Dee Estuary.

Nearest decent pub/café/tea room
At the slipway, there's a kiosk selling coffee and ice cream. For something more substantial, West Kirby's self-styled 'premier coffee lounge and bistro' **Lattetude** (0.1 miles; lattetude.moonfruit.com; 0151 6253986) is at the railway station end of Dee Lane.

Nearest shop
West Kirby has a plethora of small shops, including **Palms Fine Foods** (0.2 miles; 0151 625 6776) on Banks Road, where you could knock yourself up a posh picnic to eat on one of the islands.

Rules
Permits must be sought in advance for groups of six visitors or more (0151 648 4371). Dogs must be kept on a short lead. No overnight stays. No alcohol.

Things to do
Try a three-hour 'have a go' session on **West Kirby Marine Lake** with the Wirral Sailing Centre (next to Dee Lane slipway; . tinyurl.com/97evjrq; 0151 625 3292) – you can choose from sailing, windsurfing and kayaking.
Two-hour **'Dee Tours' boat trips** around the Hilbre Islands leave from the Dee Lane slipway and are also run by Wirral Sailing Centre (tinyurl.com/9yhrbaq; 0151 625 3292).

Hornsea Mere, Hornsea
East Yorkshire
OS Landranger map 107
Grid reference: TA 194 472
Size: 1.5 acres
Population: 0

18. Swan Island

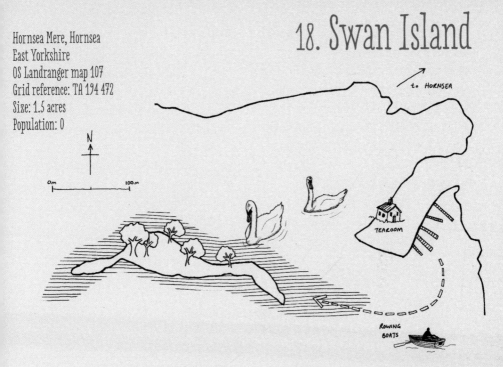

Swan Island is remarkable not so much for its history – indeed, as far as is known, no one has ever lived here, nothing has ever been built here and nothing of any consequence has happened here – but for the fact that it exists at all.

Hornsea Mere, the shallow lake on which it finds itself in solitary splendour, is the largest freshwater lake in Yorkshire. Two miles long and covering 467 acres, it's one of what was once a gathering of lakes so numerous that the land hereabouts was simply a collection of islands in a freshwater ocean. However, once the North Sea had battered its way inland, ripping out the coastline south of Bridlington, the waters from the Yorkshire Wold no longer filled the lakes south to the Humber but escaped out east into Bridlington Bay. Gradually, the meres became carrs (boggy marshy areas)

or disappeared altogether as they dried out and silted up. Hornsea Mere is the last one of any great size to have survived, a final outpost among the low wooded slopes less than a mile from the sea.

Swan Island is the only isle upon this solitary mere. There used to be another one though, further to the west, called Lady Island. A summer house was built upon it by the owners of Wassand Hall, on whose estate Hornsea Mere lies, and while the name Lady Island still exists on maps, the silting up of the lake has attached it to the shore and it is an island no more.

It's only a short row out to Swan Island, so it's handy that rowing boats can be hired from the tip of Kirkholme Nab, a little peninsula on the east of the mere. Swan is a long, thin, densely wooded isle that so perfectly forms the shape of a flamingo that you wonder how it didn't take on that bird's name instead. At least the swans, from whom the island does take its name, have the decency to remain there today, nesting in large numbers. It's because of their presence that landing on the island is not permitted. The mere is a designated Special Protection Area for birds (as well as being a Site of Special Scientific Interest), though most people's experience of swans, particularly when there are cygnets about, is that they can protect themselves pretty efficiently. While it's unlikely that they can actually break a man's arm with a blow of their wings, only a fool would volunteer to find out for certain.

It is possible to row around the island and enjoy peering into the mysterious thickets growing from soil that feels the tread of no man's boot. Plenty of birds aside from the swans have probably toddled about here though – the mere is a haven for greylag and Canada geese, little gulls, gadwalls, goldeneyes, reed and sedge warblers, pochard, shoveler and tufted ducks.

However, it would be wrong to think of Swan Island merely as a bird sanctuary that history has shunned, for it has borne witness to three events of note. The first occurred in the 13th century when a dispute flared up between the rival abbots of Meaux and St Mary's over how much of the mere – and its valuable fish stocks – each owned. To decide the issue, the two good Christian clergymen each put up their own champions who fought all day until those of the Abbot of Meaux were defeated.

Just as the island was getting over the excitement of the duelling-by-proxy clerics, on 23 December 1723 a hurricane blew in, destroying 24 houses and toppling a windmill.

The third incident concerned another extreme natural phenomenon. In 1838 the mere froze solid for six weeks or more, allowing the locals to organise an ice carnival upon it. They went skating, indulged in curling, played a rudimentary form of ice hockey, and even danced reels on the mere. Come February, they were confident enough to build fires on the ice, over which they roasted whole sheep. On one evening things became very jovial and a group of doubtless well-oiled merrymakers bearing flaming torches processed singing and dancing around Swan Island and Lady Island (still an island back then).

Perhaps their ceremony was an attempt to atone for a crime that was committed on the mere less than a decade beforehand. In 1829, Edward Anderson of Kilham described Hornsea Mere and Swan Island in *The Sailor*, a poem that helped establish the reputation of tiny British islands for inspiring somewhat lacklustre poetry (see also p113 and p237):

Many go there to fish for pleasure's sake,
But they always pay for what they take;
When caught, they weigh it at the
New Inn door,
The money it is given to the poor.
The lake is two miles long, and one
mile broad,
And both with fish and fowl it is well
stor'd;
And in the midst of it an island lies,
Where sea birds breed, for miles you
hear their cries.

And they say that William McGonagall had all the best lines.

How to get there

Take the train to Beverley (northernrail.org; 0844 241 3454) then the 246 bus (eyms. co.uk; 01482 222222) to Hornsea. From the western edge of the town, turn down Queens Gardens and then along a track to the shed where rowing boats (John; 01964 533277) are hired out. The boats are available to hire (weather permitting) from April to October – adult £3, child £1.50 per hour. The mere opens daily from 9am to 5.30pm (or dusk if earlier). A small steamboat – a replica of those that used to ferry tourists around Windermere – leaves from the same place as the rowing boats and sails past Swan Island.

Admission price/landing fee

Free.

View

Look out in most directions and you'd think all of England was one great wood. The only thing to spoil this illusion is the sight of a few houses peeping between the trees at the eastern end of the mere.

Swans dutifully circling their eponymous island

Facilities

None. However, there are public toilets next to the café by the jetties.

Accommodation

The **Albert and Victoria Guest House** (1 mile; albertandvictoria.co.uk; 01964 533310) is a smart traditional establishment near the seafront at Hornsea.

Nearest decent pub/café/tea room

The people who hire out the rowing boats also run the pleasingly **old-fashioned café** (01964 533277) next door to it.

Nearest shop

Hornsea (0.5 miles) has a selection to satisfy the eye and delight the pocket.

Rules

None.

Things to do

The rowing boat people who run the café are also the proprietors of an **18-hole putting green** (01964 533277) just a few strides from the jetties.

The innovative **Hornsea Museum** (0.5 miles; hornseamuseum.com; 01964 533443) contains many fascinating vernacular articles and is set in and around a farmhouse that was lived in for over 300 years by generations of the Burn family.

Wassand Hall (2.8 miles; open on 'selected days during the summer'; wassand.co.uk; 01964 534488) is an elegant Regency house with fine walled gardens and footpaths through woods and parkland. There are also views of Hornsea Mere, which belongs to the estate.

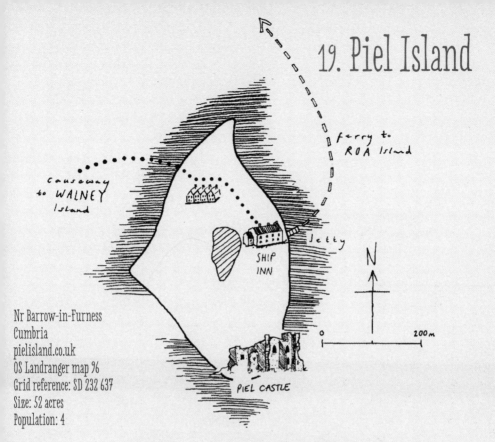

19. Piel Island

ferry to ROA Island

causeway to WALNEY Island

Jetty

SHIP INN

N

0   200 m

Nr Barrow-in-Furness
Cumbria
pielisland.co.uk
OS Landranger map 96
Grid reference: SD 232 637
Size: 52 acres
Population: 4

PIEL CASTLE

If you were going to design an ideal island from scratch it's very likely you'd come up with Piel. It comprises one pub, one short terrace of Victorian houses, a beach, a lake, plentiful seabirds and, naturally, one medieval castle. It's accessible via a 10-minute ride on a tiny ferry or a mile-and-a-half walk over the sands at low tide from another island, Walney.

The view from Piel is nothing short of extraordinary: a panorama stretches all the way from Barrow up to the Lake District's forbidding Black Coombe, around a panoply of hills to the Old Man of Coniston, down to the long sweep of the Fylde coast and all the way to the Blackpool Tower. If all this were not enough, the island also happens to have been the scene of the last invasion of Britain.

Jumping off at Piel's impressively slippery jetty, the first sight is the welcoming one of the Ship Inn. The pub underwent a renovation that lasted several years, re-opening at last in 2010, much to the joy of the regulars. And difficult though it is to believe on an island with a population of four, there are regulars here. Kayakers and the crews of an assortment of boats moor up throughout the evening and stride in,

Rowing boats named after common local wildlife

as though paddling or sailing to one's local were the most natural thing in the world. Another thing treated as perfectly normal in these parts is that the landlord, Steve, is also the King of Piel.

The tradition of crowning the landlord of the island's pub is a slightly murky one. As far as can be established it began in the early 19th century in mocking reference to the attempt to put Lambert Simnel on the throne of England. On 4 June 1487, the pretender to the throne – a lad just 10 years old – landed with several thousand mercenaries under the command of Colonel Martin Schwartz. Though of course they didn't know it at the time, they were en route to ignominious defeat at the hands of Henry VII's army at the Battle of Stoke Field in Nottinghamshire.

To commemorate this rather dismal chapter in English history, each successive landlord of The Ship is sat on a special wooden throne wearing a ceremonial helmet and brandishing a sword. A large quantity of alcohol is then poured over him and he is proclaimed king. It's really rather moving. Steve's wife Sheila is thus queen and their daughter Nicola a princess. Until fairly recently it was possible to become a Knight or Baroness of Piel by the simple expedient of sitting on the throne and buying everyone in the bar a drink. 'But it became a bit frivolous,' according to Steve, 'so now we're only making knights or baronesses of people who have performed some service for the island.'

The castle – a motte and bailey affair with an impressive curtain wall – is a ruin today, though much of its keep has survived. It began life as a fortified warehouse when constructed by monks under the Abbot of Furness in the 12th century, with the idea of keeping pirates and Scots raiders at bay. If this seems a humble beginning, it should be kept in mind that at the time it was the second largest building in Britain after the Tower of London. The current remains date mainly from the early 14th century and are in the care of English Heritage. It's permanently open and free to visit.

Later generations of the holy order seem to have strayed rather, for on realising that their fortification kept their prized goods from the prying eyes of customs officials, they turned their hand to smuggling.

The monks were not the earliest visitors to Piel by any means. Celts and Romans are thought to have visited, while Vikings actually settled on the island, providing it with its first known name, Foudray. It derives from 'fire island' in Old Norse and suggests that a beacon to guide seafarers was kept alight here. The modern name Piel Island comes from 'Pile of Fotheray', as the fortress was known in medieval times, 'pile' or 'pele' being a common term for a castle keep. The ruins on the green, almost treeless island are a captivating sight. William Wordsworth certainly thought so. After spending a month in a house with a view of Piel he was inspired to the giddy heights of doggerel:

*I was thy neighbour once, though
rugged Pile!
Four summer weeks I dwelt in sight
of thee:
I saw thee every day! and all the while
Thy Form was sleeping on a glassy sea.*

King Stephen gave the island to the
monks of Savigny in Normandy in 1127,
little knowing what japes they would get
up to here in later years. However, the
poacher was to turn gamekeeper some
centuries later, when Piel became an
outpost for customs officers. As for the
Ship Inn, it's believed to be 300 years old
or more, though the first solid evidence
of its existence dates from only 1746. A
lease granted that year to a certain Edward
Postlethwaite records his occupation as
'innkeeper from the Pile of Fowdrey'. The
pub would have to wait until 1875 and the
building of the little terrace of cottages (to
house pilots for ships coming into the port
of Barrow) for its first bona fide locals.

In 1920, at the instigation of the mayor
of Barrow, the Duke of Buccleuch presented
the island to the town of Barrow-in-Furness
as a memorial to the dead of World War I.
The name of the mayor was Alfred Barrow.
Gone are the days when every mayor had
to bear the name of his home town and
we're all the poorer for it.

How to get there

Take the train to Roose (northernrail.org;
0844 241 3454, firstgroup.com; 01709
849200) then the 11 bus (blueworksph.
com; 01539 531995) to Roa Island. The
Piel Island Ferry (adult £4 return, U14
£2, U4 free; John Cleasby 07798 794550;
John Warburton 07817 043385; or Steve
Chattaway 07516 453784) sails from 11am
to 6pm, weather permitting. Alternatively,
travel to Barrow-in-Furness station and
board the 2 bus from Duke Street to Walney
Island, hike the 6 miles to Snab Point and
walk to Piel at low tide. There were areas
of sinking sands reported in 2012, so do
consult Steve Chattaway before attempting
the crossing from Walney (possible for
about four hours every day). Otherwise,
the friendly local guide and nature expert
(and former mayor of Barrow) John Murphy
(01229 473746) will take groups across.

Admission price/landing fee

Free.

View

Barrow, the Lake District, the Fylde
coastline – it's not one you'll tire of quickly.

Facilities

A pub, bunkhouse, campsite, toilets, cold-
water showers. A small visitors centre is
planned for 2013.

Accommodation

There's a B&B at the island's own **Ship
Inn**, while a **bunkhouse** offers extremely
economical lodgings (bring your own
sleeping bags). **Camping** is also allowed
more or less anywhere on the island within
reason (pre-booking essential). Contact
Steve Chattaway (pielisland.co.uk; 07516
453784) for any of the above.

Nearest decent pub/café/tea room

Clearly, the only game in town is the island's **Ship Inn** (pielisland.co.uk; 07516 453784). Landlord/king Steve is a trained chef so you can expect something tastier than your everyday pub grub.

Nearest shop

The **Co-op** (4 miles from Roa Island; 01229 822730) in Roose is a small supermarket that covers all likely needs.

Rules

No camping in the inner bailey of the castle. Dogs on leads.

Things to do

Walney Island (1.5 miles at low tide; walney-island.com), aka 'Wet and Windy Walney', has two nature reserves and is home to the largest colony of lesser black-backed and herring gulls in Europe.

The Dock Museum, Barrow (6 miles from Roa Island; free; dockmuseum.org.uk; 01229 876400) is an innovative exploration of local life housed in a former dry dock.

The Piel Island Great Bath Race is held every third Saturday of July. Bring that rudimentary sailing boat you made out of a bath tub and join in or look on as others attempt to sail theirs around the island.

20. Chapel Island

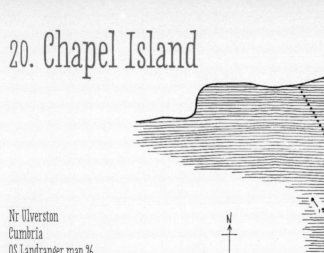

MARKER 1
MARKER 2
1 500m
N
0m   100m
FAKE CHAPEL RUINS

Nr Ulverston
Cumbria
OS Landranger map 96
Grid reference: SD 321 758
Size: 7 acres
Population: 0

The short but steep clamber up onto craggy Chapel Island through hawthorn, bramble, nettle and elder to ruins barely poking above a clutch of sycamore trees is one that follows no path. It's a sign of how relatively little visited the island is that its one notable feature is all but unreachable. And when you do at last come face to face with the grey-stone remains of the rudely built edifice, there's a surprise in store.

The island's chapel was built in the 14th century by monks from nearby Conishead Priory, which had been established as a leper colony under the Normans. Nearly a mile off the coast, the skittle-shaped isle pointing more or less north and south along the Leven estuary had long been a place of sanctuary for those crossing the Morecambe Bay sands from Cartmel to Conishead, a short cut that avoided an arduous 10-mile trek around the coast. It was, however, a very dangerous crossing, with swift tides and shifting sands ready to claim the lives of the unwary or the foolhardy. Given these circumstances, some spiritual sustenance was probably most welcome, as was a place to get out of the weather brought in off the Atlantic by the prevailing westerly wind.

However, the broken stone walls on Chapel Island are not the chapel, all semblance of which has now disappeared. They are instead a ready-ruined mock-medieval chapel built by Colonel R G Braddyll in the 1820s to make the view from the deconsecrated Conishead Priory (whose modern buildings he also had constructed) more romantic. Since there's nothing on the island to warn of the deception, the ruins are doubtless triumphantly declared to be those of the chapel by hundreds of visitors every year. Try not to be one of them.

Gothic novelist and travel writer Ann Radcliffe is partly to blame. In her book *Tour to the Lakes* which arose from her 1794 journey around Lakeland, she coined the name Chapel Island. Up until then it had been known as Harlside or Harlesyde Isle.

The fake ruins had slowly been falling into actual ruin for over 30 years – thus at least rendering themselves ruins of a sort – when a 54-ton sloop called the *Delight* grounded on a sandbank on Chapel Island on 6 October 1858. A 'handsome and substantially-built vessel', according to a report in the *Carlisle Patriot* newspaper, the poorly maintained ship sprang a leak, filled with water and capsized in the night. While the mate and a sailor managed to get away in the ship's lifeboat using a coat as a sail, two elderly seamen doggedly clung to the rigging and were rescued in the morning exhausted but otherwise unharmed.

Ironically, it's the sandy beaches that are Chapel Island's most attractive feature. Since the trees and undergrowth have rendered the greater part of the island inaccessible to all but the eider who nest here, the greatest joy comes from the western shore, which, when the wind drops and the sun shines, provides a strand exclusive enough to rival any private beach in Monaco.

Meanwhile, on the rocky face of an inlet on the eastern shore, there is a mysterious small plaque. By the font in which it is written, it would appear to date from the 1950s, and proclaims 'GDWA Private Shooting'. However, since the island can be seen from the estuary shore for miles around, it cannot be recommended as a place to have someone privately shot and no doubt this oversight caused a swift end to the enterprise. The other explanation for the sign, that the local Grange and District Wildfowlers Association once owned the rights to shoot birds here, is far too preposterous to contemplate.

It's no surprise to learn that a visit was paid by William Wordsworth, the self-appointed poet to the nation's tiny islands (he also suffered his pen to portray Staffa (p237) and Piel Island (p111) in words). In Book X of *The Prelude* – an account of his early travels – he writes:

As I advanced, all that I saw or felt
Was gentleness and peace. Upon a small
And rocky island near, a fragment stood,
(Itself like a sea rock) the low remains
(With shells encrusted, dark with
briny weeds)
Of a dilapidated structure, once
A Romish chapel, where the vested priest
Said matins at the hour that suited those
Who crossed the sands with ebb of
morning tide.

Wordsworth relates that he was on the island 'longing for skill to paint a scene so bright' when he saw a procession of travellers on horse and foot wading across the sands, one of whom cried out to him, 'Robespierre is dead!' Travellers were the internet news sites of the day, sometimes delivering reports of the latest events within months of their occurring.

This detail also clears Wordsworth of accusations that he too made the schoolboy error of mistaking the ruined folly for the ruined chapel, for Robespierre was executed in 1794 – decades before Colonel Braddyll made his mark on the island. Sadly, although Wordsworth and Radcliffe managed to visit Chapel Island in the same year, they didn't manage to coordinate their diaries sufficiently to arrange a meeting here, or England might have been blessed with its first gothic novel in plain verse.

There has only ever been one house on the island in recent history: a cottage built in the first half of the 19th century to accommodate a succession of fishermen and their families. The ruins of the dwelling are now buried under a sea of nettles.

Rather improbably, Chapel Island did nearly get its own railway station. In 1837, George Stephenson proposed slinging a railway line across the sands of the Leven estuary from Cartmel to the Furness peninsula, using Chapel Island as a halt. However, the scheme never got up a proper head of steam and was eventually reckoned to be too expensive.

Of all the tidal islands around Britain, Chapel Island attracts the most safety warnings, on account of the sinking sands hereabouts and Morecambe Bay's notoriously quick and deadly incoming tides. Despite this, the route to the island is a simple one, as Ray Porter, an official guide to the sands of the Leven estuary, points out: 'Start 50 yards to the right of the two pylons near Canal Foot, cross the Ulverston channel and head in a straight line for the island. Then take the same route back.' He also gives some other sage advice: 'If you feel yourself sinking, don't stop walking.'

How to get there
Take a train to Ulverston (northernrail.org; 0844 241 3454) then either walk or cycle the 2.5 miles along the Ulverston Canal towpath to Canal Foot or, if you arrive on a Tuesday or Thursday, board the 60 bus (Lecks Travel; 01539 531220) to Canal Foot. It's a 1.25-mile amble to the island and the time available to cross over at low water varies greatly depending on the height of the tide, though usually you should have between three and four hours. Tide timetables are available from the Tourist Information Centre in Ulverston (01229 587120). Don't go to the island if you're likely to become anxious about sand that is less than firm or in poor visibility.

Admission price/landing fee
Free.

View

Long stretches of Cumbrian coastline to both the east and the west. To the north, a railway viaduct, the Hoad monument and, it cannot be denied, some factories.

Facilities

None.

Accommodation

The Bay Horse (1.25 miles; thebayhorsehotel.co.uk; 01229 583972) at Canal Foot has some rooms with views across the estuary to the island.

Nearest decent pub/café/tea room

Try the classy and popular **Gillam's** (2 miles from Canal Foot; gillams-tearoom.co.uk; 01229 587564) tea room in Ulverston.

Nearest shop

Ulverston (2 miles from Canal Foot) has some gorgeous specialist shops and an indoor market.

Rules

No dogs during the bird breeding season.

Things to do

The **Sir John Barrow Monument** (2 miles; sirjohnbarrowmonument.co.uk) on Hoad Hill at the back of Ulverston was modelled on the Eddystone lighthouse and enjoys astonishing views of the Cumbrian coast. Look for the monument's flag – if it's flying, it's open.

Down in Ulverston, the **Laurel and Hardy Museum** (2 miles; laurel-and-hardy.co.uk; 01229 582292) celebrates the town's favourite sons.

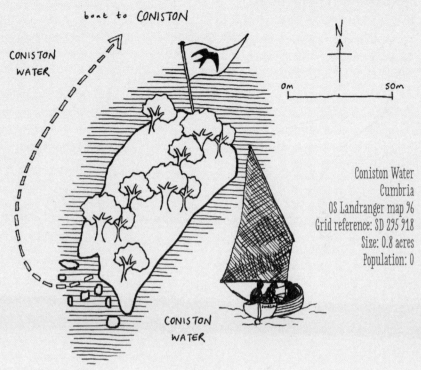

boat to CONISTON

CONISTON WATER

N

0m   50m

CONISTON WATER

Coniston Water
Cumbria
OS Landranger map 96
Grid reference: SD 295 918
Size: 0.8 acres
Population: 0

Although you might never have visited Peel Island, there's a chance you may already have been there in your imagination.

If you have read Arthur Ransome's description of Wild Cat Island – with its one pine standing proud of rowans, oaks and beech trees; its rocky shore repelling landings to all vessels whose captains did not know the secret of the island's one safe passage; and its pleasant glades where picnics could be enjoyed and stratagems hatched – you have seen Peel Island. Give or take the odd flight of fancy, anyway.

Those who are better acquainted with *Swallows and Amazons* than perhaps they'd

like to let on will know that no sooner has Arthur Ransome described the island than he has one of his characters declare her desire to camp there, as is only right and proper really.

And so begins the adventure for Swallows Susan, John, Titty and Roger, and Amazons Nancy and Peggy. Except that the Swallows didn't call their home from home Peel Island, of course, but gave it a name that was much more enthralling and dangerous. They were right to do so because Wild Cat Island was not a carbon

Left: The island's exposed western beaches; Right: The fake ruins beneath an actual sun

copy of Peel, but Ransome's amalgam of the island with something of Blake Holme (p129), an isle on Windermere. This was to set the trend for their world, which was a curious fusion of Coniston Water, on which Peel Island sits, and Windermere. While the latter can lay claim to the basic framework of their surroundings, Coniston gets to contribute several locations, including the Kanchenjunga mountain (the Old Man of Coniston), Trout Tarn (Beacon Tarn), the boathouse used by the Amazons, and, of course, Peel Island, which, unlike Blake Holme, has a handy harbour into which *Swallow* could sail.

As a child, little Arthur came to Coniston every year with his family, and his father Cyril would sometimes row them across to Peel Island for a picnic, which is no doubt when the seed for his children's story was sown. However, Ransome nearly didn't live to write the book that made his name.

In 1913, he left for Russia – ostensibly to collect folk tales, but largely to escape an unhappy marriage – and ended up reporting on the October Revolution as a correspondent for the *Daily News*. He fell in love with Trotsky's personal assistant Evgenia and set about smuggling her out of the country to save her falling into the hands of the White Russians. He put himself at considerable risk in so doing and ultimately it was only his love of chess that saved him: he avoided being executed by the Reds through mentioning that he had played chess with Lenin, and when he fell into the hands of the Whites he again avoided being executed because he had once played the game with the unit's commander.

During his time in Russia, Peel Island was obviously a place very dear to Ransome's heart. In a letter to his mother in 1917, he wrote: 'Your two pictures of Coniston hang on the wall beside a bit of Peel Island and an ikon of St Nicholas. They give me great pleasure every day...Joyce [Ransome's sister] and I MUST some day do a book just as full of lake country as ever it can.'

Just what bit of Peel Island Arthur had on his wall in St Petersburg isn't clear. However, he did make good his yearning to capture the region in written form when *Swallows and Amazons* was published by Jonathan Cape in 1930, the series eventually running to a dozen books.

The island is still popular with children today, though they're more likely to come over in organised groups learning how to handle kayaks or canoes than on their own in a dinghy. As on Wild Cat Island, Peel's natural harbour is at the southern end, with a jumble of rocks barring entry to all but those rowing, paddling or, at a pinch, sailing the smallest of dinghies, which is very much in the Ransomean spirit. Snuggled down beneath the thickly wooded southern shores of Coniston Water, the isle hides itself from prying eyes beneath its own cloak of trees and thus is a wonderful place to become a child again and imagine yourself into a daring escapade. Happily, there's no chance of children and wannabe children being warded off any time soon either because it belongs to the National

Canoeists sliding between the rocks to the landing place

Trust, which received it as a gift from the 7th Duke of Buccleuch back in 1932.

Such is the heady scent of adventure that hangs around Peel Island that *Swallows and Amazons* wasn't even the first book in which it featured. W G Collingwood, a family friend of the Ransomes who became something of a mentor to Arthur, first put Peel on the map with a novel called *Thorstein of the Mere: A Saga of the Northmen in Lakeland*. It followed the exploits of a Viking settler called Thorstein, his name taken from the ancient description of the lake as Thurston's Mere. The book was one of Ransome's favourites during his childhood and in later life he gave sailing lessons on Coniston Water to Collingwood's grandchildren, three of whose names – Susan, Titty (a pet name for a child called Mavis) and Roger – made their way into *Swallows and Amazons*.

For all the jolly questing and derring-do with which Peel Island is associated, there is one dark shadow that throws itself across its bright and cheery little copse: the death of Donald Campbell. On the morning of 4 January 1967 he had just passed the island, travelling at a speed of 320mph, when his jet-propelled boat, *Bluebird K7*, suddenly reared up and crashed.

Donald's father was Sir Malcolm Campbell, who also famously broke world land and water speed records, including one in *Bluebird K4* on the very same stretch of water 28 years earlier. His son's final words from the doomed *K7* were: 'Pitching a bit down here... Probably from my own wash... Straightening up now on track... Rather close to Peel Island... Tramping like mad... Full power... Tramping like hell here... I can't see much... and the water's very bad indeed... I can't get over the top... I'm getting a lot of bloody row in here... I can't see anything... I've got the bows up... I'm going...'

The reason usually cited for the disaster is Campbell's decision not to re-fuel at the end of his first run but to turn around immediately and go for another. It is assumed that he thought he could race back up the lake before the wake from his previous run had rebounded off the shores to disturb the water, and that this miscalculation cost him his life. However, it has been pointed out that the surface of the lake is calm at the spot where *Bluebird's* nose suddenly lifts into the air before the craft turns a somersault and disintegrates as it hits the water. The best part of half a century later, the black-and-white Pathé News footage of the crash hasn't lost its power to send a chill up the spine. When the waters were still again, all that was left was a scattering of débris, in which Campbell's teddy bear, Mr Whoppit, was found floating about in a daze.

The remains of *K7* were eventually discovered on the bed of the lake in 2001 and Campbell's body was recovered and buried in the churchyard in Coniston village. The lake is still used once a year for the Coniston Power Boat Records Week. The rest of the time there's a prudent 10mph speed limit, which, one has to say, is much more Peel Island's thing.

How to get there

Take the train to Windermere station (virgintrains.co.uk; 01709 849200, tpexpress.co.uk) and then bus 505 (stagecoachbus.com; 01228 597888) to Coniston. It's a half-mile walk to the Coniston Boating Centre

(conistonboatingcentre.co.uk; 015394 41366) where you can hire a traditional rowing boat, a kayak, a canoe, a paddleboard or an electric motorboat. It's a 6.5-mile round trip down Coniston Water from the boating centre to Peel Island, so be prepared for a very long row or paddle. Electric motorboats make the journey there and back in around two hours but unfortunately their drafts won't allow you to land on the island, which is only possible with a self-powered boat. Rowing boats cost £30/four hours; kayaks, canoes and paddleboards are £25/four hours; sailing dinghies start from £40/two hours; and electric motorboats cost £35/two hours. Shorter and longer hire periods are available.

Admission price/landing fee
Free.

View
Truly scrumptious – the green wooded shoreline of Coniston Water with the Old Man of Coniston rising above it to the northeast and sundry other peaks looming elsewhere.

Facilities
None.

Accommodation
Coniston's vegetarian **Beech Tree Guest House** (0.75 miles from boating centre; tinyurl.com/9ukzmuk; 015394 41717) is a charming 18th-century villa in its own gardens. Meanwhile, almost on the shore of the lake lies the rambling and spacious **Coniston Hall Campsite** (1.6 miles; 015394 41223).

Nearest decent pub/café/tea room
The **Bluebird Cafe** (thebluebirdcafe.co.uk; 015394 41649), right on the shore by the boating centre, boasts a glassed-wall patio allowing fantastic views of the lake.

Nearest shop
Coniston has a little flurry of shops including the **Coniston Co-operative** (0.5 miles; 015394 41247), which has a decent spread of basic necessities.

Rules
None.

Things to do
The **Ruskin Museum** (0.5 miles; ruskinmuseum.com; 015394 41164) in Coniston not only charts the history of the area but also throws light on the life of the eponymous local art critic as well as telling the story of the ill-fated Donald Campbell. If that's still not Ruskin enough for you, there's his home **Brantwood** (brantwood. org.uk; 015394 41396), which can be reached on the steam yacht *Gondola* (nationaltrust.org.uk/gondola; 015394 32733) from Coniston Pier (or stay on the yacht to enjoy a *Swallows and Amazons* tour of the whole lake).

Alternatively, on Wednesday afternoons there's a 2-hour *Swallows and Amazons* **cruise** in a 1920s solar-electric boat run by the Coniston Launch Company (conistonlaunch.co.uk; 017687 75753).

22. Islands of Windermere

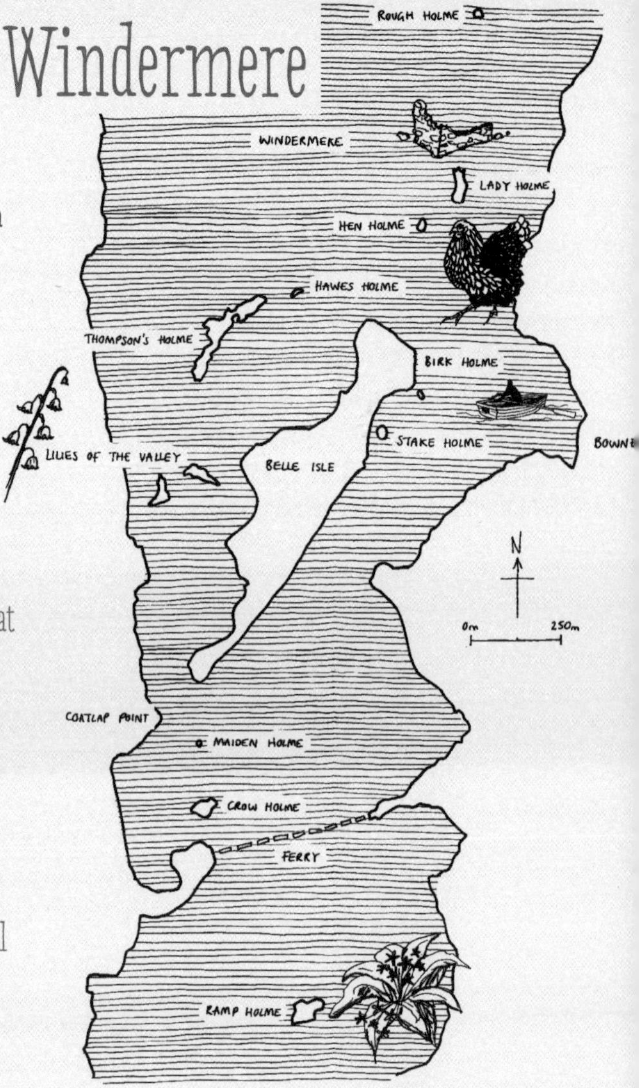

Windermere
Nr Bowness-on-Windermere, Cumbria
OS Landranger map 97
Grid reference: SD 395 972
Size: Various, from 0.01 to 2 acres
Population: 0

Close your eyes and imagine the happy occupants of a rowing boat scudding from one tiny island to the next across a still lake. The chances are that the scene that drifted before your mind's eye looked an awful lot like Windermere, the quintessential lazy sunny afternoon island-hopping lake.

ROUGH HOLME
WINDERMERE
LADY HOLME
HEN HOLME
HAWES HOLME
THOMPSON'S HOLME
BIRK HOLME
LILIES OF THE VALLEY
STAKE HOLME
BOWN
BELLE ISLE
N
0m   250m
COTCLAP POINT
MAIDEN HOLME
CROW HOLME
FERRY
RAMP HOLME

It is also England's largest natural lake, a 10.5-mile snake creeping through the Lakeland fells from Waterhead in the north to Lakeside in the south. The majority of its score or so of islands – the exact number depends on what you count as an island and what's merely a rock – lie about two-fifths of the way down in a group that is intimate enough to facilitate easy exploration and is also slap bang opposite a mighty fleet of little hire boats patiently awaiting punters. Frankly, it would be rude not to take one out (though don't bother asking for a punt – the lake is really deep).

Long before the day-trippers and tourists (a term coined in the late 18th century specifically to describe sightseers doing a tour of the Lakes) came Vikings who settled around the shores and named the lake after one of their leaders, Vinandr. The suffix 'mere' is an Old English word for a lake. The name didn't become Windermere until the 19th century and those early tourists would have known the place as some variation on Winander Mere. When Daniel Defoe dropped by in the early 1700s on the voyage of discovery that was to become his three-volume A tour thro' *the whole island of Great Britain*, he wrote: 'But I must not forget Winander Meer, which makes the utmost northern bounds of this shire, which is famous for the char fish found here and hereabout, and no where else in England.' The area was clearly a little less tourist-friendly than it is today, for he also noted that the Lake District was: 'The wildest, most barren and frightful part I have passed over in England, or even Wales.'

This image of the Lake District as a grim and frightening place was quashed for good in 1847 when the Kendal and Windermere Railway brought holidaymakers into the heart of the region and to within a mile of the lake, and boats have been on hire here ever since.

Half a dozen of the islands lie so far to the north or south that they are beyond the reach of all but the most fanatical Sunday afternoon rower. However, that still leaves a generous sprinkling within oar-shot, all of them tree-covered to a greater or lesser extent, with the smaller ones such as Rough Holme and Hen Holme little bigger than the circle inside a football pitch.

If we were to begin our exploration by heading north, we would come to Rough Holme, whose mystery, if it has one, comes from the fact that we seem to know nothing about it at all.

Heading back south, we arrive speedily at Lady Holme, about which we do know something, for it is named after a chantry (a small chapel used to celebrate mass for the soul of a rich benefactor) that once stood here. At some point in the Middle Ages, a pair of priests or monks were cooped up on this half-acre islet where, between praying for the local lord's deceased relatives, they would go out onto the lake to fish. Their chickens were kept on the scrap of an island next door, which is now called Hen Holme. Tradition has it that the clerics also cared for lepers who would live among the hens, though how much of a life this would have constituted is debatable. Some flagstones were discovered here once, leading some people to call this rocky place Chair and Table Island, though that seems unnecessarily clunky. Anyway, yacht races are started from here, so keep your wits about you if you're on the water on a regatta day.

Off to the west, waving as we pass tiny Hawes Holme, we come to Thompson's Holme, often shortened to Tommy's Holme (the 'holme' being derived from the Old Norse for 'river island'). It's the second largest isle on Windermere, though it still only clocks in at a far from steppe-like 2 acres. It's difficult to believe this fragile

little crescent of trees has had anything whatsoever to do with industry, but there was a time when gravel and sand would be extracted from around the island for use in construction.

A little to the south sit a pair of islands whose past role in the life of the lake is evident from their name. The Lilies of the Valley (East and West) are where the eponymous wildflowers proliferated, the scent of them in spring carrying across the waters. In the 18th century, tourists would row over specifically to pick a bunch or two. Sadly, they lifted rather too many and there are barely any left today. In Book II of *The Prelude* (see also Chapel Island, p116), William Wordsworth takes in not only the Lilies of the Valley but also Lady Holme and some other unnamed island thick with crooning birds:

When summer came,
Our pastime was, on bright half-holidays,
To sweep along the plain of Windermere
With rival oars; and the selected bourne
Was now an Island musical with birds
That sang and ceased not; now a
Sister Isle
Beneath the oaks' umbrageous
covert, sown
With lilies of the valley like a field;
And now a third small Island,
where survived
In solitude the ruins of a shrine
Once to Our Lady dedicate, and served
Daily with chaunted rites.

On the other side of Belle Isle lie two islets whose main claim to fame is that their names are wrong on OS maps. Birk (or Birch) Holme is rendered as Fir Holme (which appears to be just a straightforward

An island-hopping couple beneath Cumbria's perpetually gathering clouds

misidentification of trees), while Snake Holme appears as Stake Holme, which seems all the more egregious for its whiff of careless Friday afternoon typo.

Further south, Maiden Holme looks like a bit of a careless error itself. It's barely more than a smudge on the water, consisting of a single rather brave tree and almost nothing else. The island is actually moving, but at the time of writing is a little to the east of Coatlap Point. A *Blue Peter* presenter was abandoned on the islet once for the televisual entertainment of children. She was rescued though, cruelly denying the viewership some useful lessons in self-reliance.

Crow Holme was the curious choice for kennels to house the hounds of the Windermere Harriers. One would have thought the bother of getting dogs on and off the island would have been greater than whatever advantage was derived from keeping them there, but perhaps the men and women who wear the pink live by a different logic to the rest of us.

Keen or abnormally dogged rowers can carry on south from here – across the east–west path of Windermere's vehicle ferry – to Ramp Holme, an island whose name suggests it might once have been wreathed in ramsons (wild garlic). This little copse-on-the-water is owned by the National Trust and in its time has also answered to Roger Holme and Berkshire Island.

Deep in the far south lie five further isles, including Silver Holme, which became Cormorant Island in Arthur Ransome's *Swallows and Amazons*, and Blake Holme, which the children's author combined with Peel Island on Coniston to create Wild Cat Island (see p121). Meanwhile, way up at the northern end are Bee Holme, which is only an island when the level of the lake is high enough to cut it adrift from the shore, and Green Tuft Island, whose commendably succinct name provides the alpha and omega of all you will ever need to know about the place.

Which leaves us with the elephant in the room: Belle Isle. Even as elephants go, this one is huge, for it is not only the largest island on Windermere by a factor of 20 – its 40 acres all but slicing the lake in two – it is also the island burdened with the greatest number of interesting goings-on. However, it is in private hands and landing here is forbidden, which is a great pity. No discussion of the islands of Windermere would be complete without mentioning it though, so here are some snippets from its history.

The Romans were the first on board. They built a fort called Galava in AD80 at the northern tip of Windermere and the commander had a villa constructed on Belle Isle, probably around the same time. During the War of the Three Kingdoms, the island was held for the king and was duly attacked by Roundheads firing cannons from nearby Cockshott Point. A hundred years or so later, in 1774, work was started on the striking circular house (inspired by the Pantheon in Rome and believed to be the first Italianate roundhouse ever built in Britain) that still graces the island today. Wordsworth, who liked to have an opinion about housing on tiny islands (see p113) was unconvinced by it, describing it as 'a tea canister in a shop window', which is about as enigmatic an insult as you're ever likely to hear, while his sister Dorothy more famously called it 'a pepperpot', as if that were a bad thing.

That wasn't the last excitement Belle Isle was ever to see, however. The current owners, one of whom is a fixture on the *Sunday Times Rich List*, were both given short prison sentences in 2007. They had tried to get their son off a charge of speeding by denying that the notices of intended prosecution had ever reached Belle Isle, and were sent down for perverting the course of justice.

But it would be wrong to snigger as you row past.

How to get there

Take the train to Windermere station (virgintrains.co.uk, 01709 849200; tpexpress.co.uk) and then walk 1.5 miles or catch the 599 bus (stagecoachbus.com; 01228 597888) to Bowness-on-Windermere. There are many boat hire companies here including Windermere Lake Cruises (rowing boats and motorboats; windermere-lakecruises.co.uk; 015394 43360), Windermere Quays (electric boats; windermerequays.co.uk; 015394 42121), Bowness Bay Marina (electric boats; bownessbaymarina.co.uk; 015394 45535) and Low Wood Bay (rowing boats,

sailing dinghies, keelboats, kayaks, canoes and motor boats; englishlakes.co.uk/watersports; 015394 39441). These are open daily during the season. Windermere Lake Cruises hires motorboats out at weekends from November to March. Hire charges start from £12/hour for rowing boats, £18/hour for motorboats and £27/hour for electric boats.

Admission price/landing fee

Free.

View

From the islands near Bowness-on-Windermere, Wansfell Pike lurches up behind the lake to the north, to the west the shore is guarded by the steep and wooded Claife Heights, while to the south, there's Belle Isle.

Facilities

None.

Accommodation

Bowness-on-Windermere is awash with little B&Bs and guesthouses, including the excellent value **Annisgarth Bed and Breakfast** (annisgarth.co.uk; 015394 43866), a Victorian terraced house in the middle of town.

Campers should head towards the north of the lake near where there are several sites, including **Tarn Foot Farm** (7.5 miles; 01539 432596) at Loughrigg.

Nearest decent pub/café/tea room

There are cafés, pubs and tea rooms

Ducks manoeuvring into position prior to an assault on a moored yacht

aplenty in Bowness-on-Windermere. **The Elephant and Camel Café** (015394 88707) on Lake Road would be a good place to start.

Nearest shop

The Siamese-twin towns of **Bowness-on-Windermere** and **Windermere** fair creak beneath the strain of shops, many of which insist on trying to sell you outdoor gear.

Rules

Belle Isle is private. The other islands, most of which it is possible to land on with care, are owned by the National Park Authority, the National Trust or the Royal Windermere Yacht Club.

Things to do

Peter Rabbit and his chums do sometimes appear to be in a three-way wrestling bout with Wordsworth and Wainwright for the soul of the Lake District, and in Bowness they've forced a submission out of their opponents with the establishment of **The World of Beatrix Potter** (0.2 miles; warning – great website address ahead: hop-skip-jump.com; 0844 504 1233). All 23 of the tales told by Harry Potter's spiritual grandmother are brought to life 'with sights, sounds and even smells'.

23. Derwent Isle

Derwent Water
Nr Keswick, Cumbria
OS Landranger map 90
Grid reference: NY 259 212
Size: 7 acres
Population: 1 family

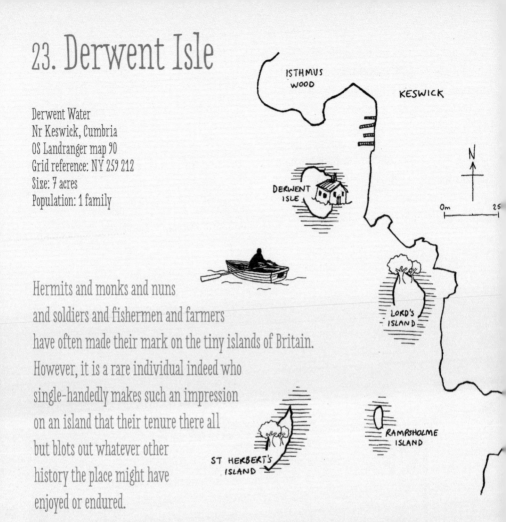

Hermits and monks and nuns and soldiers and fishermen and farmers have often made their mark on the tiny islands of Britain. However, it is a rare individual indeed who single-handedly makes such an impression on an island that their tenure there all but blots out whatever other history the place might have enjoyed or endured.

Such is the case with Derwent Isle – the man who made it his own being the otherwise entirely obscure figure of Joseph Pocklington. Derwent Isle (sometimes also known as Derwent Island) had already been through a number of incarnations before Pocklington arrived in the Lake District and fell in love with Derwentwater, the lake close to whose eastern shore it resides. The Vikings knew the island as Hestholm ('horse island'). It then became Vicar's Island – though whether this is due to its sometime ownership by the monks from Ripon's Fountains Abbey is unclear.

In 1564, with Pocklington's arrival still 200 years away, it unexpectedly played host to a small German colony. Elizabeth I invited miners from Germany over to what was then Cumberland to work the copper from the Newlands valley. Hundreds came, many of them setting up camp on Vicar's Island, where they also became smallholders and even brewed a little beer to remind themselves of home. They ended up building England's then largest smelting works and marrying into the local population (apparently bigamously at times).

The island's year of reckoning came in 1778 when Joseph Pocklington, the son of a banker from Nottinghamshire, paid £300 for it. Vicar's Island became Pocklington Island and its middle-aged owner with the silver spoon in his mouth was duly nicknamed King Pocky by the locals. He was to remain monarch for the next 17 years.

He immediately set to work transforming the 7-acre island. He employed people from nearby Keswick and beyond to build him a small mansion, a church, a boathouse disguised as a Nonconformist chapel, a porter's lodge and a miniature fortress with its own battery of small brass cannons that he named Fort Joseph (not that he was self-obsessed in any way). His tour de force, however, was the island's 'Druid's Circle'. It was based on the prehistoric circle at Castlerigg, not far from the lake, and Pocklington claimed that he had not erected it himself but discovered it. It was, he said (without a word of a lie), 'The most compleat and last built Temple in Europe.' It was not compleat for very long. The stones were dislodged by waves whipped up in a storm soon afterwards.

King Pocky was, to say the least, an eccentric character. His constructions were considered tasteless by many locals, including William Wordsworth, who took particularly badly to the mansion, judging it to be a blot on the landscape.

Undaunted, Pocklington, in league with his good friend Peter Crosthwaite, organised a regatta – something that was to become a red letter day in the Keswick calendar. Some of the events in their regatta would be unlikely to make the bill today, such as the horse swimming race. This involved a group of horses being towed out into the middle of the lake on a raft. The raft was then sunk. Spectators had, by then, placed bets on which animal would reach the shore first.

The highlight of each regatta, thankfully, was less injurious to equine stock, it being the mock invasion of Pocklington Island. An announcement from the 21 August 1781 edition of the *Cumberland Pacquet* advertised that year's carnage in advance: 'Pocklington's Island (late Vicar's Island) will be attacked by a formidable Fleet, when a stout resistance is to be made, especially from the Half Moon Battery; and it is to be thought the circling Mountains will bear a part in this Tremendous Uproar...'

Crosthwaite, the self-proclaimed 'Admiral of the Keswick Regatta', would command a flotilla of small boats. This was a task he claimed he was more than equal to, having previously – so he said – captained a gunboat in Malay whose duty was to ward off pirates from East India Company ships. Meanwhile Pocklington – fully living up to his King Pocky image – was in charge of the forces defending the island. To simulate the ensuing bombardment, both sides let off prodigious amounts of fireworks and bangers. The noise was so deafening it was reportedly heard as far away as Appleby-in-Westmorland, some 25 miles distant.

Derwent Isle has been in the hands of the National Trust since the 1950s and it remains the only inhabited isle on the lake. Pocklington's creations, such as the mansion and the Nonconformist boathouse, are still very much going concerns on what is now a thickly wooded isle in parts.

Although access to the island is restricted to a mere five days a year, the good news is that Derwent Water has three other main islands on which people can land at any time. They are all grouped in the northern half of the lake and are all covered by dense thickets.

The largest, at about 4.5 acres, is St Herbert's Island (or Isle), named after the missionary and hermit who lived here in the 7th century. The island became a fixture on the medieval pilgrimage trail and apparently the remains of his cell can just be discerned, though it has to be said that you really need to know what you're looking for and where. The isle faded back into the shadows until 1903 when Beatrix Potter refashioned it as Owl Island for *The Tale of Squirrel Nutkin*, in which it becomes the objective of a little flotilla of twig rafts captained by squirrels.

Lord's Island was once graced by an imposing home built sometime around 1460 and which belonged to successive Earls of Derwentwater. There is said to have been a drawbridge across to the mainland, though if this is true it must have been a colossal affair or the distance from the

Derwent Isle in its summer finery, with Cat Bells behind

shore considerably closer, for today there is some 75yd of water to cross.

It was a fondness for the Jacobite cause that proved the family's downfall. In 1716, following the first rebellion, the 3rd Earl was arrested, had his title stripped from him and then – which must have been the bitterest blow of all – beheaded. The family continued to use the title despite the attainder but the 5th Earl was to meet the same fate 30 years later in the aftermath of the second Jacobite rebellion. A stirring tale is told of how his wife, the countess, fled Lord's Island in order to avoid arrest. A wafer-thin cleft in the face of Walla Crag on the mainland is said to have facilitated her escape and is called Lady's Rake in her honour.

The last of the major islands, and at roughly 200ft long by 100ft wide it only just scrapes into that category, is Rampsholme. Named after the wild garlic that grows here in profusion (*hrafns holmr* being the Old Norse for 'garlic island'), its claim to fame is that it is the setting for the play *Neville's Island* by Tim Firth (he of *Calendar Girls*) – a dark comedy about four middle-aged men who are stranded on the island after a team-building exercise goes disastrously wrong.

The remaining islands – little more than rocky outcrops in reality – are Otterbield Island, Otter Island and a little scattering near the northwestern shore called the Lingholm Islands. However, if certain local people are to be believed, Derwent Water does occasionally lay claim to one extra isle that doesn't appear on maps. Towards the end of the summer, keep your eyes peeled for a sizeable floating island of vegetation that is said to bob about on a cushion of methane. Just don't leap out of your boat onto it in a bid to claim it as your own.

How to get there

Take the train to Windermere station (virgintrains.co.uk; 01709 849200, tpexpress.co.uk) followed by the 555 bus (stagecoachbus.com; 01228 597888) to Keswick bus station. Then walk 0.75 miles to the landing stage to take the ferry to Derwent Isle (only possible for five days a year – see 'Rules'). To visit the other islands on Derwentwater, you can hire rowing boats and small motorboats from Keswick Launch Company (keswick-launch. co.uk; 017687 72263) from March to the third week of November. Alternatively, take the 77 bus for the short journey to Portinscale and the Derwent Water Marina (derwentwatermarina.co.uk; 017687 72912) where there are kayaks, canoes, rowing boats, sailing dinghies and windsurf boards for hire all year round (but for a fortnight around Christmas). The Keswick ferry landing stage is a few hundred yards closer to the islands than is the marina at Portinscale. Only non-motorised boats are able to land at the islands. At Keswick, rowing boats cost from £12/hour and motor boats from £27/hour. At Portinscale, prices range from £8/hour for a kayak to £30/hour for a Laser 16 sailing dinghy.

Admission price/landing fee
Free.

View

The wooded shores of Derwent Water with a huddle of fantastically scowling hills crowding around behind (it's all right, they're suddenly all smiles again as soon as the sun comes out).

Facilities

None. There are public toilets by the car park next to the Theatre by the Lake, near the Keswick ferry landing stage.

Accommodation

Campers have **Castlerigg Farm** (1.8 miles from Keswick landing stage; castleriggfarm. com; 017687 72479) just around the corner. It comes with a terrific panorama of the fells and down towards Derwent Water. If you prefer a firm roof over your head, try **The Lookout** (1.4 miles from Keswick landing stage; thelookoutkeswick.co.uk; 07786 547459), a 1920s house with its own astonishing vistas from a large balcony.

Nearest decent pub/café/tea room

Opposite the Keswick landing stage, the **Lakeside Tea Gardens** (017687 72293) has plenty of outdoor seating and a pianola playing tea dance melodies inside.

Nearest shop

Keswick is a compact town overflowing with shops, one or two of which sell things other than walking and camping gear.

Rules

Derwent Isle is inhabited, owned by the National Trust, and accessible just five days a year (there are special boat trips organised when this occurs; tinyurl. com/8zvonol). Landing is possible on the other three main islands but no overnight stays are permitted. Be careful not to disturb any nesting birds.

Things to do

In Keswick, a major draw is the **Pencil Museum** (pencilmuseum.co.uk; 017687 73626) which makes the history of the Cumberland Pencil Company more interesting than it sounds, as well as putting on family fun days and drawing classes. Meanwhile, Keswick's **Theatre by the Lake** (theatrebythelake.co.uk; 017687 74411) is extremely highly regarded and it's well worth catching a show there.

24. St Mary's Island

nr Whitley Bay
Tyne and Wear
friendsofstmarysisland.co.uk
OS Landranger map 88
Grid reference: NZ 353 755
Size: 0.75 acres
Population: 1 family

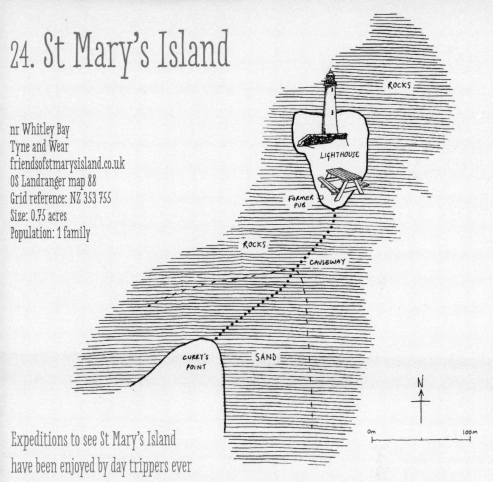

ROCKS

LIGHTHOUSE

FORMER PUB

ROCKS

CAUSEWAY

CURRY'S POINT

SAND

N

0m   100m

Expeditions to see St Mary's Island have been enjoyed by day trippers ever since the railway came to Whitley Bay in 1882. Back then the iconic lighthouse had yet to be built but there was the even more compelling pull of an inn.

Today there's a jolly collection of buildings – the bright white lighthouse, a red-roofed cottage, a larger handsome house behind. A wide concrete causeway leads over to them and the 300 million-year-old sandstone rock on which they stand. Touring cyclists weave cautiously around ice cream-licking holidaymakers while, during term time, primary school children out on a trip gabble their way excitedly across. Doubtless their teachers aren't quick to tell them that Curry's Point, at the mainland end of the causeway, is so called because that's where Michael Curry was strung from a gibbet for the murder of Robert Shevil, landlord of the nearby inn at Old Hartley. Or perhaps that's the sort of thing that gets taught all the time nowadays in primary schools. Anyway, this is definitely not one of those islands to which only the adventurous and the bold obtain access.

The boathouse on Derwent Isle

In the Middle Ages, you were in fact most likely to spend time here if you were dead. Monks from Tynemouth Priory used the islet as a burial ground and founded a chapel dedicated not to St Mary, as might be imagined, but to St Helen. This place of worship served as an unofficial lighthouse since sailors were alerted to the presence of the rock by a light that was kept burning in a window. This was traditionally known as a 'St Mary's light', which is how the island eventually came by its name. However, after Henry VIII's dissolution of the monasteries, the islet became known as Bates Hill, Hartley Bates or Bates Island after one-time owner Thomas Bates. This mutated to Bait Island due to a mix-up that occurred when surveyors for the first Ordnance Survey maps paid a visit and leapt to the conclusion that the name had something to do with the island's fishermen digging for worms. Fabulously, over 150 years later, the OS still hasn't corrected the error, with some present-day maps continuing to give 'Bait Island' as an alternative name.

Space on the island that has not been colonised by buildings is at a premium, but has largely been used for the benefit of visitors. There's a grassy section for picnics, an area with benches for those who would just sit and stare, and a raised sensory garden filled with herbs and plants to delight the nose and fingertips as well as the eyes. Just beyond this garden, a channel in the rocks known as Smugglers' Creek was the scene of something rather less

delightful. In 1722 the Surveyor of Customs, Anthony Mitchell, was foully murdered here, reputedly by a pair of brandy runners.

There was more death to come in 1799 when Russian soldiers en route to the Napoleonic Wars were stricken with cholera and swiftly quarantined on the island. As with those who found themselves holed up on St Helen's (p31) or Inchcolm (p274), only the very fortunate survived. Those who didn't were buried alongside the long-dead monks. The cemetery itself is now buried and human bones are sometimes unearthed in the course of building works.

The chapel has gone too, though it continues to live on in essence since its stones were used in a small croft constructed in 1855 by a fisherman called George Ewen. When laws governing salmon fishing changed, Ewen had to diversify and he turned the croft into an inn called The Freemason's Arms (though known to regulars as The Square and Compass), which proved an instant hit due to the fact that, when the tide was in, the local constabulary was kept at bay.

Ewen was eventually evicted after a dispute with a local farmer and a Mr and Mrs Crisp turned the alehouse into a temperance hotel, which is all very worthy but doubtless made St Mary's a duller place. It's a private residence again nowadays and last changed hands as recently as 2012. The two former lighthouse keepers' cottages now house the visitor centre and shop, so, when the causeway is covered, the island's sole inhabitants have the place to themselves.

This must make up for the decided lack of seclusion at low tide on hot summer days when happy sightseers come to climb the lighthouse. Inside, its steps cling on to the wall as they spiral upwards. From a floor just below the light, a further flight of almost vertical steps rises to the lamp room itself. There's no chance of being blinded up here since the lighthouse was decommissioned in 1984 – modern navigational technology having made it redundant. As one might expect, there are some wondrous views out to sea and along the coast if the weather's good.

Unfortunately the weather, even in sunny England, is not always good and there are estimated to have been over 300 shipwrecks around these parts. Work on the lighthouse was begun in 1896 to replace an ineffective light on the mainland and completed two years and 750,000 bricks later at a cost of £8,000. Unhappily, the light couldn't save every passing ship, as is only too evident at low tide when part of the keel of the *California*, a Russian four-masted iron barque, can be seen. The ship was driven onto the rocks in a storm in January 1913 with the loss of eight lives. It's safe to say that St Mary's hasn't been a happy place for Russians. However, at least the captain, who was rescued when at death's door, managed to pull through after spending a week being tended to by the Crisps. In gratitude he gave them

the ship's figurehead. This did not depict some fearless blonde maiden in a state of *déshabillé* as is usually the case but was a carving of the ship's architect, Walter Wilson, in evening dress. Their response to this gift is, sadly, unrecorded.

How to get there
Hop off the train at Newcastle, then take the Metro (nexus.org.uk; 0191 203 3199) to Whitley Bay, from where the 308 (arrivabus.co.uk; 0191 244 5695) or 309 bus (simplygo.co.uk; 0845 606 0260) will take you as far as Whitley Bay Cemetery from where it's a half-mile walk to the causeway. The island is open only for a few hours a day (and not every day) between May and September. It is also usually open most Saturdays and Sundays from October to April, as well as on certain other dates. Before setting out, it's best to check here: friendsofstmarysisland.co.uk.

Admission price/landing fee
Free, but entrance fee charged (adult £2.60, child £1.35) if you want to climb the lighthouse and visit the visitor centre.

View
From the top of the lighthouse there's Whitley Bay to the south, with Seaton Sluice, spartan Blyth and some inshore wind turbines to the north.

Facilities
Souvenir shop, visitor centre, toilets (there are more toilets by the car park on the mainland), a sensory garden, cycle stands, picnic tables, a birdwatching hide and, should you suddenly feel the need to have a meeting, a conference room.

Accommodation
Try the popular and inexpensive **Sunholme Guesthouse** (2.4 miles; sunholme.co.uk; 0191 251 1186) in Whitley Bay.

Nearest decent pub/café/tea room
If you're absolutely desperate, there's usually a **refreshment trailer** and an **ice cream van** opposite the island in summer. Otherwise, head for the incandescently bright lights of Whitley Bay (2 miles).

Nearest shop
For a whole new retail experience, try the shop inside the **Whitley Bay Holiday Park** (0.5 mile). For a whole old retail experience, Whitley Bay (2 miles) is just down the road.

Rules
Dogs must be kept on a lead. The last admission up the lighthouse is half an hour before the island closes.

Things to do
18th-century **Seaton Delaval Hall** (3 miles; nationaltrust.org.uk/seaton-delaval-hall; 0191 237 9100) claims to be 'the finest house in the northeast of England' and has some pretty spectacular gardens to boot. Whitley Bay's **Playhouse** (2 miles; playhousewhitleybay.co.uk; 0844 277 2771) is the jewel of the town's regeneration and hosts a steady stream of live events rarely seen outside seaside towns.

The causeway to St Mary's at low tide

25. Inner Farne

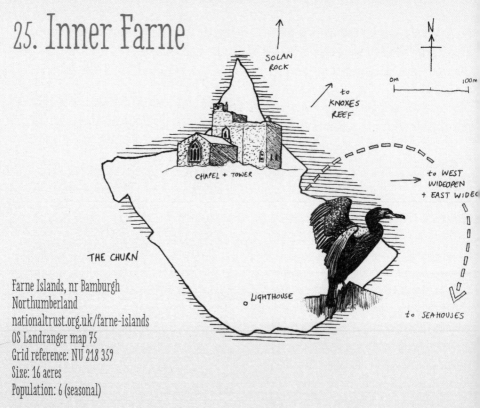

SOLAN ROCK

to KNOXES REEF

N

0m   100m

to WEST WIDEOPEN + EAST WIDEO

CHAPEL + TOWER

THE CHURN

to SEAHOUSES

LIGHTHOUSE

Farne Islands, nr Bamburgh
Northumberland
nationaltrust.org.uk/farne-islands
OS Landranger map 75
Grid reference: NU 218 359
Size: 16 acres
Population: 6 (seasonal)

Few things look more vulnerable than a low-lying island in the midst of the waves, and many of the 28 Farne Islands look ripe for disappearance at the slightest rise in global sea levels. Indeed, some are even now only visible at the lowest of tides. In this respect, Inner Farne can count itself fortunate, for although it slides precariously into the North Sea on one side, its western cliffs rise to the highest point in the entire island group – a nosebleed-inducing 62ft above sea level.

It was not their apparent fragility that first brought St Aidan to these isles in around AD640 but the lack of human activity upon them. He came to Inner Farne to meditate, away from the hustle and bustle of Lindisfarne (Holy Island), which was then the centre of all things Christian in Britain and where he served as bishop for 16 years. The deserted Inner Farne was only a little over 5 nautical miles away but may as well have been on a different planet. However, Aidan found he couldn't entirely escape from the world even here. One day in AD642, he was apparently jolted from his meditations by the sight of King Penda and his Mercian army attacking the royal city of Bamburgh on the mainland. He instantly set about praying and lo, the wind changed, blowing flames from the burning city into the faces of the marauders.

The islands are split into two clusters separated by Staple Sound. The many boats that ply the waves from Seahouses, 30 minutes away, sweep up to the more southerly federation – of which Inner Farne is quite obviously the top dog – and more often than not pass through a guard of honour composed of grey seals. Around 6,000 of these amiable souls live around the islands, forming one of Europe's most important colonies.

However, it is not so much the seals that draw visitors to these islands as the birds. Inner Farne glories in thousands of them, including puffins, guillemots, shags, cormorants, razorbills, eiders, Sandwich terns, common terns and roseate terns. It is the Arctic terns, though, that the summer visitor first becomes rather acutely aware of on landing at the small jetty on the eastern side of the island. Those incomers who forgot their hats or who did not know to bring one soon create a makeshift one with their arms as they scurry to all that remains of St Mary's chapel, a little shelter that now acts as the National Trust's visitor centre. On their way they pass through a busy Arctic tern nesting area and the birds, fearful for the safety of their eggs or young, dive-bomb the heads of interlopers. Their bills, as sharp as any dentist's drill, can deliver a jab of surprising ferocity to the exposed pate, and visitors who consider themselves too cool to cover their heads rarely feel the same way after the first retributive assault.

It means that the first feature of interest on the island is frequently overlooked. The Fishehouse, right by the jetty, is the last remnant of a guesthouse that St Cuthbert built for those coming to visit him. For all that St Aidan got here first, it is St Cuthbert who has made the greatest mark on the island. The chapel just across from the visitor centre (through yet more Arctic terns) is named after him and it was he who first built a cell here in AD676. His story is one of 7th-century social mobility. Growing up as a shepherd boy, he entered the monastery and ended up being begged by the Archbishop of Canterbury to become the Bishop of Lindisfarne.

Cuthbert was merely the Prior of Lindisfarne and had reached the grand old age of 39 when he came to live on Inner Farne as a hermit. Angels helped him build the walls of his cell so that they shut out all earthly distractions. However, he was soon at work putting up a wooden cross to scare away the demons that inhabited East and West Wideopen, the neighbouring islets used for burying locally shipwrecked sailors. According to Cuthbert, the demons were 'clad in cowls and riding upon goats, black in complexion, short in stature, their countenances most hideous, their heads long, the appearance of the whole troop horrible', so it's just as well he got rid of them really.

After a short spell as Bishop of Lindisfarne, Cuthbert returned to Inner Farne to die, which thing he did on 20

March 687. The beautiful little 14th-century chapel, which was restored in the 1800s, is dedicated to him, and the remains of his cell are believed to lie beneath the grand Castell Tower next door. Although it was built around 1500 to defend the island, this pele tower owes its name not to any fortress-like characteristics but to the man who had it built, the Prior of Durham, Thomas Castell. Although it did boast a small garrison, it mainly served to house monks, before going on to become a primitive lighthouse. It's now home to the half-dozen National Trust rangers who live on the island for up to nine months a year.

Although there were other hermits who came to live here after Cuthbert – including Bartholomew, who stayed from 1150 to 1193 and wrote the Farne Meditations – not all those called to the religious life were as upright as the great saint. The 15th century was a particularly rum one for the monastery, with John de Rypon sent away for 'extravagance', John Harom discovered to have pawned the chapel's chalice and some fine robes, and John Kirke caught in the pursuit of women. Such unbecoming behaviour would have shocked the institution's earlier benefactors, albeit that Alexander II of Scotland had granted the brotherhood an annual sum of only eight shillings, which perhaps did not help assuage his nation's reputation for parsimony. Not that the English monarchs were any better – Edward III passed the duty of paying the monks to the city of Newcastle, while Henry III merely gave them a plot on the mainland for the construction of a storehouse.

A path marks out a circuit of the island from the chapel and tower to the lighthouse, taking a longer route back via the western coast. In summer you are rarely more than a few yards from something feathered and great care must be taken to stay on the path and to avoid treading on the tiny balls of fluff and incomprehension that make their way onto it. The air is filled with the squawking and shrieking of birds on a constant mission to be somewhere else. The ground is carpeted with pensive puffins – known locally as 'tommy noddies' – the scrub-covered earth pockmarked with their burrows. The cliffs are crammed with preening shags and statuesque cormorants. This is a place where total and intimate immersion in birdlife is not only possible but unavoidable, and can have few rivals anywhere in Britain. It's fitting that when St Cuthbert was here he laid down decrees protecting the island's birdlife – what were possibly the first such regulations anywhere in the world. In Northumberland, eiders are known as 'cuddy ducks' (from 'Cuthbert's ducks') to this day.

At the landward end of the island sits a squat white lighthouse and keeper's cottage in a neat white-walled enclosure. The light was built in 1809, replacing an earlier one that supported a beacon where coal and wood was burnt. However, it was not the Farne lighthouse that would be catapulted to fame. That fate befell Longstone light,

Clockwise from top left: Inner Farne from the south; Seahouses harbour with a boat that sails to the island; shags

at the far seaward end of the group. From here it was, on the morning of 7 September 1838, that lighthouseman William Darling and his youngest daughter rowed out into the teeth of gale-force winds and lashing waves to save the few survivors among the 63 passengers and crew of the steamer Forfarshire as it languished on the rocks of Big Harcar. Grace Darling became a heroine to her nation, the popular press of the day happily exaggerating reports of her actions, and she received £700 from public subscriptions. Even Queen Victoria gave her a gift of £50 in recognition of her bravery. It was not to end well though. The media frenzy and public interest in her (from marriage proposals to requests for locks of her hair to unannounced

visitors arriving on Longstone just to touch her) quickly became burdensome. The intrusions into her life – she couldn't leave the lighthouse without causing a furore – lasted all the way up to her death four years later from tuberculosis. She was 26.

How to get there

From Alnmouth railway station (eastcoast. co.uk; 08457 225225) take the X16 bus (arrivabus.co.uk; 0844 800 4411) to Alnwick then the 418 (travelsure.co.uk; 01665 720955) to Seahouses. Four companies offer various trips that land on Inner Farne, and their booking office booths are in a sweet little row on the harbour front. They are Billy Shiel MBE (farne-islands. com; 01665 720308); Golden Gate (01665

Left: An Arctic tern fledgling wanders across a walkway; Right: Stained-glass window in St Cuthbert's chapel

721210); Serenity (farneislandtours.
co.uk; 01665 721667); and Hanvey's
(farneislands.co.uk; 01665 720388). The
fare is around £13 (£9 for children) for a
landing trip, which often includes a cruise
around the other Farne Islands. The island
is open to the public from 1 April to
31 October.

Admission price/landing fee
Adult £6.20, child £3.10. National Trust
members free.

View
The other Farne Islands, Bamburgh Castle
and Holy Island.

Facilities
Toilets, a small visitor centre that sells a
few, largely puffin-centric souvenirs.

Accommodation
The excellent **Beadnell Bay campsite**
(1.75 miles from Seahouses; tinyurl.
com/92a8epy; 01665 720586 – no
calls after 8pm) has views over the
sea. Meanwhile, there are wigwams, a
bunkhouse, a campsite and cottages to
let at **Springhill Farm** (1.3 miles from
Seahouses; springhill-farm.co.uk; 01665
721820).

Nearest decent pub/café/tea room
The 18th-century **Olde Ship Inn** (0.1
miles; seahouses.co.uk; 01665 720200),
has nautically themed bars that teeter
precariously on the tightrope between
charming and tacky.

Nearest shop
Seahouses has plenty of shops, albeit that
a high proportion sell gifts, mementoes and
other of life's unnecessities.

Rules
No dogs. Keep to the walkways and, in the
breeding season, make sure you don't step
on any chicks.

Things to do
Just up the coast, **Bamburgh Castle** (3
miles from Seahouses; bamburghcastle.
net; 01668 214515) is the royal seat of the
Kings of Northumbria and one of Britain's
largest inhabited fortresses.
The **Grace Darling Museum** (3.6 miles
from Seahouses; free; tinyurl.com/8jm5vvh;
01668 214910) in Bamburgh tells the story
of the courageous young woman's big night
and its unforeseen aftermath.

Bird-friendly cliffs with the lighthouse behind

GLASGOW
EDINBURGH
ARRAN
NORTHERN IRELAND
NEWCASTLE
ISLE OF MAN
LEEDS
KINGSTON UPON HULL
IRISH SEA
ANGLESEY ISLAND
MANCHESTER
LIVERPOOL
35
34
33
32
31
NOTTINGHAM
BIRMINGHAM
WALES
CAMBRIDG
30
OXFORD
LONDON
26
27
28
CARDIFF
29
BRISTOL
BRISTOL CHANNEL
SOUTHAMPTON
PLYMOUTH
ISLE OF WIGHT
ENGLISH CHANNEL

WALES

26. Skokholm

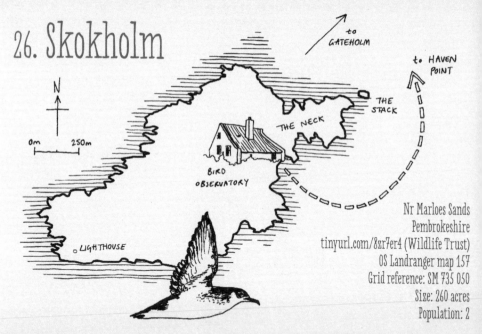

N
0m 250m

to GATEHOLM
to HAVEN POINT
THE STACK
THE NECK
BIRD OBSERVATORY
LIGHTHOUSE

Nr Marloes Sands
Pembrokeshire
tinyurl.com/8zr7er4 (Wildlife Trust)
OS Landranger map 157
Grid reference: SM 735 050
Size: 260 acres
Population: 2

Poor Skokholm. If only it had somehow drifted further up the Welsh coastline – to Cardigan Bay perhaps, or Milford Haven – it might have found fame and fortune. As it is, it's doomed to play second fiddle to its larger neighbour Skomer, an island that can offer a stone circle, prehistoric houses, a standing stone and a more easily pronounceable name.

However, being much less accessible than Skomer, Skokholm can at least claim to be the more exclusive of the two islands. And when it comes to birdlife, Skokholm (or Ynys Sgogwm to give it its seldom-used Welsh name) is certainly a match. Huge numbers of Manx shearwater and storm petrel congregate around the island, while puffins, razorbills and guillemots breed on its high old red sandstone cliffs. Add in the large colonies of gulls along with plentiful oystercatchers, skylarks, wheatears and the rare chough, and choice blown-in visitors such as the purple heron, golden oriole and glossy ibis, and you begin to realise why

the Wildlife Trust was so keen to buy the island back in 2006.

The outline of Skokholm would bear an almost perfect likeness to the grey seals that haul out on its rocky foreshore if it weren't for the trunk-like peninsula that bursts out of its eastern flank. On one side of this promontory is South Haven, where an unassuming stone pier greets visitors to the isle. The name Skokholm comes from the Old Norse for 'wooded island' but there are very few trees left here now. This leaves an almost uninterrupted view across the island as it rises gradually from the 70ft cliffs in the northeast to the 160ft cliffs in the southwestern corner. And you don't have to look very far for a clue as to how Skokholm lost its 'skok' – on the path between South Haven and the island's only cottage stands a wonderfully preserved lime kiln. Here limestone would have been burnt with culm (a mixture of clay and coal dust) to produce fertiliser. For hundreds of years, from the Norman era up until Victorian times, any time-travelling Vikings rowing past would have surely have renamed the place Býrholm – 'farm island'.

The cottage – a farmhouse built around the early 1700s – was renovated from top to bottom in 2012 and now provides very smart accommodation for the island's warden, as well as volunteers and visitors. Sporting toothpaste-white walls and roof, it's named after naturalist Ronald Lockley who leased Skokholm in 1927, painstakingly repaired the buildings and founded a bird observatory. Next door, a low outbuilding also decked out entirely in white (either coloured paint is unobtainable in the locality or the decorators decided to create their own somewhat misplaced tribute to Leeds United) has also been converted into basic but comfy lodgings for visitors.

The land between these former farm buildings and the lighthouse on Skokholm's southwestern tip belongs to the birds and the rabbits, the latter having been introduced by the Normans. The island's flora, managed by these peaceable mammals, is surprisingly diverse and includes relatively unusual specimens such as three-lobed water crowfoot, rock sea spurrey and small nettle. The island also has areas of wetland and saltmarsh in which mudweed (surely one of the least complimentary names ever given to a living organism) and sea milkwort grow. Fans of rare lichens and nationally rare invertebrates are in for a treat too.

The attractive lighthouse, another vision in white, was built during World War I and now runs automatically on solar power. The difficulty of getting supplies the mile from the island's quay to the lighthouse was solved by the creation of a narrow-gauge railway and sections of the line can still be seen here and there. The railway's two small trucks were initially pulled by a donkey. A pony then took over duties until eventually made redundant by a tractor. The lighthouse was snapped up by the Wildlife Trust in 2012 and there are plans afoot to convert it into Skokholm's third lodging house. Should this come to pass you'll almost certainly have to do battle for a room with hordes of writers, artists and other creative types because it's hard to imagine a more inspiring location to hole up in for a week.

Just along the cliffs is the crater left by the island's disused quarry. From here you can keep a lookout over the waves for harbour porpoise – daily visitors in late summer – as well as common, bottlenose and Risso's dolphins, all of which are somewhat less prolific in number.

But Skokholm's twin jewels are its Manx shearwater and storm petrel. Around 15 per cent of the world population of the former are found around Skokholm and Skomer. Like the storm petrel, the hardy little birds spend most of their lives at sea, only coming on land to breed and then only after dark. With burrows to defend and pair bonds to re-establish, the nocturnal hours during the breeding season (roughly April to August) are busy ones. A moonless night full of the unceasing cries of unseen Manx shearwater is an experience not readily forgotten.

How to get there

From Milford Haven railway station (arrivatrainswales.co.uk; 0870 900 0773) take the somewhat sporadic 315 (Edwards Bros) to Marloes. It's a 2.5-mile walk to Martin's Haven, from where the Wildlife Trust ferry sails to Skokholm. At the time of writing, a decision had yet to be made as to whether day trips would recommence in 2013. If they do, sailings will be between mid-April and October (there may even be some evening trips thrown in too). If not, it's still possible to visit if you stay on the island (see 'Accommodation'). The boat fare is £25 return.

Admission price/landing fee

Free.

View

Skomer, Gateholm (p154) and the Pembrokeshire coastline.

Facilities

Compost loos and a small shop that stocks tinned food suitable for those staying overnight.

Accommodation

The **two dwellings** on Skokholm (tinyurl. com/8ctnws5; 01239 621600) were entirely refurbished in 2012 and are available to let from April to October. They have a combination of single, twin and double rooms and can accommodate up to 20 people for three-day, four-day or week-long stays at very reasonable rates. (Wildlife Trust members get first dibs at bookings, which is yet another good reason for joining the organisation.)

Nearest decent pub/café/tea room

Head for Dale and the much lauded **Griffin Inn** (4.5 miles; griffininndale.co.uk; 01646 636227) on the waterfront.

Nearest shop

For anything other than tinned goods, which are available in the tiny island shop, there's **Marloes Village Store and Post Office** (2 miles; 01646 636968).

Rules

Keep to footpaths. No dogs.

Things to do

Rather conveniently, sailings to neighbouring **Skomer** leave from Martin's Haven up to three times a day from April to October, weather permitting (tinyurl. com/8oygej7).

Gateholm (p154; 1.5 miles along coastal path from Martin's Haven) is accessible at low tide from Marloes Sands.

The **Milford Haven Heritage and Maritime Museum** (11 miles; milfordhavenmuseum. org.uk; 01646 694496) provides an interesting and inexpensive examination of the area's history.

Clockwise from top left: Manx shearwater burrows at Purple Cove; Skokholm puffin with sand eels; the lighthouse

27. Gateholm

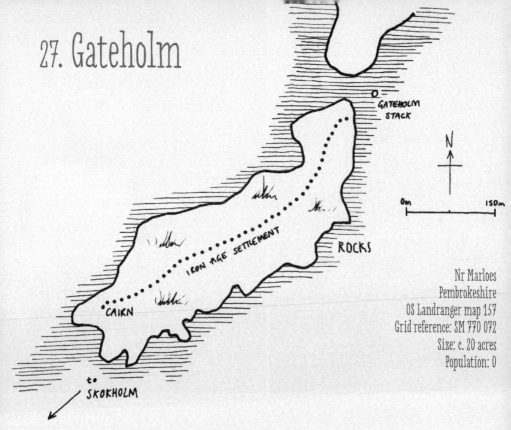

GATEHOLM STACK

N

0m — 150m

IRON AGE SETTLEMENT

ROCKS

CAIRN

to SKOKHOLM

Nr Marloes
Pembrokeshire
OS Landranger map 157
Grid reference: SM 770 072
Size: c. 20 acres
Population: 0

Gateholm is not an island that gives up its secrets willingly. The 100ft flanks of this flat-topped sentinel rise almost vertically from the Irish Sea. Once upon a time it formed a lengthy promontory thrusting out from the Pembrokeshire coast and the good people who lived here could simply stroll out along it.

However, since its conversion into an island by the ever-clawing waves sometime in the last millennium or two, a visit to this wild National Trust-owned outpost has entailed something a little more taxing. Indeed, unless you're a climber or happy grappling with almost sheer rock faces, you may have to content yourself with enjoying the vertiginous descent from the mainland to Marloes Sands and colonising Gateholm's bouldery foundations at low tide. At least

you'll have the wonderful crimson rocks of old red sandstone to gaze upon.

If you are confident about going up, by far the best option presents itself at the southeastern corner. A precipitous slope, doubtless caused by part of the island falling into the sea, leads up to the southern tip. The first 10ft of this incline will prove the trickiest to overcome since the rock face offers minimal hand and foot holds. The next section consists of further steep rock but with vegetation on the left-hand side. The final section is the easiest and it's possible to clamber up this onto the top of the island.

When Channel 4's *Time Team* came here they got Tony Robinson and his crew of archaeologists onto the island by means of a long zip wire from the mainland. Despite being on Gateholm for only three days, they did some invaluable work, proving that not all television is mind-numbing pap broadcast for the specific purpose of tearing the souls from the bodies of its sofa-bound audience and beating them to a pulp with a cudgel bearing the legend 'Dante was right'.

Although finds made on previous digs in the 1920s and 30s, including a small bronze stag, suggested that Gateholm had been inhabited during a number of different periods, the prevailing wisdom was that the existing archaeological remains were of an early Christian monastery. The *Time Team* established that the truth was something quite different.

The reward for scrambling up onto the island is a view of a thin, flat curve of clumpy grass ungrazed by rabbits. A narrow path, now much overgrown and difficult to make out, winds its way to the far end, where an apologetically small cairn provides the island's only notable feature. Ordnance Survey maps of Gateholm display the word Settlement and the symbol for a church. Furthermore, aerial photos show a vast number of circles and squiggles and curves across the length of the island. However, on the ground it takes a very sharp pair of eyes indeed to discern anything other than tussock after tussock after tussock.

This is not necessarily a bad thing. It just means that you will need all your powers of imagination to conjure up the generations of communities who, if Tony Robinson is to be believed, once called this exposed plot of land home.

The first known settlers arrived in the Bronze Age and created half a dozen smallholdings here. By the Iron Age there was double that number of roundhouses dotted about. However, Gateholm really came into its own during the Roman occupation of Britain, when a huge slew of buildings was erected and a road laid to connect them. A lot of the structures were very small, akin to the cells of monks, which is what led to the belief that a Christian monastery had been founded here. During the 2nd and 3rd centuries as many as 200 people may have lived on the promontory, making it a very important community.

Why did they come here? One of the reasons is obvious at first glance: it's an admirably defendable position, even back in the days when it was part of the mainland. But there's more to Gateholm than that. It was once the Heathrow of its day – a hub at the centre of a busy network of transport routes, with ships sailing between here and Scotland, Ireland, Cornwall, the Isle of Man and other parts of Wales. Also, the site was very likely to have been of religious significance. Without putting too fine a point on it, to ancient humans the promontory would have resembled the male member, making it an obvious choice of location for the performance of all-important fertility rites. A phallus and an amber bead found on Gateholm would seem to bear this out.

At some point after these thousands of years of activity, a section of the promontory closest to the mainland began collapsing into the sea, and Gateholm was born. This gives it a curious distinction: it is younger than the history scarred upon it. It's fitting too that a promontory on which fertility rituals were carried out should give birth to an island. No doubt the ancient priests would have chuckled over that.

How to get there

Alight at Milford Haven railway station (arrivatrainswales.co.uk; 0870 900 0773) and board the infrequent 315 (Edwards Bros) to Marloes, from where it's a 2-mile walk to Gateholm. From the Marloes Sands National Trust car park, take the track past the YHA hostel to the end, turn left along the footpath, then right along

the cliff path. Opposite Gateholm turn left down the cliffs, forking left halfway down. It's a scramble over boulders to the foot of Gateholm. Alternatively, after passing Marloes Court, follow the signposts to Marloes Sands and walk west along the beach and over the boulders.

NB: There's no path up from the beach onto Gateholm, so unless you're a climber or happy grappling with steep rock faces, you'll have to make do with colonising the island's rocky bottom. Should you go up, remember that coming down will be trickier. If you fall off and break your ankle, wrist, neck, etc, you've only yourself and gravity to blame. Accessibility is very variable but if you reckon on there being an hour either side of low tide in which to cross you shouldn't find yourself stranded.

Admission price/landing fee
Free.

View
Skomer, Skokholm (p150) and the Pembrokeshire coastline.

Facilities
None, though there are some loos provided by the National Trust next door to the YHA (see 'Accommodation').

Accommodation
YHA Marloes Sands (0.2 miles; yha. org.uk/hostel/marloes-sands; 0845 371 9333) could hardly be better placed for an assault on Gateholm and has private rooms as well as dorms. There are campsites at **West Hook Farm** (2 miles; westhookfarm-camping.co.uk; 01646 636424), which has great views but is rather exposed to the elements, and **Foxdale** (2 miles; foxdaleguesthouse.co.uk; 01646 636243), the latter also offering B&B and a self-catering apartment. Further accommodation can be found at marloes.org.uk.

Nearest decent pub/café/tea room
From Easter to autumn head for **The Clock House** (2 miles; clockhousemarloes.co.uk; 01646 636527) in Marloes, where you'll find a licensed Mediterranean-style café/bar.

Nearest shop
Marloes Village Store and Post Office (2 miles; 01646 636968) stocks groceries, fresh fruit and veg, and a small selection of alcoholic beverages.

Rules
None.

Things to do
The **Marloes Mere Britton hide** on the track between the youth hostel and Gateholm offers the possibility of spotting yet more feathered wildlife.

Boats run by the Wildlife Trust (1.5 miles by coastal footpath; tinyurl.com/9skrhgk) to Skomer and Skokholm (p150) leave from Martin's Haven.

28. Worm's Head

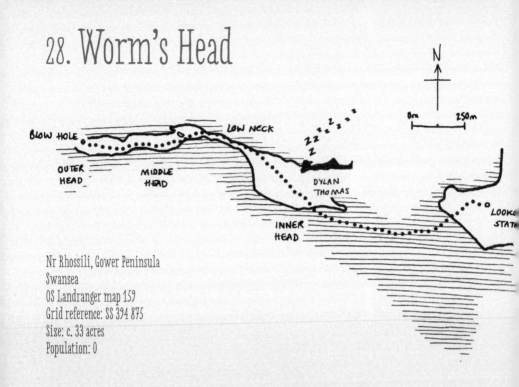

Nr Rhossili, Gower Peninsula
Swansea
OS Landranger map 159
Grid reference: SS 394 875
Size: c. 33 acres
Population: 0

The English language is an incorrigible thief but sometimes its sins do find it out. Such is the case with Worm's Head, an extraordinary tidal island whose constituent parts bear little resemblance to any section of a worm (though, let's face it, all the sections of a worm look alike anyway, probably even to other worms).

They do, however, call to mind what the top of a scaly dragon's neck and head might look like if it chose to poke itself up from under the waves. It's no surprise to learn then that the Worm in this case is a corruption of the Old English *wyrm* – meaning dragon – which was probably stolen from the Old High German *wurm* or the Old Norse *ormr* or both. A mile-long rollercoaster jutting out into the Bristol Channel, it's not only one of the most exhilarating islands to visit but also

one of Britain's most visually impressive chunks of landscape. The National Trust must hug themselves every time they remember it's in their care. The gentle walk from the village of Rhossili along the coast to the Old Coastguard Lookout offers up views to be savoured and stored away for later use when your soul needs refreshing. The lookout is now staffed by volunteers belonging to Coastwatch and it's immediately apparent why their presence is a good thing. The causeway far below is a long and jagged one and strandings are fairly common occurrences, despite their best efforts. A large board outside the little Victorian building displays the safe crossing times and there's a siren that can be sounded to warn stragglers.

There's no track across the wide curved causeway, so visitors are faced with a choice of 100,000 routes over the rocks. At first there are mussels underfoot, then a variety of smaller crustaceans, then finally a whole new landscape complete with miniature rift valleys and lochs to be negotiated. The whole thing takes around 15 minutes if you don't dawdle or spend too long looking for grey seals.

On the far side is the largest hump of the island, the Inner Head, on whose 150ft ridge an ancient promontory fort once stood, though there's nothing left now to indicate just how long ago it was built. It was on the slopes of the Inner Head that a young Dylan Thomas fell asleep, missed the tide and had to wait until the next one, fortified by only a bag of sandwiches and a book.

He later recalled: 'I stayed on that Worm from dusk to midnight, sitting on that top grass, frightened to go further in because of the rats and because of things I am ashamed to be frightened of. Then the tips of the reef began to poke out of the water and, perilously, I climbed along them to the shore.'

The Worm's Head featured in Thomas' short story *Who Do You Wish Was With Us?*, which described a rather happier visit: 'The sea was out. We crossed over on slipping stones and stood, at last, triumphantly on the windy top. There was monstrous, thick grass there that made us spring-heeled and we laughed and bounced on it, scaring the sheep who ran up and down the battered sides like goats. Even on this calmest day a wind blew on the Worm.'

The sheep have gone, which is probably just as well, because the grass on the Worm's Head is so much to the liking of ovine stock that they apparently develop a sort of mania for it. In 1932, farmer Wilfred Beynon claimed that his flock had escaped from one of his fields on the mainland and attempted a desperate crossing over to the Worm, where they had previously grazed. All 70 were caught by the tide and drowned.

Leaving aside thoughts of why there is no memorial to these sheep on the island, we press on. Between the Inner Head and the small Low Neck there's an eye-catching natural rock crossing called Devil's Bridge. There's some more clambering to be done to reach Middle Head, soon after which comes journey's end, the spiralling Outer Head. This is a popular breeding ground for guillemots, herring gulls, razorbills, kittiwakes and a puffin or two, and as a consequence is off limits to humans from March to mid-August.

Outside these times, visitors can peer over the far edge of the Outer Head to observe a blow hole called the Worm's Head Cave. According to antiquarian John Leland, writing in the 1530s, 'Few dare enter it and Men fable there that a Dore within the spatius Hole hathe be sene with great nayles on it.' However, just 50 years later, the rather more level-headed William Camden was recording in his book *Britannia*, 'Toward the head itself, or that part which is farthest out in the sea, there is a small cleft or crevice in the ground, into which if you throw a handful of dust or sand, it will be blown back again into the air. But if you kneel or lie down, and lay your ears to it, you will then hear distinctly the deep noise of a prodigious large bellows. The reason is obvious; for the reciprocal motion of the sea, under the arch'd and rocky hollow of this headland, or promontory, makes an inspiration and expiration of the air, through the cleft, and that alternately; and consequently the noise, as of a pair of bellows in motion.'

The distinctive noise made by the blow hole led to the apparently once popular but rather clunky local saying, 'The old Worm's blowing, time for a boat to be going.' Excavations revealed human bones and the remains of mammoth, rhinoceros and bear in the cave, so presumably it was once rather more accessible than it is today.

For an island that is such a conspicuously dragon-like shape, there's surprisingly little folklore of the Leland kind surrounding it. One would have thought at the very least that St George could have taken time off from his duties guarding the Emperor Diocletian to perform some heroic deed here, possibly involving a wimple. As it is, there's merely a largely forgotten tale about St Cenydd being cast adrift in a wicker cradle and being rescued and taken to

Worm's Head by seabirds, something we've probably all experienced at some point. But then again, perhaps the island reckons it can provide enough spine-tingling moments for its visitors without wrapping itself in myths and legends too.

How to get there

Take the train to Swansea (arrivatrainswales.co.uk; 0870 900 0773, firstgreatwestern.co.uk; 08457 000125) then the 118 bus across the Gower Peninsula to Rhossili. Passing the National Trust shop, there's a mile-long track to the coastal lookout that marks the start of the walk down the cliffs and across the rocks to Worm's Head. The island is usually accessible for around four to five hours at each low tide. Crossing times are clearly displayed at the coastal lookout.

Admission price/landing fee

Free.

View

The magnificent sweep of Rhossili Beach; the island of Lundy on a clear day.

Facilities

None, though there are public conveniences in Rhossili (1 mile).

Accommodation

There are several campsites around, the best being at **Eastern Slade Farm** (9 miles; easternsladecampsite.freeservers.com; 01792 391374) just west of Oxwich, which commands synapse-snapping views out over the Bristol Channel.

Devil's Bridge

Nearest decent pub/café/tea room

Try Rhossili's **The Bay Bistro & Coffee House** (1 mile; thebaybistro.com; 01792 390519) which has a varied menu. Look out for their laverbread burgers on the specials board.

Nearest shop

The **National Trust shop** in Rhossili will sell you gifts, sweets and biscuits. For groceries, there's a convenience store in **Scurlage** (4.5 miles), though most of the locals seem to go to the well-stocked shop at **Knelston petrol station** (5.75 miles; 01792 390903).

Rules

Keep to paths to avoid trampling the wild flowers on the island. The Outer Worm (the far end of the head) is out of bounds between 1 March and 15 August each year in order to protect nesting birds.

Things to do

Lie on **Rhossili Beach** (1 mile), rightly famed for its glorious arch of amber sand. **Oxwich Castle** (8 miles; open daily April to September; cadw.wales.gov.uk; 01792 390359) is a stunning Tudor manor that would doubtless be far more celebrated if it were not hidden away on the Gower.

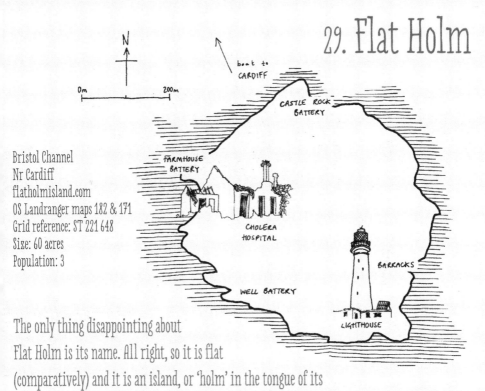

N

0m   200m

boat to CARDIFF

CASTLE ROCK BATTERY

FARMHOUSE BATTERY

CHOLERA HOSPITAL

WELL BATTERY

BARRACKS

LIGHTHOUSE

Bristol Channel
Nr Cardiff
flatholmisland.com
OS Landranger maps 182 & 171
Grid reference: ST 221 648
Size: 60 acres
Population: 3

The only thing disappointing about Flat Holm is its name. All right, so it is flat (comparatively) and it is an island, or 'holm' in the tongue of its Scandinavian visitors, but if we always followed that literalist scheme of nomenclature, we'd be left calling Glasgow 'Big City', Snowdon 'Tall Mountain' and Milton Keynes 'Mistake'. Ynys Echni ('flat island'), its Welsh name, sounds better but hardly gets the pulses racing either.

Someone (possibly you) should launch a campaign to return the island to the moniker given it by its Anglo-Saxon settlers: the much more mellifluous Bradanreolice. That's a name that would do justice to a place whose many achievements include the hosting of a technological breakthrough that changed the way the world communicated.

Who cares if Bradanreolice means nothing more exciting than 'broad burial ground'?

Flat Holm has been sucking in history since before history began, or at least before it began to be written down. An axe head found here dating from the late Bronze Age suggests that people were making their way out to the island nearly 3,000 years ago, and presumably chopping down trees on it. There's little call for axes on Flat Holm today, for it is populated by one stunted sweet chestnut tree, a solitary baby oak tree in a gully and some shrubs that aspire to forming the odd copse without harbouring any realistic hope of doing so. They squat down as low as they can to avoid the worst of the wind

Worm's Head rising dragon-like from the sea

and glower at the buildings thrown up in clumps around them.

Flat Holm is only about 550yd across and yet it plays host to several tiny townships, each of which throws light on a different chapter of the busy history of the island, and one of which, the lighthouse, throws a welcome light out to sea as well. However, their presence has done nothing to deter the lesser black-backed gulls that nest on Flat Holm's relatively low cliffs and have formed the largest colony of their species in Wales.

None of today's buildings were around to welcome the island's first named visitor. In the late 6th century, St Cadoc frequently sailed over to Flat Holm to seek solitude and refresh himself spiritually. Perhaps his mind was on higher things when he absent-mindedly left a book behind here. He sent two of his disciples, Gwalches and Barruc, to retrieve it, but their boat capsized and they were drowned. Of such intimate personal tragedies is so much of history formed.

It was hubris that brought the Danes here in AD918. Ohter and Hroald, two earls who moonlighted as anagrams, brought a fleet of ships over from Brittany to ravage the Welsh coast. They bit off more than they could chew when they ventured south and encountered the natives of Watchet and Porlock in Somerset. As the *Anglo-Saxon Chronicle* records with some glee: 'There was a great slaughter each time; so that few of them came away, except those only who swam out to the ships. Then sat they

out there on an island called the Flat-holms; until they were very short of food and many men had died of hunger because they could not obtain any food.'

It would be wrong to infer from this, however, that Flat Holm is some sort of barren desert. For 800 years until 1942 the island was farmed (at one point by Augustinian monks) – a farmhouse still stands today, though now serving as a hostel. Indeed, Flat Holm would no doubt have lived out a purely agricultural existence were it not for two reasons: its strategic position guarding the approaches to Bristol and the River Severn, and its relative remoteness – the island of Steep Holm being its only neighbour.

The first fortress on the island was completed in 1869 and was a key link in the Bristol Channel coastal defences built in fear of an attack by Napoleon III. The Franco-Prussian War that broke out the following year put paid to any putative French plans for an invasion, but threw Britain into feverish speculation that the Germans might invade instead (one must always have an enemy, after all). However, the German fleet never came and the nine guns on Flat Holm remained silent. This must have been something of a disappointment to the inventor of the ingenious Moncrieff Disappearing Carriages that housed them. To counteract the lack of cover on Flat Holm, the gun in each carriage was forced down into a pit whenever it fired. When it was to be fired again, it raised its head back over the parapet, so to speak, with the aid of a counterweight. The carriages have been dismantled and removed from the island but the pits and most of the guns remain. The barracks, meanwhile, are now home to a museum and the island's bar, The Gull and Leek, the most southerly pub in Wales.

It was in 1883 that the quality for which St Cadoc (and 18th-century smugglers) so prized the island came into its own again. Flat Holm's isolation made it ideal as a location for a cholera hospital. Ships carrying passengers or crew with the disease could drop them off at the island, thus protecting mainland Britain from contagion. At its peak, the hospital had 16 beds and its own laundry. It also possessed a crematorium, which could hardly have been an encouraging sight for incoming patients.

The hospital was condemned by the Department of Health in 1935, but that was not the end of its useful life. World War II put Flat Holm back onto a martial footing: 350 soldiers were stationed here to man a radar station and various Lewis, Bofors and anti-aircraft guns. In the true spirit of 'make do and mend', one ward of the former hospital became a NAAFI while another served as a cinema and concert hall. Sadly, the hospital buildings are now roofless and dilapidated, though there are plans to restore them should enough money be raised.

It was the loss of life among troops from a previous generation that brought about the building of Flat Holm's lighthouse.

In 1736, 60 soldiers were drowned in a shipwreck near the island. A year later, the first light shone out, somewhat feebly by today's standards, since it was merely from a brazier, albeit one that got through nearly a ton of coal a night. Today's elegant lighthouse is now thoroughly up to date, having been converted from electricity to solar power. Its flashing beams were supplemented until 1988 by a foghorn, established here in the Edwardian era. Its keeper's cottage is now a holiday let.

The light can be seen 15 nautical miles away, but it's a signal that travelled a mere quarter of that distance that put Flat Holm on the map. On 13 May 1897, the 23-year-old Italian Guglielmo Marconi, aided by his assistant George Kemp, transmitted the very first wireless message to travel across the waves. The Morse Code communication was sent to Lavernock Point on the coast of south Wales. It read: 'Are you ready?'

The inanity of the message is in keeping with a proud tradition of opening gambits conveyed over pioneering media. The first words ever spoken on the telephone were: 'Mr Watson, come here – I want you.' (On picking up the receiver, Alexander Graham Bell had managed to knock a jar of acidulated water over himself.) The first tweet ever posted on Twitter was founder Jack Dorsey's 'just setting up my twttr', a message which also dispensed with punctuation.

Happily, there's nothing banal or ungrammatical about the patter of the guides as they show visitors around the island. Should you prefer to explore by yourself, there are self-guided packs explaining the buildings, flora and fauna (look out for the rare wild leek and slow worms). Furthermore, while there you have the opportunity to do your bit for a tiny island by joining the Flat Holm Society (not to be confused with the Flat Earth Society, which is somewhat less estimable).

How to get there
Take the train to Cardiff Central (arrivatrainswales.co.uk; 0870 900 0773, firstgreatwestern.co.uk; 08457 000125) and either stroll or cycle along the footpath/cycle path to Cardiff Bay and out to the Barrage South car park from where you'll be taken to the boat (adult £24, child £12, family £65; flatholmisland.com; 029 2087 7912). Most trips allow three hours on the island. Alternatively, there are slightly less frequent trips from Weston-super-Mare (adult £24, child £12; mwmarine.org; 01934 636734).

Admission price/landing fee
£6 per person.

View
Steep Holm (p63), Cardiff to the northwest and Weston-super-Mare to the east.

Facilities
Loos, a museum, a shop and a pub.

Accommodation
You can stay in the island's **hostel** or, more luxuriously, in the newly renovated Grade II-listed **Fog Horn Cottage,** which even runs to its own little garden (flatholmisland.com; 029 2087 7912).

Nearest decent pub/café/tea room
In 2011 the island acquired its own pub, **The Gull and Leek**, situated in the Victorian barracks, though at present they don't serve food.

Nearest shop
The **little shop** on the island sells souvenirs and fair trade snacks.

Rules
None.

Things to do
The Welsh capital fair pulsates with amusements (see visitcardiff.com) including: Cardiff Bay (visitcardiffbay.info) – now the home of the devolved Welsh parliament and, perhaps more importantly, the **Dr Who Experience** (doctorwhoexperience.com; 0844 801 3663), among other attractions.
In the city itself, **Cardiff Castle** (cardiffcastle.com; 029 2087 8100) is a hugely impressive hunk of Norman stronghold-cum-Victorian Gothic fantasia.

30. Llangors Crannog

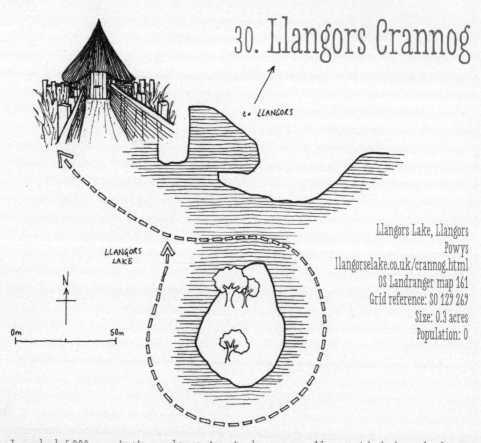

to LLANGORS

LLANGORS LAKE

N

0m   50m

Llangors Lake, Llangors
Powys
llangorselake.co.uk/crannog.html
OS Landranger map 161
Grid reference: SO 129 269
Size: 0.3 acres
Population: 0

Jump back 5,000 years in time and try to imagine how you would cope with the hazards of everyday life. Not only were there wild animals roaming about that could kill or maim, you were also at the mercy of anyone who had a notion to deprive you of your goods, your family members or your life, and could back up such an impulse with force.

It made sense, therefore, to build a homestead where you could defend yourself and your loved ones. A lake or a loch whose waters served as a natural moat not only guarded against the possibility of being caught unawares, but also deterred those would-be assailants who could neither swim nor had the means to sail.

So it was that crannogs began to be built. Derived from the Old Irish *crannóc* – literally 'young tree' but expressing the idea of a wooden structure – these small artificial islands were typically held together by a palisade comprising a ring of timber piles on a reef or other high point of the loch bed. Where no wood was available, the crannog was created by piling rocks on top of each other until they breached the surface of the loch, or by making use of a rocky outcrop that had already formed an islet. A stone building was then constructed on top. Where the crannog was built close enough in to the shore, a wooden walkway was often put in place (presumably with the idea that it could be dismantled or defended in some way in an emergency) or a causeway built.

There are literally hundreds of crannogs in Scotland but the one on Llangors Lake is the only one in Wales. Furthermore, we can be certain that an Englishman's home was not his crannog, for not a single one has ever been discovered there. However, the most extraordinary thing about crannogs is not that our prehistoric ancestors were building them up to 5,000 years ago, but that they were still being built in the late 17th century.

Tree-ring dating of this particular one on Llangors Lake – the largest natural lake in south Wales – has established that it was put together in several stages between AD889 and 893. The builders probably came from Ireland – a nation with a tradition of crannog construction – and used sandstone boulders, brushwood and timber. Once completed, the crannog served as a royal residence for the Welsh kingdom of Brycheiniog. There's a splendid artist's impression of it in the replica crannog built close by for visitors – it imagines several single-storey thatched houses behind a sturdy wooden fence and a walkway to the shore on which men, women, children and mules pass the time

of day, while a couple float by in a dug-out canoe (one such was retrieved from the lake in 1925 and is now displayed in the Brecon Museum). Sadly, the dream was not to last: the crannog was destroyed by fire in AD916.

The *Anglo-Saxon Chronicle* appears to reveal how this came to pass: 'Æthelflæd ['The Lady of the Mercians'] sent an army into Wales and stormed Brecenanmere [Llangors Lake] and there captured the wife of the king and thirty-three other persons.' It's not inconceivable that they set light to the island afterwards.

Identified as a crannog in the 1860s by two antiquaries called Edgar and Henry Dumbleton, the island is now thickly wooded. It's also an archaeological site and too fragile to receive visitors, but it is possible to give it a close inspection by hiring a rowing boat or kayak and circumnavigating it. Further consolation comes in the shape of the simple modern replica crannog built a short distance away and crammed with information about the crannog and the lake that surrounds it.

There's certainly no shortage of tales that have attached themselves to Llangors Lake. The chronicler Giraldus Cambrensis (Gerald of Wales), who visited in 1188, wrote that local people had reported the water turning green – which they interpreted as a portent of impending invasion – and that sometimes this phenomenon was accompanied by scarlet streaks in the water 'as if blood were flowing along certain currents and eddies' which did not bode well at all. These are now thought to have been caused by algal blooms or sediments.

Gerald also told of another marvel related to him by local people – that a mysterious city existed below the waters and that at times the surface could be seen covered with buildings and gardens. With the level of the lake no doubt rising and falling in flood and drought, covering and revealing the crannog, it seems quite likely that their eyes were not deceiving them (but that perhaps their imaginations *had* got a little carried away).

How to get there

From Abergavenny railway station (arrivatrainswales.co.uk, 0870 900 0773) take the 43 or X43 (stagecoachbus.com; 01633 485118) to Brecon and nab a taxi (Lakeside Taxi; 07836 500933) across to Llangors Lake. The crannog can be approached by boat at any time (see 'Things to do'), although landings are not permitted. However, a nearby replica crannog is open daily except Wednesday from 11am to 4pm from March to October.

Admission price/landing fee

No charge for the replica crannog.

View

Allt yr Esgair (a hill and Iron Age fort), the Brecon Beacons.

Facilities

None, but there are loos on the road between the 'information crannog' and the campsite reception.

Accommodation

There are two campsites right next door, with **Lakeside Park** (llangorselake.co.uk; 01874 658226) being slightly closer. The owners also look after the crannog. **Pen-y-Bryn Guest House** (0.5 miles; tinyurl.com/cyvogh4; 01874 658606) in Llangors offers B&B as well as a self-catering apartment.

Nearest decent pub/café/tea room

The **Lakeside Park campsite** (0.1 miles) has a café as well as its own bar (food at the latter restricted to a barbecue on a summer Saturday). In Llangors (0.5 miles), both the **Red Lion** (01874 658825) and **The Castle** (01874 658225) serve meals.

Nearest shop

The **Lakeside Park campsite shop** (0.1 miles) stocks a few basic supplies, otherwise there's a small convenience store in **Bwlch** (5 miles) and several shops in **Talgarth** (5 miles).

Rules

None.

Things to do

Take to the lake – rowing boats, kayaks, Canadian canoes, pedalos and something called 'funboats' are available for hire (llangorselake.co.uk; 01874 658226). At the **Llangorse Multi Activity Centre** (1.25 miles; activityuk.com; 01874 658272) you can go skytrekking (think zip wires), horse-riding, BMXing, climbing or get muddy, wet and gloriously disorientated tackling the dingle scramble.

Clockwise from top: The crannog, now obscured by trees; replica crannog in winter; entrance to the replica crannog

31. Ynys Gifftan

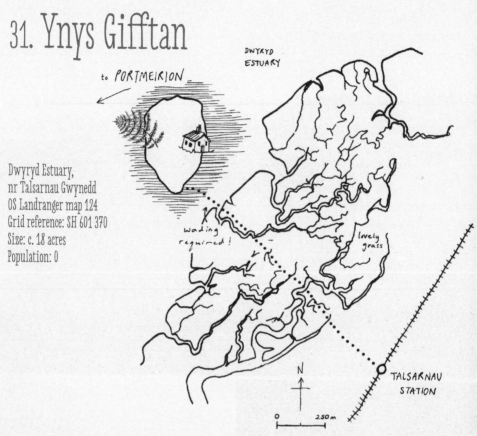

to PORTMEIRION

DWYRYD
ESTUARY

wading
required!

lovely
grass

N

TALSARNAU
STATION

0   250 m

Dwyryd Estuary,
nr Talsarnau Gwynedd
OS Landranger map 124
Grid reference: SH 601 370
Size: c. 18 acres
Population: 0

It's a sad truth about Britain that not everyone is given their own island by the monarch. Furthermore, history would suggest that to be in with the slightest chance of some free island action you need to be ennobled. That would certainly explain Lord Harlech's good luck when he was graciously presented with a tiny isle in the Dwyryd estuary in the early 1700s.

The island in question became known as Ynys Gifftan ('Anne's Gift Island') since the hand that bestowed it upon the noble lord belonged to Queen Anne. However, her royal highness doesn't seem to have been convinced that it would be wholly appreciated because she added the caveat that it could never be sold on. Three centuries later, the island is in the hands of Francis David Ormsby-Gore, 6th Baron Harlech.

For most of those 300 years, Ynys Gifftan has been inhabited by tenant farmers scraping a living off this little hump cast adrift in the sands. It's also open to any day-tripping commoners who might care to visit an island that offers views not only of Snowdon but also of Portmeirion, Clough Williams-Ellis' fantasy village.

The walk to Ynys Gifftan, though relatively short, is something of an adventure. A track passing through fields from Talsarnau station leads to a flat sweep of grass shot through with rivulets like the blue veins of a cheese. These must be stepped across, leapt over or worked around to get to the shore. One can well imagine the nightmare this must have been for those living on the island who had to cross here on dark winter evenings.

Anyway, try not to get so caught up with negotiating your way across that you forget to study the grass. It is of such high quality that from 1953 to 1962 a small turfing industry was established. Talsarnau grass was sent to Wembley stadium and even graced the courts at Wimbledon. This was certainly a step up from World War II, when the area suffered the indignity of being used as a rifle range.

Ordnance Survey maps baldly state: 'Public Rights of Way to Ynys Gifftan can be dangerous under tidal conditions.' However, the short passage over the sandy estuary to the southern end of the island presents only one difficulty at low tide – a channel right at the start that is rarely completely dry and will need to be paddled or waded across. Ponder if you will, as your footprints trail behind you in the amber sand, just how different was the scene at this gentle estuary when a devastating tsunami swept up here in 1927. Having relatively little low ground, Ynys Gifftan was saved from the worst of its wrath but the village of Talsarnau found itself ripped apart while the railway line along the coast was destroyed. Happily, the village recovered, and briefly became a popular seaside resort before fading back into obscurity. It was the most exciting thing to happen in the estuary until the late 1960s when Patrick McGoohan brought the television series *The Prisoner* to Portmeirion and filmed scenes of sinister Rovers (actually large meteorological balloons) bouncing across the sand to recapture escapees. There are several episodes in which Ynys Gifftan can be glimpsed in the background, trying not to draw attention to itself.

The island comprises a more or less circular hillock, much overgrown nowadays with bramble, gorse and bracken, with a narrow sill in places, meaning that a circuit around it involves as much walking on rocks and sand as on the island itself. Time your visit right, however, and you can go for a swim afterwards in one of the little lagoons that form just off the southwestern end at every low tide.

The island's small house still stands and indeed was occupied until a decade or so ago when the last tenant upped sticks. Accounts written by members of the family who lived on Ynys Gifftan for much of the 20th century portray a difficult life spiced with occasional compensations. Surprisingly, they had no boat – the water was never deep enough for long enough to warrant one – so the times at which they could leave and return were determined

by the tide. While this proved the perfect excuse for a late arrival at school, it also meant that it was hard to invite friends over. It kept nosey inspectors away during the war (butter remained plentiful on the island for the duration) but could also impede the local doctor in an emergency. Huw Williams, who was born on Ynys Gifftan sometime around 1910, kept sheep on the island for 60 years but had to work as a shepherd on a neighbouring farm as well. His father before him had had to double up as a quarryman but injured his leg in an accident and died young.

A local teacher interviewed about 1930s life on the island in the now defunct monthly newspaper *Llais Ardudwy* recalled a story an aunt had told her about the creation of Ynys Gifftan. During the last Ice Age, an explosion had catapulted into the estuary the landmass that forms the island. The hole it had left behind then filled with water, creating the lake now known as Llyn Tecwyn Uchaf.

However it came to be (and I think we can be fairly sure that the explosion theory is a little wide of the mark), Ynys Gifftan's position was very convenient for smugglers. Ships arriving to pick up slate from nearby Porthmadog would take a small detour up the Dwyryd estuary to the island to drop off certain illicit goods – spirits, salt and soap were common items of contraband here – for confederates to transport ashore. It was a practice that continued from the 18th to the mid-19th century, when changes to revenue laws obviated the need to smuggle.

Ynys Gifftan is silent now, awaiting a new tenant who may never arrive. Unless, of course, you yourself fancy realising those dreams of a new life on an island...

How to get there

Talsarnau railway station (arrivatrainswales. co.uk; 0870 900 0773) gives a very good impression of having been built specifically to serve Ynys Gifftan. It's just a half-mile walk from the station to the point where you can cross over to the island at low tide. The channel immediately closest to the mainland never dries completely so be ready to roll up your trouser legs. Depending on how much you're prepared to wade (and the tide races in here so you should never go too deep), the island can be accessible up to three hours either side of low tide.

Admission price/landing fee
Free.

View
Portmeirion, the Afon Dwyryd estuary and Snowdon.

Facilities
None.

Accommodation

Estuary Cottage (estuarycottage.com; 01766 771778) is one of the very few houses that has a view of the island. You can also stay in their caravan in the garden. If you can afford it, **Portmeirion** (see 'Things to do') is a most otherworldly place to stay.

Nearest decent pub/café/tea room

There's an okay-ish pub in Talsarnau called **The Ship Aground** but it doesn't serve food, so try **The Lemon Tree** (01766 770283), a highly rated Bangladeshi restaurant in Penrhyndeudraeth (3 miles).

Nearest shop

There are a few small shops in **Penrhyndeudraeth** (3 miles) which should see to any immediate needs.

Rules

None.

Things to do

Portmeirion, the dream-like village created by Clough Williams-Ellis, brings *un pezzo di Portofino* to the Welsh coast, and really has to be visited to be believed (5 miles; portmeirion-village.com; 01766 770000). The recently created **Taith Ardudwy Way** footpath (taithardudwyway.com) covers 24 miles of coastline from Barmouth up to Llandecwyn, passing Ynys Gifftan near the end.

Portmeirion and the sands of the Dwyryd estuary, where once Rovers played

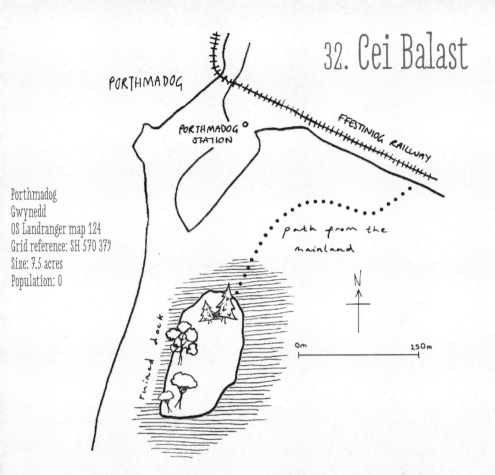

PORTHMADOG

PORTHMADOG STATION

FFESTINIOG RAILWAY

path from the mainland

N

0m   250m

ruined dock

Porthmadog
Gwynedd
OS Landranger map 124
Grid reference: SH 570 379
Size: 7.5 acres
Population: 0

If any British island can be said to have been an accident it's Cei Balast. Perhaps 'accident' is too strong a word. When ships docking at Porthmadog offloaded the ballast they had been carrying in their holds, their crews would have known that the cumulative effect over the years would be to form a new island.

Indeed, Cei Balast (pronounced 'kay bal-ast' and meaning 'Ballast Quay') is not even the first bit of new land created at Porthmadog. Stones were originally dumped at a place called Rotten Tare (now part of the harbour's existing quays). The pile rose to a height of 18ft above low water and in 1862 the new site was chosen. By then,

The Cob, a mile-long sea wall created in 1811 by William Madocks (he built the port too – hence Porthmadog) to reclaim land for agricultural use, had redirected the Afon Glaslyn and scoured a deep channel that allowed ships to dock.

So, how come we don't have little ballast islands all around the coast? The answer

lies in the dense nature of slate. Triple-masted ships – many of which were built in Porthmadog or at shipyards nearby – carried the slate mined at Blaenau Ffestiniog (hitting a peak in 1873, when 116,000 tons were exported). When they returned home empty, or with substantially lighter cargoes, from Europe, the Americas or Asia, their captains had to take on board a quantity of large stones in order to maintain stability at sea.

Cei Balast started from humble beginnings as a mere sandbank. A retaining wall was built to stop the discarded ballast from spreading and, once enough rocks had been piled up, a steam crane was installed to help with the unloading. A track was then laid, up and down which the crane trundled. As the island grew apace – in the 1870s more than 1,000 ships were sailing into Porthmadog – a house (now sadly gone) was built for the crane operator and his family. His name was Lewis, and the isle on which he lived became known as Lewis's Island. Over the years, the doughty crane operator faded from the town's collective memory and the island took on its current prosaic name or, occasionally, Ynys y Balast ('Ballast Island' – the English name by which it also hails).

Crossing the tracks of the Ffestiniog Railway as they stretch out along The Cob, and clambering down over the rocks of the sea wall, it's a brief walk over the sands to the island, often with oystercatchers, curlews and redshanks as companions. To the right trickles the Afon Glaslyn on its reluctant way out to the big bad sea at Tremadog Bay. Rising above the river, Porthmadog's modernist South Wharf estate ably demonstrates why 1970s concrete developments have yet to worm their way into the hearts of the nation.

There's a girdle of strewn stones and then a pronounced lip as you step up onto the island. However, at this northern end it's all but impossible to make any further headway into the dark heart of the beast on account of the bramble-and-thorn-tree thickets that create battlements more effective than anything built in stone. However, at the southern end, the vegetation relents and it's possible to penetrate far enough to deduce that, although the island may have been created by humans, it now belongs to shrubs and trees and bracken and brambles (and rabbits). Long gone are the days when the island rang to the cries of local boys playing football or the bleats of grazing sheep.

An unforeseen consequence of this gathering of stones from around the world was that the island became garlanded with exotic plants grown from seeds that had hitched a ride on the rocks. Sadly, these appear now to have been choked out of existence. A pair of inaccessible conifers are the only obvious display of anything one might count as exotica. However, there's evening primrose on The Cob and Welsh mudwort on the Glaslyn marsh. Both plants are believed to have been borne here from the United States (despite the latter's rather misleading name).

Happily, the island's industrial heritage has proved much less evanescent. Some of

A tiny sample of the many stones that have created Cei Balast

the island's rocks were recycled for local construction. The more attractive stones were also used to adorn the façades of Porthmadog's buildings and can still be seen today. Fire bricks from the demolished Glaslyn Foundry litter the western foreshore of the island beneath a tall row of rotting wooden pylons that rage against the dying of the light. They clearly trace the line of the quay wall, whose jet black interlocking stones are still visible in parts. Together they created a monument that will remain long after they themselves have disappeared into that great night.

How to get there

Take the train to Porthmadog (arrivatrainswales.co.uk; 0870 900 0773) from where it's a five-minute walk to the Ffestiniog Railway station. The least muddy route to the island begins just beyond the new platform on The Cob. Cei Balast is accessible for up to three hours at low tide and for longer on a big tide. However, there is usually a shallow and narrow channel to wade or jump across as you start off. Consult the harbourmaster for the tide times and best crossing routes.

Admission price/landing fee

Free.

View

Porthmadog, the Glaslyn estuary and the mountains of Snowdonia.

Facilities

None.

Accommodation

Harbour Court (tinyurl.com/cdx9jd7; 01766 513980) has both self-catering cottages and a B&B very close to the island. There's further accommodation listed at porthmadog.co.uk.

Nearest decent pub/café/tea room

Porthmadog (0.25 miles) is a busy tourist resort with plenty of places to eat and drink. The closest is **Spooner's** grill, café and bar (festrail.co.uk; 01766 516032) on the platform of the Ffestiniog Railway station.

Nearest shop

Porthmadog (0.25 miles) is teeming with retail outlets keen to take your money.

Rules

None.

Things to do

The **Ffestiniog Railway** is one of Britain's most scenic steam lines and runs from Porthmadog up into Snowdonia, ending in Blaenau Ffestiniog. The **Welsh Highland Railway** now also starts at Porthmadog and charges north to Caernarfon (both festrail. co.uk; 01766 516000). Porthmadog is also the starting point of the rather humbler **Welsh Highland Heritage Railway** (whr. co.uk; 01766 513402).

For those not so much into steam engines, the **Maritime Museum** (01766 513736), when open (it's staffed by volunteers), gives an insight into the ships whose ballast ended up at Cei Balast.

Top: The old wharf rots away; Bottom: Looking back down the island to Porthmadog and Snowdonia

33. Ynys Llanddwyn

Newborough Bay
Anglesey
OS Landranger map 114
Grid reference: SH 388 630
Size: 60 acres
Population: 0

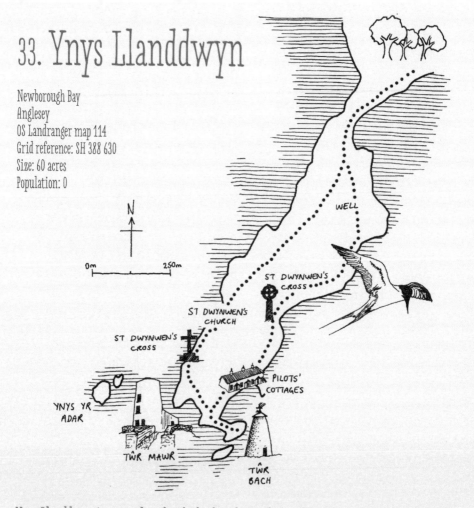

Ynys Llanddwyn is not a place for the broken-hearted. It's a place for those still woozy with love's first intoxicating draught. It's a place for couples whose relationship is in danger of foundering on the rocks of cold sobriety and who yearn to be drunk with affection once more. It's a place for lovers whose mutual regard has stood the test of time and has deepened with the years. It's also a place for people who like cormorants.

So, why should a remote island off the southwest coast of Anglesey have taken on the unofficial name Lovers' Island and become a Mecca for those so insecure about their own personhood that they've succumbed to the degradation of attaching themselves limpet-like to another human being? Ironically, it's all down to someone who devoted herself to a life of chastity: Saint Dwynwen. This patron saint of lovers has in recent years become a rival to St Valentine. In several parts of Wales, St Dwynwen's day (25 January) has supplanted the hearts-and-flowers fest that is 14 February.

The place on which Dwynwen established her hermitage is very nearly not an island at all. Only at very high tides does the sea reach far enough up the sandy beach of Llanddwyn Bay to cut it adrift from the densely wooded Newborough Forest. The isle is very much a creature of the sea, however. It was created back in the absurdly ancient Precambrian era by small volcanic eruptions. When the molten lava hit the cold seawater above, it formed a small blob, which dropped onto other small blobs that had already cooled. The resulting oddly shaped 'pillow lavas' give Ynys Llanddwyn the look of a billowing sheet. Further outcrops appear to have burst out of the island's grassy skin, hurling themselves into the sea as if they knew the fate that's coming to us all.

A walk around the island's long finger of land is a gentle one, conducive to a quiet stroll taken hand in hand. Aside from the odd glimpse of a Soay sheep or a wild pony, the half of the island nearest the shore offers up no sign that it had been inhabited for the best part of 1,500 years. It's only when a 14ft-high Celtic cross and the bare ruins of a church heave into view that human activity here begins to reveal itself. The cross is a newcomer, having been installed in 1903 as a tribute to the island's saint. The ruins of Llanddwyn ('Dwynwen's church'), which lend the island its name, are of rather greater vintage and it's a pity that so little has survived.

The church came into being some time in the late Middle Ages when Benedictine monks arrived to found an abbey. Built on the site of St Dwynwen's cell (or perhaps the church she founded), the abbey was an important place of pilgrimage – the faithful came from as far away as continental Europe – and hence became extremely wealthy. The days of prosperity were not to last, though, being brought to an end by Henry VIII's dissolution of the monasteries. The church's missing stonework is likely to have been pilfered for buildings further up the island.

It's fair to say that the veneration of St Dwynwen (whose gilded statue had adorned the church) did get a little out of control. The renowned Welsh poet Dafydd ap Gwilym visited the island in the 14th century and wrote an entire poem eulogising her, in which he begins by talking to her statue: 'Dwynwen deigr arien degwch' ('Dwynwen, your beauty is as hoar-frost's tears'). In the Middle Ages, the tears of hoar-frost were better known for their allure than is sadly the case today, where they go largely unregarded.

As is so often the case with saints, there are conflicting stories about Dwynwen's life. She was one of a prodigious number of daughters (possibly 25 to 35) fathered by Brychan, an Irish-born ruler over the Welsh kingdom of Brycheiniog. She and a young

man called Maelon Dafodrill are said to have fallen in love. Depending on whose version of events you believe, she then rejected him because she wanted to become a nun or because her father disapproved of the match. Some stories attest that Maelon raped her. She fled into the woods, begged God for help, fell asleep, and had a dream in which an angel gave her a potion that would erase all memories of her former love. However, a side effect of the potion – one that would almost certainly see it being taken off the shelves today – was that it would turn Maelon to ice.

At this point the saintly story suddenly gets crossed with a fairytale, with Dwynwen asking to be granted three wishes: i. that Maelon be thawed out; ii. that God would make all true lovers happy; and iii. that she herself would never again yearn to be married. She moved to the island that now bears her name and soon developed a reputation as something of an agony aunt, with couples coming from miles around to ask her advice. It's unfortunate that the phrase she is best known for is the rather insipid 'Nothing wins hearts like cheerfulness.' She died around AD465, supposedly on 25 January.

Some time after her death, her duties as a relationship counsellor were taken over by some eels who lived in a well on the island. Women would toss a few breadcrumbs down for them, then lay a handkerchief on top. If the eels disturbed the handkerchief a gal could rest assured that her lover would remain faithful. This was clearly a scam run by the eels to get free bread, but since they had little else to do and had somehow got themselves trapped in a well, one shouldn't judge them too harshly.

Stride past the church and you come to another cross, again dedicated to the saint. Beyond that, down a slope, lies the relatively modern end of the island where sit two small lighthouses, Tŵr Bach ('Little Tower') and Tŵr Mawr ('Big Tower'). The latter, complete with integral keeper's cottage, was built in 1845 and modelled on the windmills that were once common on Anglesey. It was decommissioned in 1975, the light being transferred back to the much older Tŵr Bach, which it had supposedly replaced forever. That wasn't quite the end of Tŵr Mawr's story though, for it outshone near homophone Demi Moore in the ghost-based thriller *Half Light*. It was painted red for the occasion and had its light magically restored via some clever CGI.

Down below, protected by a rise in the ground, squats a terrace of four single-storey pilots' cottages, two of which are still in use, while the remainder house an exhibition about the island which is open most days from June to September. The small cannon outside had no defensive purpose, but was used to summon the crew to the lifeboat that was stationed here until the end of the 19th century.

A few years later, in 1911, the Welsh branch of the RSPB chose Llanddwyn for their first-ever action: protecting the roseate tern against egg thieves. The birds are still here – though outnumbered by their cousins the common, Arctic and little tern – along with sandpipers and turnstones. Meanwhile, one of Llanddwyn's tiny breakaway islets, Ynys yr Adar ('Bird Rock'), comes alive each spring when a full 1 per cent of the British breeding population of cormorants lands here to make sweet love. St Dwynwen, one can't help thinking, would have approved.

How to get there

Take the train to Bodorgan (arrivatrainswales.co.uk; 0870 900 0773) then the bus towards the village of Newborough, alighting at Newborough Forest. Walk 2 miles southwest through the forest to the coast. Ynys Llanddwyn is accessible from the beach and is only cut off briefly at high tide.

Admission price/landing fee

Free.

View

The vista of Newborough Forest and the Anglesey coastline is rather overshadowed by the magnetic attraction of Snowdonia on the other side of Caernarfon Bay.

Facilities

None. The nearest loos are in the Newborough Forest beach car park (1 mile).

Accommodation

Awelfryn Caravan Park (2.5 miles; awelfryn.co.uk; 01248 440230) is a couple of acres of meadow on the road to Newborough (they're open for campers too). There's another at **Penlon** (3.5 miles; whitelodgecaravanpark.com; 01248 440254) attached to the Marram Grass Café (see below). For B&Bs and hotels you'll have to head for **Llangefni** (11 miles).

Nearest decent pub/café/tea room

Newborough (3 miles) has a pub and a chippy but it's worth pushing on the extra half-mile to Penlon to sample the **Marram Grass Café** (Wednesday to Sunday; themarramgrass.com; 01248 440254).

Nearest shop

There's a **Premier convenience store** in Newborough (3 miles).

Rules

No dogs. Don't collect rock specimens.

Things to do

The site of the **Llys Rhosyr**, the royal court of the Welsh princes (2.5 miles; llysrhosyr. co.uk) is on the road south of Newborough with an exhibition on same (with café) at the Prichard Jones Institute in Newborough itself (3 miles; pjinstitute.co.uk).
Tacla Taid, the Anglesey Transport and Agriculture Museum (3 miles; 01248 440344) in Newborough is full of classic vehicles set in a replica 1940s village street.

34. Cribinau

nr Aberffraw
Anglesey
OS Landranger map 114
Grid reference: SH 336 683
Size: 0.3 acres
Population: 0

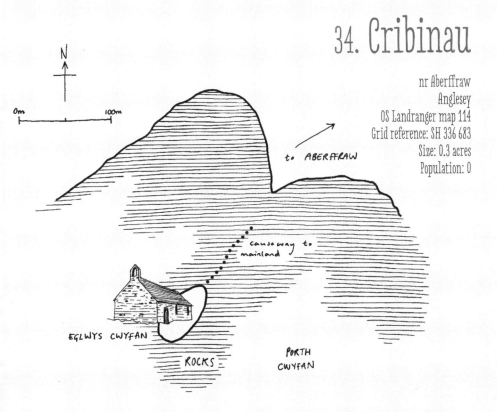

N

0m   100m

to ABERFFRAW

causeway to
mainland

EGLWYS CWYFAN

ROCKS

PORTH
CWYFAN

If there were an annual award for the British island that most resembled a cake – and it's surely a matter of some concern that there isn't – Cribinau would forever keep an acceptance speech in its back pocket. Perched on a bed of rocks, the island is an oval with smooth vertical sides all round as if a cook had run a knife around it to tidy it up.

On top of the flat greensward sits a trim church, looking for all the world like an over-sized cake decoration placed there to celebrate a vicar's birthday. The church is not just a physical presence on the island, swallowing up much of the space on it, to all intents and purposes the church *is* the island. Don't bother asking anyone from the nearby village of Aberffraw for directions to Cribinau (pronounced crib-in-eye) because they'll look at you with blank incomprehension. To them, the island is Llangwyfan or Eglwys Cwyfan (which both mean Cwyfan's church), or even the delightfully florid Eglwys yn y Môr Cwyfan Sant ('St Cwyfan's Church in the Sea').

First views of the island come from the country lane that weaves its way down to Porth Cwyfan, the little bay that harbours Cribinau. A short walk around the beach (excellent for rock pooling) leads to a rough wide path that is not so much a causeway as a strip of rocks free of seaweed. A set of stone steps cut into the flank of the island climbs the 20ft up to the grass that covers the surface like mint icing. Refreshingly, the handrail with which the steps are equipped constitutes the only safety measure on the island. Responsibility for not falling off the edge onto the rocks below is handed squarely to the visitor.

Unlike the vast majority of churches on tiny islands, this one is not a ruin. Furthermore, it's still consecrated, with three services taking place here every year, one a month between June and August. They're apparently very popular too – the novelty of going to a service on such a miniscule island, and one blessed by such inspiring views across the water to Snowdonia, drawing the faithful over from mainland Anglesey and beyond.

The origins of Llangwyfan are obscure but the earliest stonework dates from the 12th century and it may have been built at the behest of some local lord who perhaps also donated the island for that purpose. Cribinau itself may have already had some spiritual significance, either for the early Christians or the pagans who came before them, since islands were places special to both groups. The Cwyfan to whom the church is dedicated is probably St Kevin, whose base at Glendalough in Ireland is a relatively short boat trip away across the Irish Sea.

The 14th and 15th centuries saw major alterations take place, most notably the building of an aisle, parallel to the existing nave, which doubled the size of the church. An arcade of three arches gave access from one to the other, and when the aisle collapsed in the 19th century, these arches were bricked up. Their outlines can still be clearly made out along the northwest wall.

However, the church's location had proved problematic long before the demise of the aisle. Notwithstanding the loss of parts of the churchyard into the sea as the island eroded, storms and high tides often made the causeway impassable. For many years a room in the mansion house of Llangwyfan Isaf was used as a standby on such occasions, the rector leading the service being entitled to a breakfast of two eggs and a cup of small beer to compensate him for making the trip, which wasn't bad given that it's only half a mile away. Eventually, in 1870, a new parish church was built on the mainland, and a couple of decades later Llangwyfan was a ruin. Various fundraising efforts since then have helped to restore the church to its current state.

But what of those walled sides that give the island its singular appearance? Ask Bryn Fôn Jones, the barman at the Y Goron pub in Aberffraw, and he'll tell you the tale that traditionally explains them. It goes something like this. One night, local people saw a ship sailing dangerously close to the rocky coastline. To warn the crew of this, they built fires along the shore. The captain saw the lights, changed course and the ship was saved. Some time later, he asked the local people if he could do anything

Clockwise from top left: A taste of the view to Snowdonia; Cribinau stars on signage; Eglwys yn y Môr Cwyfan Sant

for them to thank them for their quick thinking. They told him that the island was crumbling and that it was putting their church at risk. He duly took the building of the wall in hand and the church, like his ship, was saved. It may not be the most exciting story ever told but the world could probably do with a few more that involve the exchange of kindnesses, so one can only hope that it is true.

How to get there

From Tŷ Croes railway station (arrivatrainswales.co.uk; 0870 900 0773), take the 25 bus (eifionscoaches.co.uk; 01407 721111) to Aberffraw. It's a pleasant 1.5-mile walk along a lane to the coast (follow signs to 'Eglwys Cwyfan') and a further 200yd along the beach. If you want to look inside the church, ring warden Roy Mearns beforehand (01407 810209) to make arrangements. In summer, the island is accessible roughly from two hours after high tide to two hours before the next high tide. In winter, especially in rough weather, the island can become inaccessible even at low tide.

Admission price/landing fee

Free (but donations gratefully received in a box on the church wall).

View

Huge dollops of Snowdonia.

Facilities

None. Nearest loos in Aberffraw (1.7 miles).

Accommodation

Llys Llewelyn Heritage Centre (2 miles; llys-llewelyn.com; 01407 840940), on the outskirts of Aberffraw, has three self-catering cottages and three studio apartments. Next door, the former pub **Prince Llewelyn** does B&B (01407 840090).

Nearest decent pub/café/tea room

Aberffraw's pub **Y Goron** (1.7 miles; 07546 020733) is open all day, serves food, and has a beer garden with a cracking view across the dunes.

Nearest shop

Storfa Plas Coch in Aberffraw (1.7 miles) is a newsagent and post office with a modest selection of basics.

Rules

None, though there is a notice suggesting that you don't go out of your way to fall off the island.

Things to do

Llys Llewelyn Heritage Centre (2 miles; open most days; 01407 840940) in Aberffraw has an audiovisual exhibition on the local history, in-house traditional chair-caning, as well as a shop and tea room. Further afield, **Plas Newydd Country House and Gardens** (15 miles; nationaltrust.org.uk/plas-newydd; 01248 714795) contains a varied collection including a military museum and Rex Whistler's largest painting.

35. Church Island

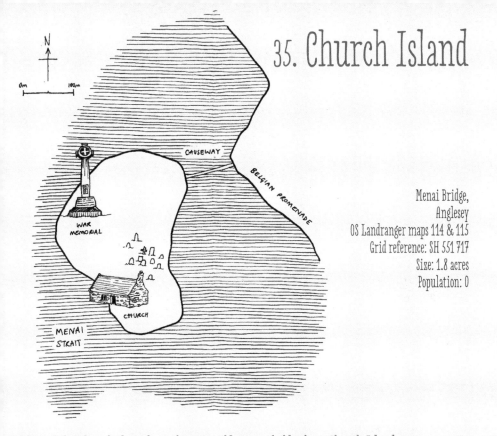

Menai Bridge,
Anglesey
OS Landranger maps 114 & 115
Grid reference: SH 551 717
Size: 1.8 acres
Population: 0

At first sight, there looks to be nothing terribly remarkable about Church Island. A small blob of rock in the Swellies – the name given to the mile of the Menai Strait between its two famous bridges – it hides beneath a steep wooded slope doing little to call attention to itself. However, it is an island that has wrapped itself in, if not a cloak, then at least a shawl of mystery.

For a start its church is named after an obscure saint called Tysilio (who also features in the lesser-used Welsh version of the island's name, Ynys Tysilio). However, he was never canonised. There's nothing too sinister in this – in days of yore the term 'saint' could refer to anyone who lived a particularly godly life. He is said to have inhabited a cell on the island and to have built a church here, though not a trace of either can be found. The current church was built in the early 1400s, but nobody knows quite why or by whom. It presumably replaced the earlier place of worship, which would explain why the new church was called Llandysilio ('Tysilio's church').

Llandysilio's stained-glass window: 'I am the resurrection and the life'

If you're wondering why 'Llandysilio' sounds vaguely familiar, it's almost certainly from the time some friend or relative treated you to a performance of their one rather unambitious party trick: viz, reciting the longest placename in Britain: *Llanfairpwllvaguewelshlikenoisesomethingsomethingllantysiliogogogoch*. The sesquipedalian village is just up the road.

The details of Tysilio's life are sketchy to say the least. He was a son of Brochwel Ysgithrog, King of Powys, and was born towards the end of the 6th century. While Tysilio was touring around founding churches, his older brother Cynan was running up a host of victories in battle against his fellow Celts, none of whom, unsurprisingly, rushed to his son's rescue in AD615 when he fought the invading Saxons at Chester. The son, Selyf ap Cynan, was killed and it's thought that his uncle Tysilio, under pressure to return to the royal court to help fill the vacuum, instead sought sanctuary on the island.

Nowadays there's a causeway across to the isle from the Belgian Promenade, a broad walkway built by Belgian refugees during World War I as a thank you to the local people for taking them in. Just how long the causeway has allowed permanent access to the island is unclear, although we do know that it was substantially rebuilt in 1963.

The island it serves is almost entirely taken up by the church, its graveyard and a war memorial on top of a steep-sided hillock. This just leaves a sliver of grass outside the containing churchyard wall where Canada geese congregate and lone herons perch among the ox-eye daisies and ragwort. What first grabs the attention is an immense spreading tree with cones shaped like sleigh bells. This is a Monterey cypress, a conifer most often found on the coast of California but which here finds itself custodian of the churchyard's obligatory yews. Beneath it, a relatively recent plaque screwed into a low wall commemorates the deaths of three men killed while building the Menai suspension bridge and who were 'buried on Church Island without a memorial'. It's hard to know whether to feel more saddened at the manner of their deaths or at whatever set of circumstances led to them being interred so ignominiously.

A tarmac path heads straight for the compact little church past slate gravestones bilingually regretting the passing of many a Jones, Hughes, Owens, Price and Williams – lucky lucky men and women with a name above their earthly remains. In some cases their full addresses are given too, which seems odd because the one thing you can be certain of is that you won't find them at home.

They weren't overly tall people in life if the church door is anything to go by, for it threatens anyone over 5ft 8in with a spell in hospital. The church itself – an unassuming rectangle of rough-hewn stones – is as unremarkable inside (the oldest windows are late Victorian) as it is outside, with one notable exception: a fine octagonal font that predates the building it graces.

A path around the island leads the visitor past two even smaller islands – Ynys Welltog ('Grassy Island') and Ynys Benlas

('Green Top Island') – the former accessible on foot at low tide and celebrated for the diversity of its marine life. Meanwhile, a trip up to the war memorial provides one of the best vantage points in the whole Menai Strait from which to see both Thomas Telford's suspension bridge and Robert Stephenson's rather less sublime Britannia Bridge.

Resume your walk clockwise around the shore and the island has one last tiny mystery in store. At low tide you can make out an abandoned causeway on which a tide mill used to sit. Today not a scrap of the mill is left – a testament if ever there was one to the superior grinding powers of the sea.

How to get there

Take the train to Bangor (arrivatrainswales.co.uk; 0870 900 0773, virgintrains.co.uk; 01709 849200) followed by bus 57 (padarnbus.co.uk; 01286 870880) or 4A (arrivabus.co.uk; 0844 800 4411) to Menai Bridge (alight as soon as you can after crossing the bridge). Follow signs to the island, which is down the hill at the far western end of the Belgian Promenade.

Admission price/landing fee
Free.

View
The Britannia Bridge, Whitebait Island, the outskirts of the town of Menai Bridge and, from the top of the hill, the Menai Bridge itself. The rest is woods and fields.

Facilities
None.

Accommodation
Menai Bridge isn't bursting at the seams with great accommodation. However, there is a gem of a B&B at Benllech called **Ysgubor Ddegwm** (9 miles; ysguborddegwmanglesey.co.uk; 01248 853471) that's well worth the journey.

Nearest decent pub/café/tea room
Try the intriguingly named **Sosban and The Old Butchers Restaurant** (0.5 miles; 01248 208131) on Menai Bridge High Street.

Nearest shop
If you fancy compiling a picnic, you'll find a very tempting delicatessen called **Stafford House** (01248 712368), which is also on the High Street.

Rules
Dogs on leads at all times. No alcohol to be consumed (your dog should probably give it up anyway).

Things to do
It pays to be wary of anywhere calling itself an 'experience' but **The Menai Heritage Experience** (open intermittently from April to October; menaibridges.co.uk; 01248 715046) at the Thomas Telford Centre is well worth a wander around if you're lucky enough to find it open.

Both the newly opened 870-mile **Wales Coast Path** (walescoastpath.gov.uk) and the rather more modest **Isle of Anglesey Coastal Path** (tinyurl.com/3zwsnjb) pass the landward end of the causeway.

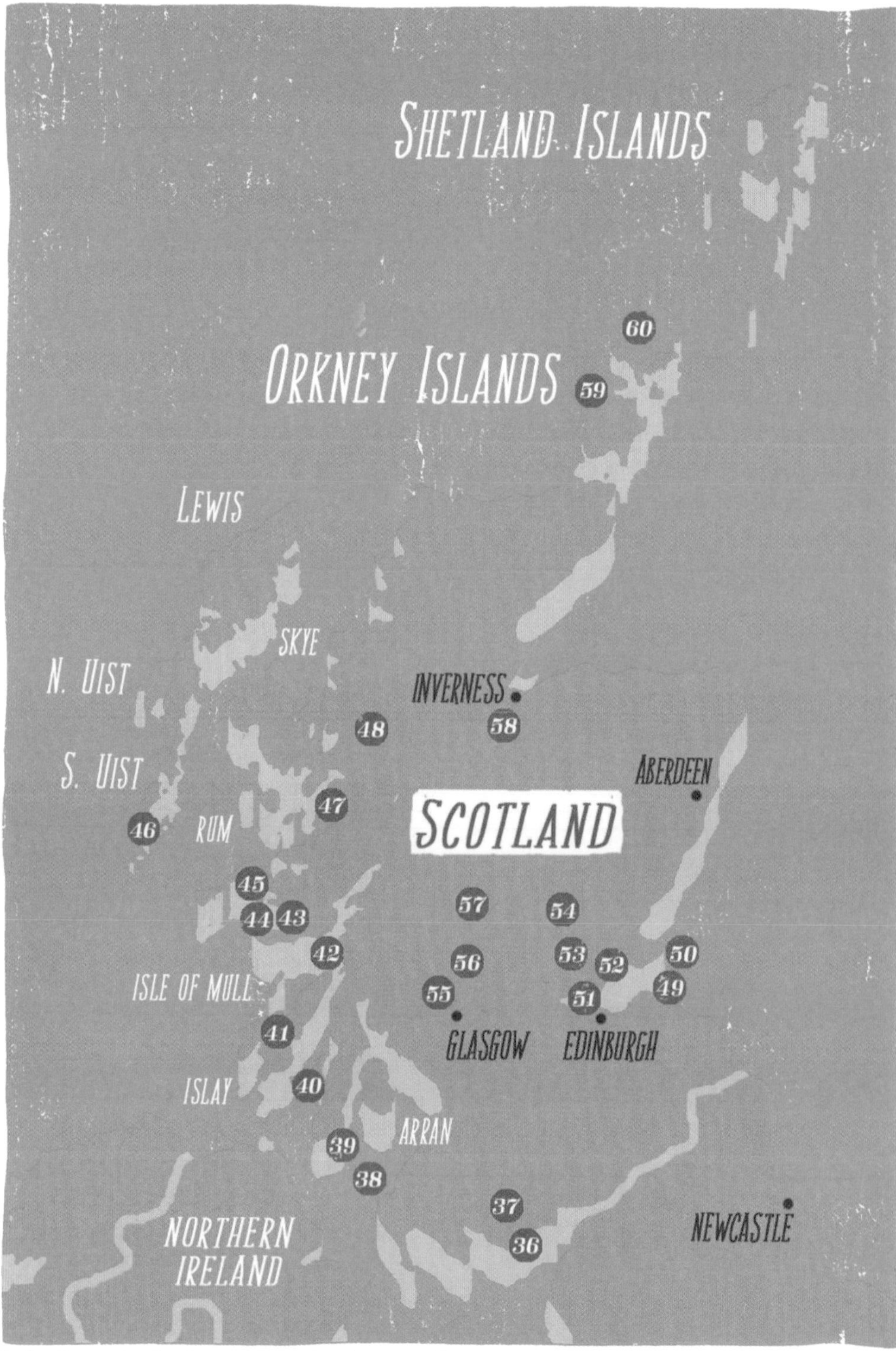

SHETLAND ISLANDS

ORKNEY ISLANDS

60
59

LEWIS

SKYE

N. UIST

S. UIST

INVERNESS

48

58

ABERDEEN

47

46 RUM

SCOTLAND

45

44 43

57   54

42

56   53 52   50

55   51   49

ISLE OF MULL

GLASGOW   EDINBURGH

41

ISLAY   40

ARRAN

39

38

37

36

NORTHERN
IRELAND

NEWCASTLE

SCOTLAND

36. Hestan Island

nr Auchencairn
Dumfries and Galloway
hestan.co.uk
OS Landranger map 84
Grid reference: NX 838 501
Size: 150 acres
Population: 0

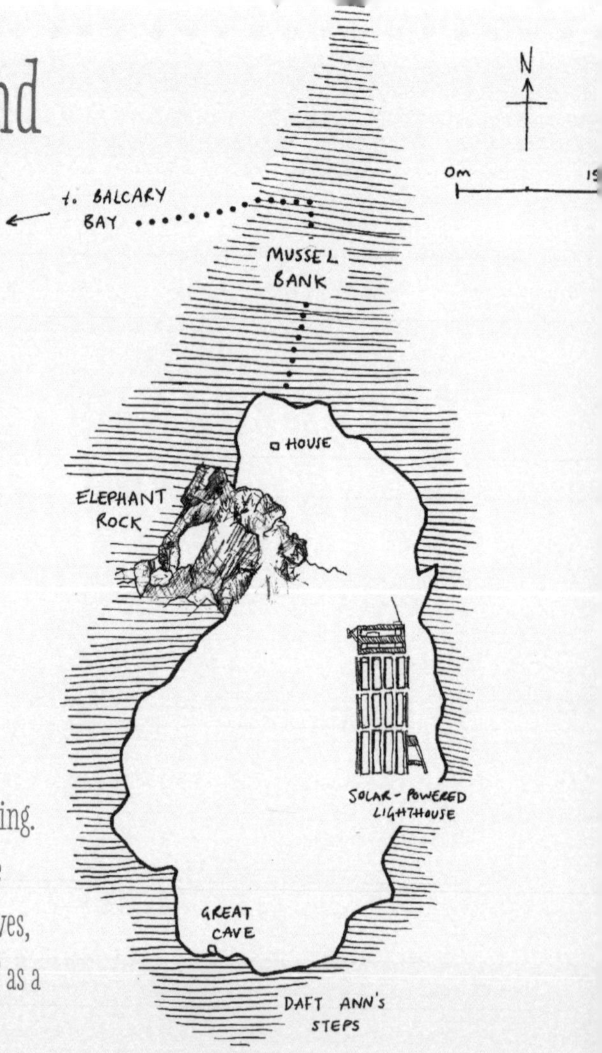

N

Om   15

to BALCARY BAY

MUSSEL BANK

□ HOUSE

ELEPHANT ROCK

SOLAR-POWERED LIGHTHOUSE

GREAT CAVE

DAFT ANN'S STEPS

Hestan Island is a deceptive little thing. From a distance it's merely a simple grassy hump emerging from the waves, 'a great whale stranded on the shore' as a 1930s travel guide once put it.

'Not much to explore there,' you might think to yourself. And indeed, it does look like one of those islands where the journey to reach it is three-quarters of the appeal, one of those places to which, as Robert Louis Stevenson said, it is better to travel hopefully than to arrive.

The route more often used for getting over to Hestan starts in Balcary Bay at the stake nets. These two manmade webs stretching out from the shore over the lustrous sands have been catching unwary fish in the receding tide for generations. One would think that here was the laziest possible means ever devised for harvesting the seas, albeit that the nets need mending and re-mending and the wooden stakes must be replaced once rotted. One fence points straight towards the middle of the island, the other to its seaward tip. However, it is a fool who takes directions from fences, so ignore these and head for the far left of the Rack, about a mile and a couple of shallow channels away.

The Rack is a wide shingle bank topped with thousands of mussels that juts out from the shoreward end of the island towards Almorness Point (from where the much shorter walk to Hestan starts, though it involves crossing a burn that can be quite deep). It forms a convenient causeway to the island, assuming you don't lose your footing on the mussels.

In the 12th and 13th centuries the island was owned by the monks of nearby Dundrennan Abbey and the wily friars saw in the Rack a means of employing an even lazier method of fishing than the stake net. At its far end they built a walled enclosure in which incautious fish would be trapped when the tide went out. It's called the Monk's Pool and can still be made out, though it's so shallow nowadays that it's a very determined fish indeed that gets to spend the hours of low tide in it.

At the other end of the Rack stands a white cottage sheltering from the sea beneath the island's hump. According to a local census it was originally built by 'three ore miners' around 1841 (when copper was mined on the island), and it has been lived in by lighthouse keepers, subsistence farmers and, perhaps most surprisingly, a church organ maker.

John Scott moved to the island in the 1950s with his church minister wife Beryl and decided to supplement their meagre income by making pipe organs. The instruments he built had to be partly dismantled before they could be shipped off the island in a small boat. (One can still be seen in Auchencairn's St Oswald's church, though tellingly it's not the one they use during services.) Needless to say, he gave up the struggle after a few years and the Scotts, who left in 1960, were the last people to live permanently on the island. The cottage, which has no electricity or running water (there's a well nearby), is now kept as a somewhat spartan holiday home by the island's current owners.

There's some dispute over who Hestan's first inhabitants were. A collection of oyster shells near the house may or may not be a Mesolithic midden. If not, the island is a blank page historically from the Big Bang right up to the arrival of the fish-trapping monks, though even they did not live here. It's conceivable that Hestan (sometimes also spelt Heston) is derived from *hesten*, the word for horse in Old Norse. With an extraordinary leap of the imagination of which J R R Tolkien would have been proud, the island can just about be made to resemble a horse with its head down. However, there is no evidence of Viking occupation.

The island's most exciting times were to come with the arrival of Edward Balliol, sometime King of Scotland. A daring opportunist, Balliol managed to get himself crowned at Scone in 1332 after Edward III of England helped him defeat the regent, the Earl of Mar, at the battle of Dupplin Moor. He was deposed twice by Scots loyal to the absent David II and restored to the throne twice (again with the help of perfidious Albion) before finally being shown the door in 1336. He made Hestan his bolt hole, building a mansion on a high plateau about 50yd from where the miners' cottage is today and having his supporter Duncan McDowell defend the island with a garrison.

On the return from France of David II, Balliol ordered that the garrison on Hestan be strengthened. In response, David's followers blockaded the island. Changing tactic, the king successfully bribed McDowell with an offer of land in return for switching sides. This led to the only military incursion in Hestan Island's history. In 1345, Englishmen William de Dyfford and Sir Thomas de Lucy sailed from Wyrkyngton (Workington) with 80 men and took Estholme (Hestan's name at the time) by storm. McDowell and his garrison swiftly surrendered and were dispatched to England, McDowell ending up in the Tower of London.

However, just two years later, Balliol made Hestan his home, though it was to become a place of much bitter brooding for him. While still claiming to be king, he saw his chances of regaining the throne of Scotland slowly melt away and he was finally forced to abdicate (a word that perhaps flatters him) in 1356, giving his crown and his lands in Galloway and northern England to Edward III in return for a pension. Sadly, the mansion on Hestan has mimicked Balliol's place in the history books and has all but disappeared, though the footings can still be seen.

Lordship of the hill is now contested by sheep and herring gulls which, if they joined forces, might just be able to repel invaders. The sheep, however, scuttle away at the advent of humans, leaving the gulls to fly around and kick up an unholy stink, particularly in the breeding season when their nests are full of large, speckled and vulnerable eggs.

Passing along the spine of the island, the square-sided toy-like lighthouse comes into view below on the left. A great deal of shipping has been lost in the area over the centuries and, as a belated response, a gas-lit lighthouse was built here in 1893. It's now powered by solar panels and looks less like a lighthouse than a scale model of an office block. However, its petite build and the fact that it appears to be hiding from the sea rather than blazing out over it make it rather fetching, like an ingénue on a huge film set.

Among the rocks guarded by the lighthouse is a series of submerged outcrops known as Daft Ann's Steps. There are conflicting stories about how they got their name. The nub of the tale concerns an Auchencairn girl of slight intelligence who believed she could get to Hestan from the mainland by walking directly to this reef and laying stepping stones out in front of her. She was duly drowned.

Just around the corner from the doomed girl's rocks is the Great Cave. This is the cavern S R Crockett made famous in his now little-read novel *The Raiders*, published in 1894, in which the hero, Patrick Heron, finds himself cast into the violent and unpredictable world of Solway Coast smugglers and Galloway gypsies. The cave on Hestan Island (appearing under its very old name of Rathan Isle) is used by the desperate smugglers to hide their kegs of brandy. Crockett had obviously done his homework because the island had actually been owned by a Patrick Heron (though not the artist of the same name, who was born rather later).

The cave, which extends about 30yd into the island, is worth a poke about in, though don't let Crockett's description of its interior be your guide, for he based that on a cavern found on Northern Ireland's Rathlin Island. However, there is evidence that real-life smugglers did use the cave on Hestan in the 18th century as a store for their contraband, so breathe in deeply as you explore and smell the tax evasion.

Hestan has one last surprise for the visitor. Make your way around the western edge of the island and down below you'll see an elephant grazing on the beach. Or at least you'll see Elephant Rock, a sculpture formed by nature that really does look impressively like an elephant. Certainly much more than Hestan looks like a horse.

How to get there

Take the train to Dumfries (scotrail. co.uk; 0845 755 0033) then the 501 bus (stagecoachbus.com; 01387 253496) to Dalbeattie followed by the 505 (ABC Travel; 01671 830284) to Auchencairn. It's a pleasant 2-mile stroll down a shoreside lane to the stake nets in Balcary Bay, from where you start your walk to the island. When there are big tides, you'll have about three hours to get across and back safely, but on smaller ones, not much more than two hours. Do check tide timetables, follow the route shown on the map and be aware that the tide here races in without a thought for your tarrying footsteps.

Admission price/landing fee
Free.

View
From the hilltop, an extensive wind farm and large tracts of the Scottish side of the Solway Firth are at your mercy. In good weather, Maryport and other points along the English shore can be seen too. Cast your eye north for a panorama of hills. On many of them you may spot the remnants of hill forts, the building of which was a popular pastime during the Iron Age.

Facilities
None. There is precious little shelter to be had either, so if you wish to take cover under a tree you'll have to bring your own.

Accommodation
For those with deep pockets, there's the 17th-century **Balcary Bay Hotel** (balcary-bay-hotel.co.uk; 01556 640217) which overlooks Hestan. Also boasting a view of the island is **Balcary Mews** (balcarymews.co.uk; 01556 640276), a B&B and a self-catering cottage. Further accommodation can be found on the Auchencairn village website (auchencairn.org.uk).

Nearest decent pub/café/tea room
The bar prices at the **Balcary Bay Hotel** are pitched with an eye to sobriety. For somewhere less committed to the temperance cause, try Auchencairn's **Old Smugglers' Inn** (2 miles from Balcary Bay; solwaysmugglers.co.uk; 01556 640331).

Nearest shop
Auchencairn Store in Auchencairn (2 miles; 01556 640385) is a friendly community shop and post office selling basic supplies and monographs about the local area. They also have a small book swap section.

Rules
None, but do respect the privacy of the holiday home's residents if they are about, and be sure not to tread on any nests. The gulls' animated cries above your head will alert you to their presence.

Things to do
Visit the disarmingly pretty town of **Kirkcudbright** (11.5 miles), with its castle (open April to September; tinyurl.com/c6jekbv; 01557 331856), fine churches, Tolbooth, old jail and historic Broughton House (open April to October; nts.org.uk/Property/14; 0844 493 2246).
Have a go at curling. The Auchencairn Curling Club (01556 640216) meets between September and March and claims that 'anyone who would like to have a go is made very welcome'. The curling stones come from Ailsa Craig (p208).

37. Threave Island

nr Castle Douglas
Dumfries and Galloway
tinyurl.com/cwg697v (Historic Scotland)
OS Landranger map 84
Grid reference: NX 739 623
Size: 20 acres
Population: 0

Ivan the Terrible, Edward the Confessor, Vlad the Impaler, Æthelred the Unready – the list of historical figures known by their defining characteristic is a long and vaunted one.

It's also one to which two tiny islands of Scotland have made a contribution, proving once and for all that major land masses do not hold the monopoly on reductive nomenclature. Kisimul (p245) gave us Ruari the Turbulent and Roderick the Gentle, among others. Threave Island, in its turn, introduced to the stage a character so morosely inimical there could be only one possible name for him: Archibald the Grim.

History is famously written by the victors, but in this case it was those

Archibald defeated who came up with his epithet. His father, 'the Good Sir James' of Douglas, had been Robert the Bruce's closest friend throughout the Wars of Independence and, like a 14th-century George W Bush, Archibald was only too keen to pick up the cudgels where his immediate progenitor had left off. It was the benighted English who gave him the appendage 'the Grim' on account of the ferocity of his demeanour on the battlefield. No doubt this delighted him, even as he was forcing them from Lochmaben Castle in 1384, thus completing their expulsion from Scotland.

While never more happy than when teaching the English a lesson, he was not averse to turning on his fellow Scots or, more specifically, the upstarts from Galloway. Fifteen years before his ultimate triumph against the Sassenachs, Archibald was granted the Lordship of Galloway by Robert the Bruce's son, David II. It was a gesture not without an ulterior motive, for it meant letting Archibald and his followers loose on the Gallovidians, with whom Scottish kings often found themselves at daggers drawn.

Archibald immediately set to work building a castle. He chose an island on the River Dee, which, so legend decrees, had already had a fortified home on it for several centuries (Threave is probably a corruption of the Old Welsh *tref* meaning homestead). Raising up a tower nearly 100ft in height also sent a message that this was not a lord with whom to trifle. Archibald then set about pacifying the men of Galloway, succeeding where various kings of Scotland had failed. He died at Threave on Christmas Eve 1400, the 3rd Earl of Black Douglas and southern Scotland's most powerful figure.

Over the next half century, it was the amassing of even more power that eventually led to the downfall of the Douglases. In 1437, the whole of the Scottish nation was, in a sense, controlled by Threave. Archibald's grandson, the 5th Earl (and also called Archibald), was appointed regent to his cousin, the six-year-old King James II of Scotland, but died two years later. By around 1450, the rich, good-looking and popular William, 8th Earl of Douglas (they were getting through earls at a heady rate, partly due to one of them being summarily executed while still a teenager) feared that the volatile king was likely to attack him and so began to strengthen Threave Castle. He demolished various outbuildings and built a state-of-the-art artillery wall, much of which has survived to this day.

By 1452, James had had enough of his rival. He asked William to Stirling Castle, sending him a letter in which he guaranteed his safety. When the two met, the king demanded that the earl dissolve a friendship pact he had made with John II, the Lord of the Isles (p221), Scotland's other great powerbroker. When William refused, James went for him with a dagger. The king's courtiers joined in and, having killed their guest, are said to have thrown him out of a window. He had been stabbed 26 times and had had his head split open with an axe.

Not unsurprisingly, William's brother James, who found himself catapulted to the title of 9th Earl, continued to fortify Threave by dint of various earthworks, a curtain wall, three corner towers and a gatehouse. Henry VI of England picked up the bill, seeing an opportunity to gain himself an ally against the Scottish throne.

James led an abortive rebellion against his brother's murderer and in 1455 Threave

Top: The Threave Island ferry putters in; Bottom: Archibald's castle lowers grimly over the River Dee

was besieged by the king's forces, headed up by the monarch himself. Legend has it that a huge cannon called Mons Meg (now on display at Edinburgh Castle) was constructed especially to overcome Threave's monstrous defences. If it was used, it was unsuccessful – the island was not to be taken by force. It so happened that the governor of the castle had left his second-in-command in charge who himself had appointed a deputy to run things. Through the negligence of all three men, the castle was lost – the garrison was simply bribed to surrender it and given safe conduct out of the country.

Reaching the island today involves a walk for the better part of a mile down a path that zigzags along the edges of fields. On reaching the Dee, visitors ring a ship's bell to alert a boatman and take what may well be the briefest ferry journey onto any tiny island in Britain. While by far the greater part of the isle is given over to a marshy wilderness kept as a wildlife sanctuary (lovers of otters and ospreys should keep their eyes especially peeled), the area around the castle is a beautifully maintained lawn that would not look out of place on the Old Course at St Andrews.

If the castle is an expression of Archibald's character, the English chose their nickname for him well. Even from a distance the ruins look forbidding, so what feelings it engendered in Archibald's enemies during the castle's pomp can only be guessed at.

The five-storey tower house is 'unadorned with architectural fripperies' as the nearby information board has it. Its walls are 10ft thick and the accommodation within included unique penthouse lodgings for men-at-arms who had instant access to a wooden gallery overhanging the top floor, from where they could fend off siege engines.

Once James II had captured Threave, the island took a bow and excused itself from further major interventions into Scottish history. The castle was briefly taken by the English in the 16th century and by the Covenanters in the 17th, and was used to house French prisoners during the Napoleonic Wars, but by its previous standards these were trifling affairs. It did, however, unwittingly give birth to a once popular proverb: Every man's man had a man, and that gar'd the Threave fa' [and that made the Threave fall]. That is, when tasks are delegated, often no one gets around to carrying them out and disaster ensues.

Phantom conversations have reportedly been heard on Threave Island, although there is no truth in the rumour that one of the voices is that of a warlike fellow proclaiming: 'I didn't get where I am today by being called Archibald the Delegator.'

How to get there

From Dumfries railway station (scotrail. co.uk; 0845 755 0033) take the 500 or 501 bus to Castle Douglas from where it's a 10 to 15-minute walk to the entrance to

Threave Island. (If travelling by bike, note that there's a cycle path from Dumfries to Castle Douglas, mainly using the Old Military Road.) The island is open daily from April to September from 9.30am to 5pm and in October to 4pm – the last ferry to the island leaves 30 minutes before closing time.

Admission price/landing fee
Adult £4.50, child £2.70.

View
The River Dee, here wide and shallow, and distant hills in almost any direction you care to turn.

Facilities
There's a hut selling guidebooks and souvenirs on the island and, on the mainland, some very nice Historic Scotland loos.

Accommodation
There's a goodly ration of places to stay in Castle Douglas, the pick of the crop being the sleek **Summerhill B&B** (1.5 miles; summerhillbandb.co.uk; 01556 502658) with its fancy spa pool.

Nearest decent pub/café/tea room
There's a licensed restaurant open to visitors of the **Threave Estate** (see 'Things to do'). However, Castle Douglas is a designated Food Town so it would be a pity not to consume something there, perhaps at the excellent café below **Designs Gallery** (Monday to Saturday 9.30am–5.30pm; designsgallery.co.uk; 01556 504552).

Nearest shop
There's a good range of shops on **Castle Douglas'** long main drag, including that evergreen favourite, a hairdresser's called A Cut Above.

Rules
The part of the island reserved for wildlife is off limits.

Things to do
Spend some time on the **Threave Estate** (open all year, daily; nts.org.uk/Property/Threave-Estate; 0844 493 2245). The **Stepping Stones hide**, 100yd away along the river from the island, is a particularly good place for spotting otters. Footpaths around the 1,600-acre estate link a handful of other strategically located hides including, satisfyingly, one on **Lamb Island**, which is even smaller than Threave. The estate is Scotland's first **bat reserve** (seven species live there) and bat detectors are available at **Threave Gardens Visitor Centre**. You're advised to book to visit the estate's focal point, the mid-Victorian **Threave House** (April to October, Wednesday to Friday and Sunday), which is a strictly 'guided tour only' property restored to its 1930s pomp.

38. Ailsa Craig

Nr Girvan
Ayrshire
OS Landranger map 76
Grid reference: NX 019 997
Size: 245 acres
Population: 0

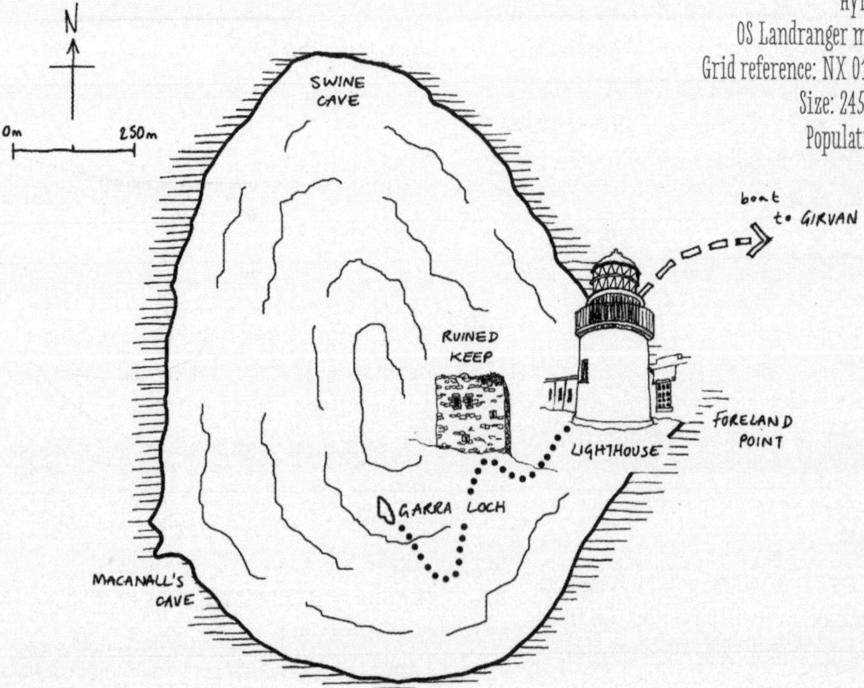

N

0m   250m

SWINE CAVE

RUINED KEEP

LIGHTHOUSE

boat to GIRVAN

FORELAND POINT

GARRA LOCH

MACANALL'S CAVE

No matter how many times you see it, there's always something a little bit shocking about Ailsa Craig. It's an island that resolutely refuses to play by the rules. Nobody would mind it having its own mountain if it had the decency to spread itself out over the sea a bit too.

But to poke out of the water like a giant's fingertip is all wrong. It simply doesn't *look* like an island ought to look. It's no wonder early sailors named it Aillse Creag – Fairy Rock – for it appears to have come from a whole other world.

Like Bass Rock (p258), off the east coast of Scotland, Ailsa Craig owes its distinctive outline to something rather more mundane than fairy magic, though no doubt the eruption of the volcano some 500 million years ago that left this plug here was quite dramatic at the time. However, although it's not evident when viewed from the Ayrshire coast, roughly 10 miles distant, Ailsa Craig does have a little lip of land sticking out on its eastern side, like a tab you might pull on to lift a lid from a yoghurt pot. It's here that boats land, and it's here too that human intrusions on the island are most evident.

A neat but stubby lighthouse – built by the Stevensons in the 1880s – pokes above a walled compound of low white buildings. A disparate collection of quarrymen's cottages sits around waiting for something to happen again, while a narrow-gauge railway line in an advanced state of decay suggests that nothing will. Only an unobtrusive helipad points to the possibility of future developments.

The railway once connected the pier with a quarry on the south side of the island, thus enabling the export of riebeckite. For those of you not up on your fine-grained micro-granites, this is the stuff of which curling stones are made. Indeed, between 60 and 70 per cent of all curling stones in existence come from Ailsa Craig. In the late 19th century, a community of nearly 30 souls lived on the island, their menfolk working the quarry (aside from three who were employed in the lighthouse). Through their labours they also extracted the riebeckite that floors the Chapel of the Thistle in Edinburgh's St Giles' Cathedral.

There's one cottage that is still used from time to time, a small white box-like affair at the foot of the cliffs. Above it, 50yd or so up a steep path, stands the Peel Tower, the only truly ancient structure on the island. There's no certainty over when it was built, why it was built or even who built it (though the Hamilton family are the bookies' favourites in this regard). It's a small, square, fortified keep that can have housed not many more than half a dozen defenders. In 1404, the island was given to the monks of Crossraguel Abbey by Robert III and they are said to have put it to use

as a retreat house. By the 16th century, however, it had gained a reputation as a hideout for pirates and smugglers.

Possibly its most exciting adventures came about during the Scottish Reformation. The ardent Catholic Hugh Barclay of Ladyland took possession of Ailsa Craig and held it on behalf of King Philip II of Spain. His plan was to use the island as a base for the provisioning of Spanish forces that would invade Britain and return her to the true faith. The plot was discovered, however, and Barclay drowned somewhere off the island, either in an attempt to escape or in an act of suicide.

Choose a fine day and climb from the tower past little Garra Loch to the summit of Ailsa Craig – its flanks, speckled white with scurvy grass, so precipitous that this southeastern ascent is the only possible way up – and you'll be rewarded with views over to Northern Ireland, some 35 miles away. Ailsa Craig's nickname, Paddy's Milestone, derives from its position about halfway between Belfast and Glasgow – a route taken by many an Irish émigré in search of work.

Also variously known as the Perch of Clyde and Elizabeth's Rock (from the Gaelic Creag Ealasaid), Ailsa Craig is perhaps best known today for its colony of northern gannets. The island is an RSPB reserve (as well as an SSSI and a European Special Protection Area) and their wardens have counted around 36,000 pairs breeding here, which is about 5 per cent of the world's gannet population. That's not to say they get the place entirely to themselves. There are also numerous guillemots, kittiwakes, razorbills and gulls, as well as non-sea birds such as wheatears and pipits.

Most satisfying of all though is the news that *Fratercula arctica* is making a comeback. Hamish Haswell-Smith, in his mammoth tome *The Scottish Islands*, records the fact that there were once at least 250,000 pairs of Atlantic puffins on Ailsa Craig and that the Victorian ornithologist Robert Gray reported that, on disturbing the birds, 'for a time their numbers seemed so great as to cause a bewildering darkness'.

It was rats that did for this puffin metropolis. They disembarked from boats that came carrying materials for the lighthouse in 1889 and over the following 90 years wiped out the entire population. A mass poisoning programme carried out in 1991 has, in turn, wiped out the rats (and rather dented rabbit numbers too, sadly) allowing the puffins to re-establish themselves. There are now over 100 pairs here, their main opponent nowadays being the tree mallow, a plant gaining a hold on the island and which bungs up their burrows. Meanwhile, lovers of the slow-worm will be thrilled to learn that the ones hiding under rocks on Ailsa Craig vie with those on Steep Holm for the title of largest slow-worm in Europe.

In May 2011, the island was put up for sale by the 8th Marquess of Ailsa, who is

asking for a mere £1.5m. At the time of writing there had been no takers, which seems surprising until you realise that this extraordinary maritime landmark isn't connected to any utilities at all, which no doubt lessens its appeal to prospective reclusive millionaires. Or perhaps it's the smell of 72,000 gannets...

How to get there

Take the train to Girvan (scotrail.co.uk; 0845 755 0033) – it's a 15-minute walk to the harbour from where the MFV *Glorious* sails (£25pp; ailsacraig.org.uk; 01465 713219, 07773 794358). The boat's website claims 'Daily sailings...all year round' but don't be fooled. It should more honestly read 'Sailings when the weather permits and enough people (at least four) turn up to make the trip viable.' Your best bet is to try the school summer holidays and pray for sunshine and calm seas. Alternatively, get a group together and try ASW Charters' boat *Rachael Clare* (visitscotland.com; 07885 474333). There's also a non-landing trip from Campbeltown (mull-of-kintyre.co.uk; 01586 552056).

Admission price/landing fee

Free.

View

On a clear day, the Ayrshire coast, the Mull of Kintyre, Arran and (when really very clear indeed) as far as Northern Ireland.

Facilities

None.

Accommodation

For a view of Ailsa Craig, and a reminder of what the 1970s looked like, there's Girvan's **Westcliffe Hotel** (westcliffehotel-girvan. co.uk; 01465 712128). Further afield, the **Walled Garden Caravan and Camping Park** near Maybole is, as its name suggests, entirely within a walled garden (11 miles; walledgardencp.co.uk; 01655 740323).

Nearest decent pub/café/tea room

Pub/restaurant **The Roxy** (01465 715261) in Girvan has won a couple of awards and been a finalist in a hatful of others, albeit that one of them was '2007 Pub Idol – Bar Person of the Year'.

Nearest shop

Girvan is full of them – imagine Rhyl but without the pizzazz.

Rules

Do stay well clear of nesting birds, particularly in the breeding season.

Things to do

The premier attraction in the area is **Culzean Castle**, 18th-century former home of the Marquess of Ailsa, with a 600-acre estate thrown in and the promise of 'an experience' (10 miles; culzeanexperience.org).

If you prefer to confect your own experiences, hop 5 miles or so up the coast to the fragmentary remains of **Turnberry Castle** (free; tinyurl.com/cl5a23s), a fortress whose origins are thrillingly uncertain.

£1.5m and this could all be yours

39. Davaar Island

Campbeltown Loch, Mull of Kintyre
Argyll
OS Landranger map 68
Grid reference: NR 758 202
Size: 140 acres
Population: 2 (seasonal)

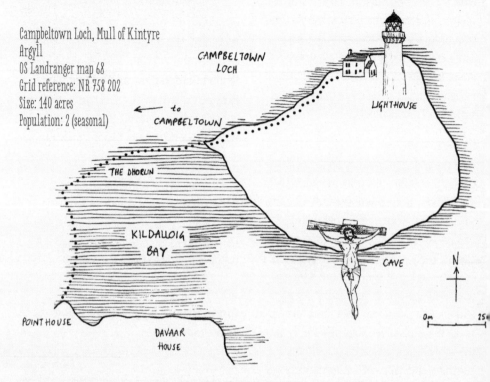

'The true mystery of the world,' averred Oscar Wilde, 'is the visible, not the invisible.' When he spoke these words, the playwright, novelist and arch aesthete clearly had in mind a curious event that occurred in a cave on Davaar when he was 33 years old.

To get to the cave you must follow in the footsteps of the major protagonist in the mystery. This means that from Campbeltown, near the foot of the Kintyre peninsula, you must strike out along the coast, wait for low tide, and make your way over the Dhorlin, a shingle causeway that doglegs across to Davaar and takes the best part of 20 minutes to walk. On reaching the island (basically a large mound resembling a tin jelly mould of a prone rabbit that has been squashed at one end, possibly by an actual rabbit), you should greet any resident wild goats or North Ronaldsay sheep that are loitering about. The latter are an extremely rare breed and apparently an absolute nightmare to control because they don't hold any truck with sheepdogs and have worked out that they can cross over to the mainland at low tide if the fancy takes them. On the plus side, they do graze a lot of plants that other sheep eschew, including seaweed, which is why their foibles are overlooked by their owners on the Kildalloig Estate, the organic farm of which Davaar is a part.

Turn right, following the directions of a large, no-nonsense sign with an arrow on it. After passing a ruined stone shelter the way around the island's coastline becomes rather narrow, with cliffs rising up to the left. The cave you are looking for is the fourth one along, as any local will tell you if asked, though that depends on what counts as a cave and what is just a sort of hole in the cliffs.

Inside, you'll find what sparked a veritable furore in Campbeltown and beyond: a passable mural of the crucified Christ. To the right of it is the head of a boy, presumably Christ again, though with what look like wings this time, and the words 'I did all this for thee/What wilt thou do for me'. On the rocks beneath the paintings, votive offerings of candles, handwritten notes and moderately artistic piles of pebbles are pretty much a permanent fixture.

So far, so unmysterious. What caught the public imagination, however, is that no one knew how the mural came to be. On 20 August 1887, the *Campbeltown Courier* reported that a passing yachtsman had sauntered into the cave, struck a match to light his pipe, and almost fainted from the shock of seeing Christ gazing soulfully down at him. At the time, Campbeltown suffered from a surfeit of artists and there was no shortage of speculation as to who might have been the perpetrator. Indeed, many people, both local and further afield,

held the belief that the mural had been painted by God himself as a sign. The picture fuelled a wave of pilgrimages, which is still a steady trickle to this day.

The truth, as with every mystery, was rather more mundane. The artist was Archibald Mackinnon, an art teacher at a local school. 'I awoke from a dream in which I beheld the body of our Saviour on the Cross,' he has been quoted as saying. In the dream he even saw the wall of the cave on which he was to paint what he had seen and he naturally felt compelled to make his dream a reality. It cost him his job, as it turned out. He left Campbeltown shortly after his mural was discovered, apparently concerned about the repercussions of having used paint belonging to his school. He ended up in Nantwich, where, among other things, he made a paintbrush using his wife's hair (with her consent, one hopes).

Although Mackinnon's departure from Campbeltown must certainly have looked suspicious, there are differing stories about how long it was before the provenance of the work was discovered. We do know that he returned to Davaar to touch up the painting in 1902 and again in 1934, the latter occasion at the behest of the town council amidst much pomp and ceremony, so the cat was clearly out of the bag by then. He died the next year at the age of 85.

A complete shoreline circuit of the island is an arduous venture, since the 1,000yd section from Mackinnon's cave to the lighthouse on Davaar's northeast corner

involves almost constant scrambling or jumping from rock to rock (though there is the reward of some fine rock pools towards the end). The lighthouse, which can also be reached by retracing one's steps from the cave, was built in 1854 by Thomas and David Stevenson, author Robert Louis' father and uncle respectively. It was automated in 1983 and two of the keepers' cottages have since been converted into holiday lets, while the third is used for six months every year by the cottages' caretakers.

They also look after a third holiday let: the Davaar Observation Post. Thrown up during World War II – a time when function evidently held the whip hand over form – this two-storey box-like structure enabled observers to receive signals from ships identifying themselves before they entered Campbeltown Loch. It was not to be Davaar's only contribution to the war effort. One of the mooring points of an anti-submarine boom protecting the loch was also based on the island – pretty close to the end of the causeway.

From here it is possible to head up the hill to experience the island's moorland and bogs, its heather and bracken. Consolation comes in the form of a view out over the sea towards Ailsa Craig. And while you're drinking it in, and wondering about what you might do for the Jesus down below, you might get lucky and spot an idling basking shark or a purposeful porpoise.

Left: Archibald Mackinnon's Christ crucified; Right: Davaar's lighthouse and cottages

How to get there

From Glasgow railway station (scotrail.co.uk; 0845 755 0033) take the 926 bus (westcoastmotors.co.uk; citylink.co.uk) and cast aside all sense of the brevity of life. A little shy of four hours later you'll be in Campbeltown and within easy walking distance of Davaar. The island is accessible for about three hours each side of low tide. Tide timetables can be viewed at the Tourist Information Centre (01586 552056).

Admission price/landing fee

Free.

View

Campbeltown, Arran and Ailsa Craig (p208).

Facilities

A litter bin.

Accommodation

Look no further than the island itself, on which you can stay in one of **two lighthouse cottages** or a **former wartime lookout** (kintyrecottages.com; 07979 296197). In Campbeltown (2 miles) there's the somewhat faded **Argyll Arms Hotel** (argyllarmshotel.co.uk; 01586 553431), where Paul McCartney and Denny Laine formed the band Wings in 1971.

Nearest decent pub/café/tea room

Try **Fresh Bytes** (2 miles; 01586 551666) on Main Street, Campbeltown, a Mecca for those with a gluten intolerance (and a minor pilgrimage site for those without).

Nearest shop

Campbeltown, a.k.a. 'Wee Glasgow by the Sea', is a place of many shops but something of a tired mien – it's evidently a long time since the town claimed, with justification, to be the richest in Britain.

Rules

None.

Things to do

Campbeltown Heritage Centre (2 miles; open April to September; campbeltownheritagecentre.co.uk) covers all things local from art to coal via farming and whisky – there were once so many distilleries in the town that it was said that fog-bound fishermen could smell their way into the harbour.

The Picture House (2 miles; weepictures.co.uk; 01586 553899) in Campbeltown was built in 1913, is the oldest working cinema in Scotland, and looks like a Bond villain's house.

The **Kintyre Way** (kintyreway.com), an 87-mile walking route from Tarbert to Dunaverty, passes through Campbeltown.

40. Cara

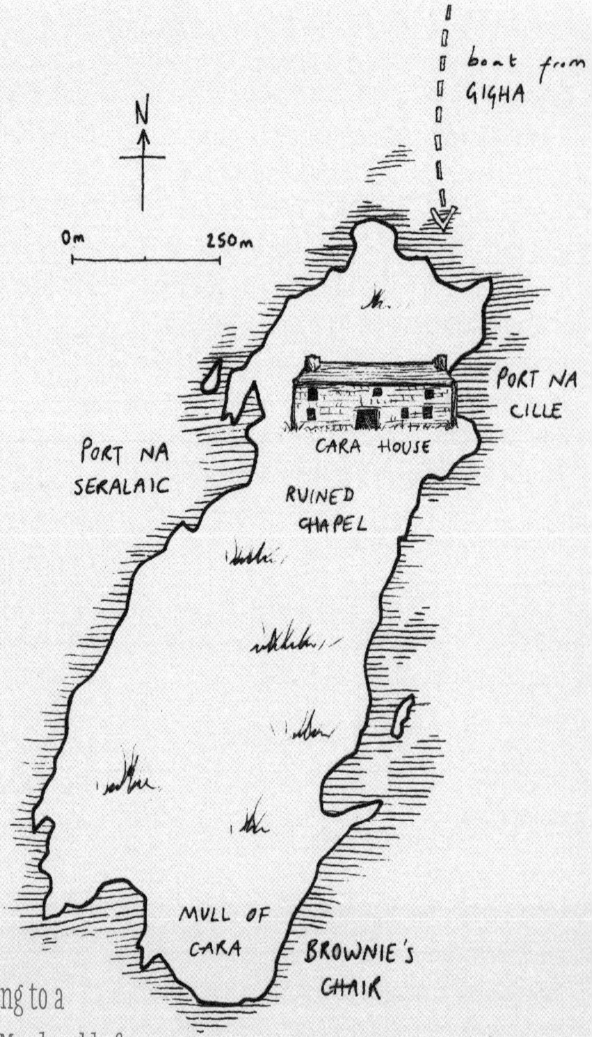

Off Gigha
Argyll
OS Landranger map 62
Grid reference: NR 639 439
Size: 163 acres
Population: 0

Cara is an island under the unofficial lairdship of a Brownie. This is not a small girl working towards her home skills badge but 'a neat little man, dressed in brown, with a pointed beard' according to a description given in 1909 by Morton Macdonald of Largie, who also pointed out that the man was 'not recorded in any census'.

As you might have guessed, he's also not like you and me but the spirit of a Macdonald of ages past who was murdered by a Campbell, the clan that gives treachery a bad name. Just off the west coast of the Kintyre peninsula, Cara (Gaelic for 'dear one' or 'dear friend') is the dot to the long exclamation mark that is Gigha ('God's Island'). At first sight, it doesn't look much – a treeless island that rises abruptly in the south before gently falling down to the sea at its northern end. There's one house that no one could describe as beautiful. Built for the tacksman (the steward for the estate) around 1733, it serves today as the holiday home for its leaseholder, one Harry Teggin.

However, scratch beneath the surface, and it's a more important and intriguing little island than its appearance suggests. For a start, it has attracted settlers for eons. The brace of interconnecting caves in the cliffs at the southern end of the isle show signs of human habitation of indistinct origin, but one can assume they're fairly venerable. We also know that Viking boots have almost certainly trodden its soil. King Haakon sailed a fleet of 120 ships from Bergen to the Hebrides in response to a threat from King Alexander III to wrest the isles from his control. The intimidating force anchored in Gigalum Sound, just north of the island, for up to three weeks before they headed off for Orkney.

Cara also became entangled in a dispute between the Macdonalds and (inevitably) the Campbells. Kinsmen who threw in their lots with Sir James Macdonald, newly escaped from prison in 1615, made Cara their base as they plotted to capture Hector MacNeill of Taynish and Gigha, who was allied to the Argyll Campbells. MacNeill duly sent a party to raid the island but the Macdonalds, warned by beacon from the mainland, saw them off, though they were routed themselves some time later. Tradition has it that MacNeill and some Campbell lords had dinner in the mansion house and for dessert hanged eight Macdonalds, burying their cadavers in the chapel. If so, they were not the only men to come to an untimely end on Cara – the brother of Flora Macdonald (she of Bonnie Prince Charlie fame) was killed in a shooting accident on the island.

Nothing remains of the mansion. However, behind the current house lie the ruins of a chapel that was abandoned during the 18th century. Its origins are vague but it appears to have been built by the monks of Icolmkill as a retreat house, its rather prolix name being the Chapel of St Finla in the Island of Kara (sic) beside the Monkshaven.

Cara is still owned by the Macdonalds of Largie (close by on the Kintyre peninsula) and is apparently the only island in the hands of direct descendants of the Lords of the Isles who, aptly enough, ruled from another tiny island, Eilean Mòr (p221). With rocks strewn about it, it has claimed more than its fair share of shipwrecks and disasters. Willie McSporran, a current native of Gigha, had his own grandfather drowned off the island in a squall. It cannot, however, be blamed for the loss of the *Aska* on 22 September 1940. The brand new ship, loaded with copra (coconut kernels), received a direct hit from a bomb dropped by a German plane. She drifted into the bay on the west side of the island and burned brightly for six long weeks. 'You could see the glow as far away as Campbeltown [about 20 miles away],' Willie recalls.

The island's precariously small population had given up the unequal struggle 10 years beforehand when the MacGougan family said goodbye to the house and took themselves off to Gigha, leaving Cara to the rabbits and the feral goats that still graze the island today.

Margaret Johnson (née MacGougan), now on the mainland, was a girl at the time, the youngest of eight children, and is the last surviving person to have lived on Cara. She remembers the hardship of keeping body and soul together by fishing, farming (they had sheep, cows and hens), cultivating a kitchen garden and making their own butter. She is also full of stories about the Brownie (pronounced 'Broonie'). This is hardly surprising, since he's said to live in an attic room in the house on Cara. 'If we heard any unexplained noises on the farm, like a knock on the front door when nobody was there – that was the Cara Brownie. Then once, after we'd left the island, a Macdonald fisherman took shelter in the house from a storm. He heard a noise outside and inexplicably, there by the front door, was a huge pile of feathers.'

Yarns about the Brownie are legion. Often he's obstructive to those who joke about him, but then extremely helpful when they see the error of their ways, like the time two disrespectful men from the mainland tried to roll a cask of wine up a plank from the cellar underneath the house on Cara. The Brownie made it immovable until they apologised, at which point, the barrel shot up the plank and careered along the shore until it set itself down next to the men's boat. He's also been said on occasion to have milked cows, lit welcoming fires in the hearth and even done the washing-up for the house's residents.

Is there anything to the Brownie tales? Rationally, one would think not. However, both Margaret Johnson and Harry Teggin report being keenly aware of the Brownie's presence. Though the people of Gigha often speak of the sprite with a wee smile playing on their lips, they are noticeably careful to speak no ill of him. And why should they? As spirits go, he seems of the better sort. I certainly came to no harm during my brief sojourn on the island, though I did doff an imaginary hat to him while there. Indeed, taking shelter from a shower under the Brownie's Chair – some outcropping rocks on the east of the island that more or less resemble a one-armed seat – I found myself gazing blankly out at a patch of sea when suddenly a dolphin leapt out of it. It flipped back under the waves in a flash and never reappeared. If I hadn't been looking at that little scrap of water right then I'd never have seen it. Now, if that's not solid proof of the Brownie's existence, I fear you'll never be convinced.

How to get there

Transporting oneself to the Kintyre peninsula is not achieved without effort. Probably the least stressful means of doing so is to take the train to Glasgow (scotrail. co.uk; 0845 755 0033) then board the 926 bus (westcoastmotors.co.uk; citylink.co.uk) with a sturdy book. Around three-and-a-half hours later, alight at Tayinloan. Here a ferry (hourly from 8am to 7pm in summer; calmac.co.uk; 0800 066 5000) will take you over to the isle of Gigha, landing in

Ardminish Bay. Enquire at the nearby post office if there's anyone on the island with a boat in the water who will ferry you over to Cara. In late spring and summer, the chances are there will be. Or, if the weather is good, you can hire a sea kayak (see 'Things to do') and make your own way over. Unless you're a Campbell, in which case you'd be advised to stay away.

Admission price/landing fee
Free.

View
To the north there's gentle low-lying Gigha, while to the east the Kintyre peninsula stretches out interminably.

Facilities
None.

Accommodation
On Gigha, the **Boathouse Café Bar**, about 300yd from the ferry slipway, offers camping on a small grassy area next to the café (and has toilet and shower facilities). Booking ahead is essential (01583 505123; info@boathouse-bar.com). The community-owned **Gigha Hotel** (gigha.org.uk; 01583 505254) at Ardminish, a short walk from the ferry slipway, boasts a dozen rooms, one more than the baronial mansion that is **Achamore House** (achamorehouse.com; 01583 505400).
For other accommodation on Gigha see gigha.org.uk/accom/other.

Nearest decent pub/café/tea room
The **Gigha Hotel's bar** (see 'Accommodation') or the **Boathouse Café Bar** if the latter remains open.

Nearest shop
The **post office at Ardminish Bay** stocks a very small supply of basic foods. Otherwise, the small **Tayinloan Stores** is half a mile from the quay on the mainland.

Rules
No, but do respect the privacy of the owners.

Things to do
At **Gigha Boats Activity Centre** (tinyurl. com/9q6kuxe; 07876 506520) in Ardminish Bay you can hire a sea kayak, rowing boat, paddleboard, wetsuit, scuba equipment or bicycle.
Achamore Gardens (achamorehouse. com; 01583 505400) is the main visitor attraction on Gigha. The estate's 50 acres around Achamore House (see 'Accommodation') include many rare and unusual plants.

41. Eilean Mòr

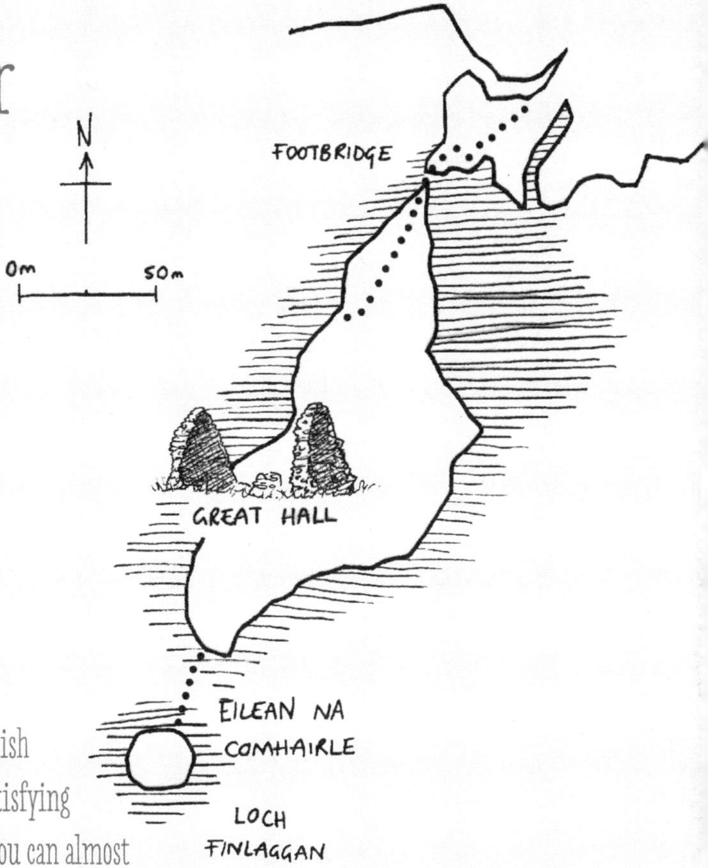

N ↑

Finlaggan, Islay
Argyll
finlaggan.com
OS Landranger map 60
Grid reference: NR 388 681
Size: 2.5 acres
Population: 0

0m — 50m

FOOTBRIDGE

GREAT HALL

EILEAN NA COMHAIRLE

LOCH FINLAGGAN

The Lords of the Isles – has British history thrown up any more satisfying name for a ruling elite? Why, you can almost taste the salt on your lips as you say the words.

These powerful Macdonald chiefs, who held sway over the Atlantic seaboard from Lewis all the way down to Kintyre, created a huge autonomous territory. Indeed, they saw themselves very much the equals of the crowned heads of Scotland, England and France. They seem to have done a good job of being lords of the isles too, their tenure coinciding with a period of unprecedented prosperity for those who lived under their sway. And of all the places they could have chosen to establish their capital, they plumped for a wee isle on an insignificant loch on the island of Islay.

To understand why they went for Eilean Mòr, we need to hurtle back over several thousand years – way before a man named John first gave himself the title Lord of the Isles around 1329. The discovery of an axe head on one of the two crannogs (man-made islands) on Finlaggan loch suggests that they were built as places of refuge in the Stone Age. What the inhabitants of the twin crannogs and the island did for the first few millennia is unknown, though presumably cleaving things in twain with axes was a popular pursuit. The islands eventually attracted the attention of a 6th-century Irish monk called Findlugan who is thought to have founded a monastery on the natural island, which was given the name Eilean Mòr (Gaelic for 'big island') to distinguish it from the two crannogs. He in turn found his name given to the loch on which it sits and, like so many of his contemporaries, he achieved sainthood into the bargain (partly for saving the life of St Columba).

Later on, Norse settlers found Eilean Mòr to their liking because it provided them with a base that was easily defendable. For several hundred years they ruled over the southern islands, known as the Sudreys, which included Islay (pronounced eye-la). It is at this point that a nobleman of Irish descent named Somerled enters our story. Local chiefs, suffering beyond all endurance under the yoke of the tyrannical Godred IV, called upon Somerled to save their people. He duly turned up with a fleet of 80 galleys he himself had designed, stealing from Norse boatbuilding techniques and improving on them. His smaller, nimbler vessels defeated the Vikings in a sea battle off the north coast of Islay on 6 January 1156, effectively transferring much of their territory into his hands. On his death (while fighting Malcolm IV of Scotland), his empire was divided between his sons Ruari and Donald. The descendants of the latter, through a series of marital alliances and canny politics, established themselves as chiefs over much of the Inner Hebrides and the mainland coast, allowing his great-great-great-grandson 'Good John of Islay' to proclaim himself the first Dominus Insularum ('Lord of the Isles'), with Eilean Mòr, a ready-made stronghold, as his seat of power.

Once accessible by a stone causeway from the mainland, today a wooden walkway takes those thrill seekers pursuing the meta-island experience (lest we forget, it's an island on an island) over the reeds to Eilean Mòr. A flat and grassy little place, it's jam-packed with the remains of 20 or so buildings.

Rather hearteningly, the first sight visitors see as they walk along the medieval paved roadway – itself a sign of how important the island was – is a purely domestic one: the low corrugations of so-called lazy beds whose cultivation helped to feed the small populace. The island's wooden fortifications are long gone, but parts of the chapel built by John I on a limestone outcrop are still here. Inside, protected from the weather by panes of glass, are eight decorated grave slabs, including those of a blacksmith (with an anvil depicted on it), a child and a man in Highland armour. Aside from the Great Hall, now almost entirely dismantled by looters, the rest of the ruins are of houses or barns, with the remnants of the building at the southern tip believed to be the Lord of the Isles' private quarters.

Pegs used for tuning harps and counters for playing games have been unearthed here, suggesting that Eilean Mòr was a place of music and gentle amusement as well as politics and power. That's not to say that the residents were content to sit by

Top: Mighty gables of the Great Hall; Bottom: Modern elevated footway above the ancient causeway

their own firesides. A 14th-century pilgrim's badge found on the shore is a souvenir of a visit to the holy city of Rome.

The crannog to the south – connected by a short causeway now submerged – was used for meetings of the Lord of the Isles with his council, which comprised thanes, armins (of lower status than a thane), and the rather unfortunately named bastards (squires of estates too small to have their own thane or armin). The miniscule islet was hence named Eilean na Comhairle ('council isle').

The decisions the Lords of the Isles made there were, on the whole, sage ones and embraced policies that avoided the debilitating conflicts that persisted on the mainland. However, the 4th Lord of the Isles, John II, was not cut from the same cloth as his predecessors and made two fatal errors: the first was to enter into a pact of friendship with William, the 8th Earl of Douglas (p203) and Alexander Lindsay, 4th Earl of Crawford, both of whom were threats to the power of James II of Scotland. Although there's no evidence to suggest any tripartite masterplan to overthrow the king, it cost the Earl of Douglas his life.

John survived, only to enter into a new and secret pact in 1462 with Edward IV. The Yorkist king agreed to help him conquer the whole of Scotland north of the Forth. In return, John would become his vassal. It's likely Edward never intended to offer any support to the venture and was merely using John to create a diversion against James III of Scotland, who was at the time in cahoots with the Lancastrian Henry IV. The islanders embarked on their conquest, taking Inverness, but the rebellion fizzled out. In 1476, Edward revealed the details of the pact to James III. The king duly stripped the treacherous John of his mainland territories, leaving him only the isles.

By 1493, James IV had lost patience with John and stripped him of the title of Lord of the Isles. He died in obscurity in the Lowlands. The Scottish Crown definitively annexed the title Lord of the Isles in 1542, and that was that. The name lives on, but only as one of the many titles bestowed upon the current Prince of Wales. It's scant consolation really.

However, the story doesn't quite end there. The tiny island of Cara (p216), just south of Gigha, is owned by the Macdonalds of Largie. Of the once mighty realm, it is the sole remaining fragment still in the hands of direct descendants of the long-lamented Lords of the Isles.

How to get there

From Glasgow (scotrail.co.uk; 0845 755 0033, virgintrains.co.uk; 01709 849200) take the 926 bus (westcoastmotors.co.uk; citylink.co.uk). After about three hours and 20 minutes, alight at Kennacraig where a ferry (calmac.co.uk; 0800 066 5000) will take you to Port Askaig on Islay. The 451 bus (timetable at argyll-bute.gov.uk) runs infrequently to the entrance of Finlaggan. It's a mile-long walk from there.

Admission price/landing fee

Adult £3, child £1.

View

The crannog Eilean na Comhairle and the low hills around Loch Finlaggan.

Facilities

None. However, the nearby information centre has a loo and a machine dispensing tea, coffee and hot chocolate.

Accommodation

The **Ballygrant Inn** (1.8 miles; ileach.co.uk/ballygrant; 01496 840277), just outside Ballygrant, makes for a good value B&B stop. Or there's the rather more expensive **Port Askaig Hotel** (3.2 miles; portaskaig.co.uk; 01496 840245) by the ferry terminal.

Nearest decent pub/café/tea room

Both the **Ballygrant Inn**, (1.8 miles) and the **Port Askaig Hotel** (3.2 miles) serve food (see 'Accommodation' for details).

Nearest shop

Ballygrant's village shop is sadly no more so the closest is now **Port Askaig Stores** in the eponymous coastal village (3.2 miles).

Rules

No dogs allowed during the lambing season.

Things to do

Despite its modest size, Islay has no fewer than **eight distilleries**. Caledonian MacBrayne (tinyurl.com/cakf25h; 0800 066

5000) offer combined ferry ticket/distillery tours. If you prefer a single malt whisky to whisky galore you could restrict yourself to nearby **Bunnahabhain** (6.7 miles; bunnahabhain.com).

If you fancy a bit of island hopping, **Jura** is just five minutes away on the ferry (islayinfo.com/jura-ferry.html; 01496 840681) from Port Askaig.

Trawl to the far north of Jura and you can see **the house in which George Orwell wrote *1984*** and the **Corryvreckan whirlpool** where he nearly inadvertently drowned himself and five members of his family.

The chapel's grave slabs, sagely protected from the elements

Off Seil Island
Argyll and Bute
easdalemuseum.org
OS Landranger map 55
Grid reference: NM 736 171
Size: 25 acres
Population: 60–70

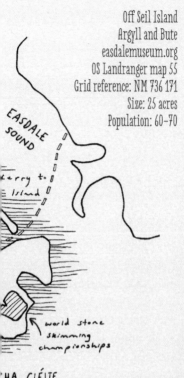

HA CLÉITE

mallest permanently inhabited

four corners of the world; its

e the scientist usually credited with

year.

most mapmakers nowadays are

gligent as to miss off this little

sea about 150yd from the island

the Argyll coast. In its heyday

d-19th century, this apparently

uential island in the Sound of

a population of around 450 living

jowl and was exporting up to 19

ofing slates every year. They were

ff to Canada, the US, New Zealand,

Australia and the West Indies among other destinations, laying the basis for the boast that Easdale's was 'the slate that roofed the world'. Had they felt the need, they could also have bragged that they had actually expanded the land mass of Scotland too. By the early 19th century, so much spoil from the slate quarries had been dumped into the sound near the mainland shore that it formed the land on which the village of Ellenabeich now stands.

There are extraordinary photographs on display in the island's museum of men descending the quarries – some of which were hundreds of feet below sea level – by means of a truly Heath Robinson collection of ropes and ladders. Inevitably, accidents happened and the island doctor was kept busy dealing with injuries. However, by the late 18th century he no longer had to treat cases of smallpox. A survey conducted in 1791 found that the community had freed itself of the disease by employing a system of inoculation. Edward Jenner's own experiments in immunisation using the cowpox virus took place a full five years afterwards.

Commercial quarrying ceased in 1911, on account of the world's newly found preference for clay tiles. The island was put on the market, but, with little to offer a buyer, it remained unsold until 1950. It is currently owned by Jonathan Feigenbaum, a dealer in stamps.

Today, the first thing you notice as you get off the little boat that carries you over in a blink from Ellenabeich is not quarries but wheelbarrows. On a small patch of grass by the harbour a battalion of them lie upside down alongside a few jaunty home-made carts. With no roads and no cars, anything that needs ferrying about on the grassy footpaths goes in a wheelbarrow, so this is the island's equivalent of a car park.

Next door is Easdale's unexpectedly funky community centre, a curvy Gaudiesque affair that no doubt raised some eyebrows at the local town council planning committee. Beyond it, whitewashed one-storey cottages of far greater vintage arrange themselves in rather haphazard lines around the inlet that serves as a harbour. Towards the middle of the isle stands a flat-topped hillock, its flanks torn off to reveal dark cliffs. Meanwhile, a wander around the outside of the island, over its millions of shards of slate, takes in all half dozen or so flooded quarries. These have an otherworldly feel to them, as if formed by a giant poking his rough fingers deep into the island from above in a misguided mission to supply its inhabitants with swimming pools.

So, why isn't the island that roofed the world elbowing for head space in the national consciousness with other famous tiny islands like St Michael's Mount and the Isle of May? Geography, for one, doesn't do it any favours, for it's in an unfashionable backwater of the Inner Hebrides. Furthermore, Easdale is not far enough out to sea to render itself exotic like Tiree or Jura. Also, the fact that its name is more suggestive of Yorkshire than Argyll doesn't help its cause. The derivation of

Easdale (Eilean Èisdeal in Gaelic) is obscure. According to the theories currently in play, you can take your pick from 'waterfall valley', 'glen of ash trees' or even 'listen to that yonder', none of which seems very likely.

Easdale has been described as a 'post-industrial wasteland' and there's some truth in that, albeit that the great bites taken out of it by the quarrymen give it more the look of a moth-eaten rag. However, since there's been no full-scale mining for 100 years now (merely the occasional hack at the rock to fulfil local orders), nature has begun to have its beautifying way with the island. The sea has turned the quarries into lagoons, while long grasses, wild fuchsia and blackthorn have covered what the sea cannot penetrate. Without being a vision of the New Jerusalem, it's clearly an extremely peaceful and pleasant place to live. By the time of the 1961 census, the population had fallen to a meagre 16 but the figure is now nearly four times that, so post-industrial community life is clearly an attractive prospect in the 21st century.

But that begs the question: what do they all *do* here? According to the folk museum's May McGillivray, there are a few builders, a web designer, a civil engineer, two fishermen, several musicians, a postwoman, some council workers, two shop assistants, some employees of the Seafari tourism company 'and some that I've not remembered off the top of my head'. Many others commute to Oban, half an hour away by road.

But all work and no play makes Jack a dull boy, and what little fame Easdale has today is down to its hosting of the World Stone Skimming Championships (stoneskimming.com). The contest, which is open to all comers, takes place in one of the flooded quarries every September. Although the event is intended first and foremost to be fun – with a big knees-up in the community centre the night before – there are proper rules and regulations and referees and everything, with a trophy for the winner of each category. If you fancy taking one home yourself, you should know that the victor in the men's competition invariably gets his smooth slate projectile to hit the back wall of the quarry, a throw of some 200ft, while the female champion usually skims her stone just over half that distance.

How to get there

Take the train to Oban (scotrail.co.uk; 0845 755 0033) then the 418 bus (West Coast Motors; tinyurl.com/ahfh6xz; 01586 552319) to Ellenabeich from where the ferry (£1.75 return, pay on way back) departs for the two-minute journey to Easdale. There are frequent sailings all year round (but with a break at lunchtime, as is only right and proper).

Admission price/landing fee

Free.

View

The island of Seil (which feels very much like the mainland thanks to the 'Bridge over the Atlantic' that has linked it to the mainland proper since 1792), Insh Island, Luing and various other islands.

Facilities

A small museum and a waiting room for the ferry.

Accommodation

You can stay on the island in a 200-year-old former **slate quarryman's cottage** (sleeps 4; lovetoescape.com; 01786 870266). Over on Ellenabeich you'll find the attractive **Garragh Mhor B&B** (garraghmhor.co.uk; 01852 300513).

Nearest decent pub/café/tea room

Just by the harbour, the island's own excellent bar and restaurant, **The Puffer** (pufferbar.com) is also a tea room.

Nearest shop

There are a couple of shelves of basic groceries in a gift shop in Ellenabeich. The nearest proper shop is **Balvicar Stores** in Balvicar (2 miles).

Rules

None.

Things to do

You cannot leave Easdale without visiting the one-room **Easdale Island Folk Museum** (open April to October; easdalemuseum. org; 01852 300173) with its homespun but fascinating look at the lives of the island's people.

Over in Ellenabeich on the mainland, **The Slate Islands Heritage Centre and Museum** (open daily; free) focuses on the slate mines of Easdale, Belnahua, Luing and Seil.

nr Balnahard, Isle of Mull
Inner Hebrides
OS Landranger map 48
Grid reference: NM 438 355
Size: 136 acres
Population: 0

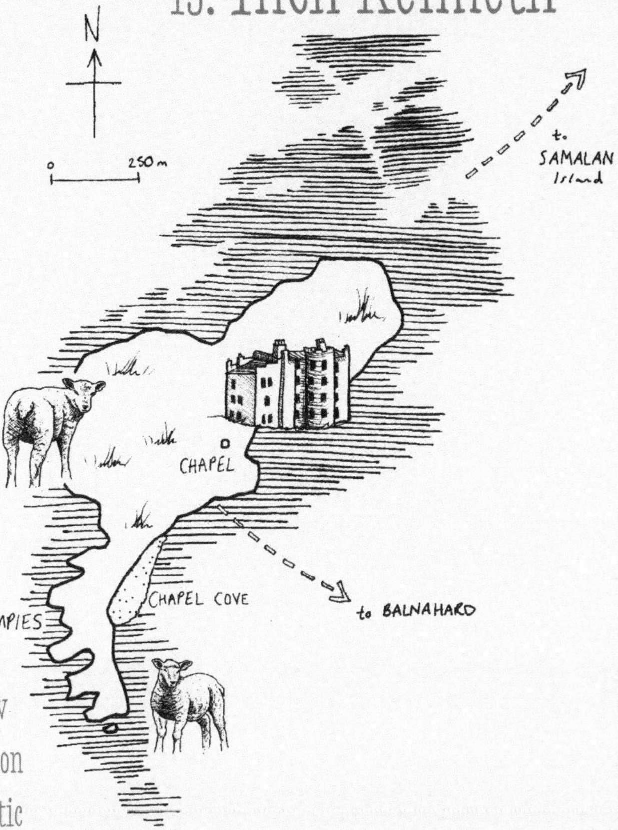

Inch Kenneth is an island in perpetual shade: not from any shadow cast over it by the huge Gribun Cliffs on nearby Mull, but by a single aristocratic family who owned it for less than three decades.

Ever since Lord Redesdale bought the island on the eve of World War II (the story goes that the previous owner, who had not long inherited it, asked in his London club whether anyone wanted to buy an island and Redesdale said yes), he and his wife, and more particularly their six daughters, the infamous Mitford sisters, have proved characters larger than the island itself, habitually reducing Inch Kenneth in the eyes of onlookers to 'that island the Mitfords owned'.

It's a pity really, because prior to 1939 this little splinter off the west coast of Mull had already lived a life worthy of any biographer's pen. So, on landing at Chapel Cove, let us forget for a moment the big white house over the hill to our right, and turn instead to Inch Kenneth's chapel and graveyard.

Constructed in the 13th century and acting as the parish church until after the Reformation, the chapel is now a ruin (in the care of Historic Scotland).

The author, standing on the official World Stone Skimming Championship stone, fails to break any records

However, it does contain eight extraordinary grave slabs decorated with galleys of Lorn – symbols of Norse royalty – and the swords of warriors. The chapel is not the oldest indication of human occupation on the island: that accolade goes to an otherwise insignificant standing stone, positioned for some unknown purpose by unknown hands at some unknown prehistoric date.

We have to wait until 1400 before we come across the first record of Inch Kenneth, by which time it secures a brief mention in the *Scotichronicon* (see p277). There's no doubt, however, as to the origin of its name. Inch is a corruption of one of the many Gaelic words for island and the Kenneth in question is St Kenneth, who was a friend of St Columba and is reputed to have built a chapel on the island in AD565, though there's no trace of it today. St Kenneth seems to have had a fondness for working rather petty-minded non-essential miracles, such as banishing mice who ate his shoes and causing birds to stop singing on the Sabbath.

The island was farmed by Iona's Augustinian community just a dozen miles away. The Dean of the Isles, Archdeacon Donald Monro, recorded his visit to 'Inchekenzie' around 1548: '...half a myle in lenthe, and not fully half a myle in breadthe, a fair ile, fertile and fruitfull, inhabit and manurit, full of cunnings about the shoare of it.' Cunnings indeed – the island spreads itself out alarmingly at low tide when all the hidden rocks and ledges parade themselves like a float of famished crocodiles.

Around 1574, the last prioress of Iona, Mary MacLean, relinquished the island to Hector MacLean of Duart, chief of the clan. The history books remained blank for the next two centuries, until the coming of none other than Samuel Johnson and James Boswell. The pair visited Inch Kenneth in 1773 as guests of Sir Allan MacLean, Johnson noting that: 'Sir Allan related the American campaign, and in the evening one of the ladies played on her harpsichord, while Col and Mr Boswell danced a Scottish reel with the other.' According to Boswell, Johnson reckoned that Sunday to be 'the most agreeable he had ever passed', which is high praise indeed from one not given to kind words about the Scots.

In the following 37 years, the island appears to have been on the skids if avid island hopper Sir Walter Scott is to be believed. After visiting in 1810 with prison reformer and difficult-biblical-middle-name-sufferer Sir George Onesipherous Paul, he wrote in a letter that his companion 'showed most incredulity on the subject of Johnson's having been entertained in the wretched hovels of which we saw the ruins'.

From then on, the island changed hands many times, passing from good owners (step forward, Lt. Col. Robert Macdonald, who built a new house there and was bountiful in his relations with the locals) to indifferent ones. Famed for its fertile sandy loam, it continued to be successfully

Clockwise from top: Robert Macdonald's house; grave slabs in the chapel; view towards Ulva and Little Colonsay

farmed until disaster struck one day in the 1890s. In a fit of depression, the man kept on the island as a shepherd by the then owners took it upon himself to ferry his wife and children across to Mull before returning to burn the house down.

But we've arrived too early at the house (which was rebuilt soon afterwards, by the way, and with an extra floor to boot). Casting out to the west we come to one of Inch Kenneth's four distinct worlds. The Humpies are stubby fingers of land that claw ineffectively at the sea. They serve as a complete contrast to the tranquil eastern extremity of the island – known as the Samalan end after the minute island just off it – where a sandy shell-strewn beach spreads out towards low seaweed-covered islets seemingly flattened by the westerly winds and home to basking grey seals and ringed plovers.

The high plateau, the third of Inch Kenneth's worlds, can be accessed easily from here because it tapers gently down to rest on the beach. Its grass is so rich that lambs who graze here grow large extremely swiftly, so hastening their demise. Standing at its highest point, a humble 160ft above the foaming brine, only a small wind turbine, a rustic stone seat and the odd wooden post give any indication that humans have been on the island at all. It's the ideal place to discover just how prone Inch Kenneth is to the mutability of the local weather. Snow can tumble out of a sunny sky (indeed, it did so on me), and the four seasons compact themselves into an afternoon. It's also the best place for scanning the heavens for white-tailed sea eagles and the seas for frolicking dolphins. Walk towards the southern edge of the plateau and the

flat roof of the four-storey house quickly comes into view, along with a row of wind-battered trees where siskins aestivate, and a slew of low buildings, many of which have lived more than one life, having served as workers' quarters, tractor sheds, a meat-hanging store and a smithy (the blacksmith's huge bellows are still in situ).

The extreme height of the house is down to Sir Harold Boulton, who, on buying Inch Kenneth for £1,500 in 1934, added yet another storey and some rather half-hearted battlements, making it appear like a stately home attempting to morph into a block of flats.

Sir Harold had found fame through penning the words of the *Skye Boat Song* ('Speed, bonnie boat, like a bird on the wing'). His poem about Inch Kenneth was less inspired, its last lines tumbling into doggerel:

O green isle of Kenneth
True Lover am I
'Tis here I'd be living
'Tis here too I'd die.

He breathed his last a year after buying the island, probably before the enlargements to the house were finished. There's a servants' bell board inside that bears the legends 'Sir Harolds bedroom' and 'Sir Harolds bathroom' (both sic), though it's unlikely that he lived long enough to summon a flunky to either.

And so we come at last to the Mitfords, and in particular to Unity, the tallest sister and, appropriately enough, the one whose history casts the longest shadow over the island. Obsessed with her friend Adolf Hitler (she was conceived in Swastika, Ontario, which perhaps sealed her fate), Unity was in Munich on the day Britain declared war on Germany. She promptly shot herself in the head but survived. She arrived back home in 1940, declaring herself 'glad to be in England, even if I'm not on your side', and eventually moving up to Inch Kenneth to live with her mother. She remained there in her pitiable little world – by all accounts the shooting had left her mentally impaired – conducting services in the ruins of the chapel and planning and re-planning her own funeral. It wasn't long in coming. She died of pneumococcal meningitis in 1948 at the age of 33.

When Lady Redesdale died in 1963 the island came into the possession of her five surviving daughters. Jessica, an ardent Bolshevik, offered her portion to the Communist Party of Great Britain. They politely turned her down. She duly bought out the other sisters and hosted parties there when she was over from America. She sold it just four years later to the current owners, Yvonne and Andrew, and the island breathed a little sigh and the birds sang on the Sabbath and the mice danced and peace returned.

How to get there

Take the train to Oban (scotrail.co.uk; 0845 755 0033), then the ferry (calmac.co.uk; 0800 066 5000) to Craignure on the Isle of Mull. Bus 495 (bowmanstours.co.uk; 01631 563221) runs to Salen, where public transport more or less peters out, aside from a very infrequent bus to Gruline – attempts to catch this should only be made by trained professionals. The Tobermory-based Mull Taxi Service (mulltaxi.co.uk; 07760 426351) can usher you the rest of the way to Ulva Ferry (alternatively it's a 21-mile cycle ride from Craignure). From Ulva Ferry, Mull Charters (mullcharters.com; 01680 300444) run occasional sailings to Inch Kenneth according to demand, so the best thing to do is get a group together and give them a ring.

Admission price/landing fee

Free.

View

To the east over Loch na Keal is the raggedy hill that is the neighbouring island of Eorsa, while to the south are Mull's staggeringly impressive Gribun Cliffs. Ulva lies to the north, while to the west are Little Colonsay, Staffa (p237), the Treshnish Isles and Iona.

Facilities

None.

Accommodation

The owners of Inch Kenneth allow **wild camping** on the island but do find a discreet spot away from the house and, of course, take everything away with you. See Staffa (p237) for other accommodation options.

Nearest decent pub/café/tea room

Head for Salen (11 miles), a small village with a surprisingly good choice of eateries: the **Coffee Pot café** (argyll-house.co.uk; 01680 300555) with 'a real fire (on cold days)'; Italian restaurant **Mediterranea** (mull-cuisine.co.uk; 01680 300200); and **Bake & Take**, a take-away baguette/hot snack cabin.

Nearest shop

In Salen (11 miles) there's a well-stocked **Spar** with toy and local book sections, and a post office.

Rules

Please respect the fact that this is a privately owned island and keep your distance from the house and its precincts. The jetty is private too – boats should be landed at Chapel Cove a little to the west.

Things to do

On Yer Bike in Salen (11 miles; Easter to October; 01680 300501) hires out road bikes, off-road bikes and trailers for those wishing to explore Mull by pedal power. There are several **all-day tours** (including mullwildlifetours.co.uk and discovermull. co.uk) on which you can see Mull's internationally renowned wildlife, including golden eagles and the magnificent white-tailed sea eagles.

44. Staffa

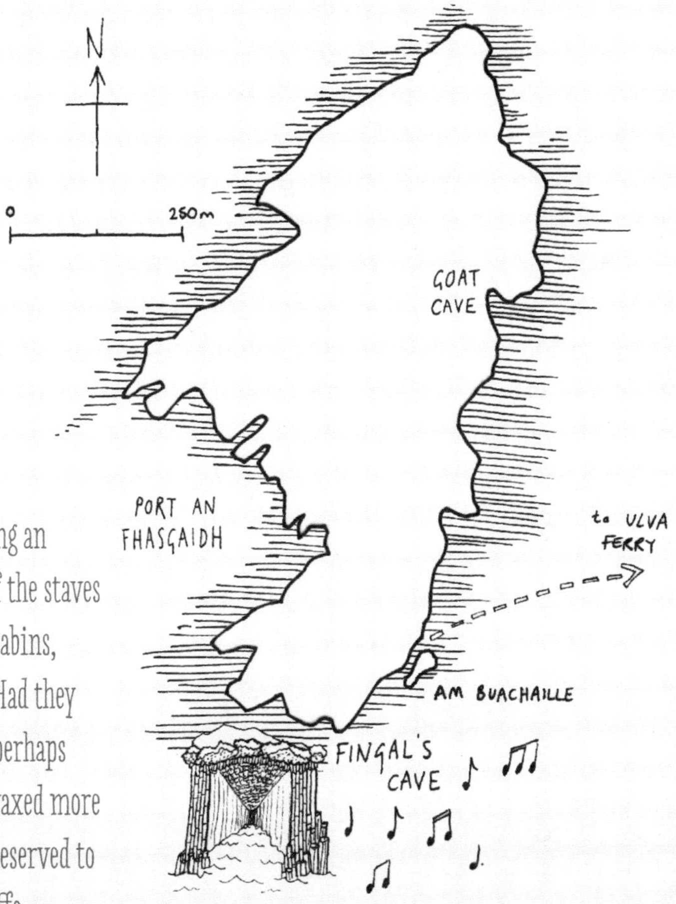

nr Gometra
Inner Hebrides
OS Landranger map 48
Grid reference: NM 324 353
Size: 82 acres
Population: 0

It was the Norse raiders, seeing an island that reminded them of the staves with which they built their cabins, who named the place 'Stafr'. Had they not been quite so prosaic, or perhaps homesick, they might have waxed more lyrical, for if ever an island deserved to take the name Muse, it is Staffa.

Poets, musicians, painters, authors – they've all felt themselves moved to create art after an encounter with Staffa. You really can't blame the island if the results have often failed to match the grandeur of their subject.

Take John Keats, if you will. The Romantic poet, after complaining in a July 1818 letter to his brother about the 'wretched walk of 37 Miles across the Island of Mull', set about capturing his experiences of the voyage from Iona to Staffa and the exploration on foot of the island's star attraction, Fingal's Cave. He coughed up a 51-line poem called *Staffa*, of which this is arguably one of the more successful segments:

> *Not St. John, in Patmos' Isle,*
> *In the passion of his toil,*
> *When he saw the churches seven,*
> *Golden aisl'd, built up in heaven,*
> *Gaz'd at such a rugged wonder.*

It's not bad, particularly, it's just not quite up there with *Ode on a Grecian Urn*. Even Keats had the grace to apologise for it: 'I am sorry I am so indolent as to write such stuff as this. It can't be helped.'

Wordsworth also drew a blank, though clearly Staffa's enormous pulling power by the time of his visit in the summer of 1833 was clouding its charm:

> *We saw, but surely in the motley crowd*
> *Not one of us has felt, the*
> *far-famed sight:*
> *How could we feel it? Each the*
> *others blight,*
> *Hurried and hurrying volatile and loud.*

Happily, although the island remains a popular destination for day trippers, it is rarely overrun with them. The fact that they go there at all is clearly not down to the stumbling poesie of Keats or Wordsworth but rather to the work of two other men: Sir Joseph Banks and Felix Mendelssohn.

Staffa had enjoyed a cameo role in Irish folklore but had been drifting in peaceful obscurity for centuries, unremarked upon by those who knew it and supporting a small population whose numbers and livestock waxed and waned.

No doubt the morning of 13 August 1772 dawned much as any other on the island. However, bad weather that day drove the Iceland-bound ship in which Sir Joseph Banks was travelling into the Sound of Mull. Passing the night on Staffa in the humble home of the island's only inhabitants (and becoming infested with lice as a result), the future President of the Royal Society was overwhelmed with what he saw and reported his findings in his *A Tour of Scotland and a Voyage to the Hebrides*. Staffa-mania broke out almost immediately.

So what makes the island so special? In four words and a hyphen: fine-grained Tertiary basalt. Staffa was created by the same volcanic activity that gave us the Giant's Causeway – basalt columns, mainly regular hexagons with some pentagons thrown in, were formed by the slow cooling of lava. Fingal's Cave – a place Keats admitted was 'impossible to describe' – really has to be seen to be believed. It's thought to be the only sea cave on the planet made up entirely of columnar basalt. It's about 80yd long and has a ceiling fully 20yd above the waves that resembles something you might see in a Gothic cathedral.

When the weather permits, boats land just around the corner, by a tidal islet called Am Buachaille. Having climbed the steep steps from the tiny jetty, visitors can prepare themselves for Fingal's Cave by having a look at Clamshell Cave, whose columns have twisted into the shape of the eponymous mollusc. A path then leads across a hexagonally paved floor around the cliffs to Fingal's Cave (named after Irish giant and folk hero Fionn mac Cumhaill). You can walk a good deal of the way in, but a small boat would be necessary to get to the very far end of the cave. Over the other side of the headland,

and almost as spectacular, is Mackinnon's Cave, which is connected by a tunnel to Cormorant's Cave.

It would be tedious to list all the notable people who came to Staffa in the 19th century when the island was a destination no self-respecting tourist could leave off their itinerary. Aside from Keats and Wordsworth, the luminaries included Sir Walter Scott, Jules Verne, Robert Louis Stevenson, David Livingstone (presumably), Queen Victoria and Prince Albert, and J M W Turner, who reported getting caught out by the weather and only making it back to Tobermory on Mull at midnight. His doggedly blurry painting of Fingal's Cave was a greater triumph than Keats' poem, though again not one of his best. It was left to Mendelssohn, whose *Hebridean Overture* was inspired by his visit in 1829, to ensure the island's enduring fame.

But arguably the most interesting insight thrown up by Staffa came a year after Banks' 'rediscovery' of the island, when Johnson and Boswell stayed with members of the MacQuarrie clan on nearby Ulva. Johnson wrote later: 'When the islanders were reproached with their ignorance or insensibility of the wonders of Staffa, they had not much to reply. They had indeed considered it little, because they had always seen it; and none but philosophers, nor they always, are struck with wonder otherwise than by novelty.'

Fingal's Cave, the geological feature even Keats couldn't describe

How to get there

Take the train to Oban (scotrail.co.uk; 0845 755 0033), followed by the ferry (calmac. co.uk; 0800 066 5000) to Craignure on the Isle of Mull. It's a 21-mile cycle ride to Ulva Ferry, or you can buy the Caledonian MacBrayne/Turus Mara's all-in ticket (01631 562244), which includes transport from Oban and across Mull. Otherwise, it's a case of taking the 495 bus (bowmanstours. co.uk; 01631 563221) to Salen and a taxi (mulltaxi.co.uk; 07760 426351) onwards to Ulva Ferry. Turus Mara (turusmara. com; 0800 085 8786) will waft you over to both Staffa (one hour on the island, if sea conditions permit) and Lunga (p241) from Easter to October. Alternatively, Gordon Grant Marine Boat Tours (staffatours.com; 01681 700338) sail to Staffa from Oban and Kilchoan on the mainland, Fionnphort and Tobermory on Mull, and Iona.

Admission price/landing fee

Free.

View

A circuit of islands: the Treshnish Isles, Gometra, Ulva, Little Colonsay, Inch Kenneth (p231), Mull and Iona.

Facilities

A refuge hut.

Accommodation

Lip na Cloiche, a family-run B&B in Ballygown, is just 2 miles along the coast from Ulva Ferry (lipnacloiche.co.uk; 01688 500257). See Lunga (p241) for further options. Wild camping is discouraged along the lochside east of Ulva Ferry but there is a **camping area at Killiechronan** (6 miles; 01680 300403).

Nearest decent pub/café/tea room

From Ulva Ferry take the eponymous boat (a sort of motorised biscuit tin that shuttles across on demand) to **The Boathouse** (theboathouseulva.co.uk; 01688 500241), a picturesque café/restaurant specialising in local ingredients. See Inch Kenneth (p231) for further options.

Nearest shop

In Salen (10 miles from Ulva Ferry) there's a well-stocked **Spar** with sections for toys and local books, and a post office.

Rules

None (though it would spoil a nice day out if you messed with Fingal's Cave and got yourself drowned).

Things to do

On Ulva, visit **Sheila's Cottage** (tinyurl. com/bnk5w3j), a reconstruction of the traditional thatched croft house in which one Sheila MacFadyen lived. It also includes a history of Ulva going back to the Mesolithic Age.

The Mull Theatre (17 miles; mulltheatre. com; 01688 302673) at Druimfin, near Tobermory, puts on a varied and high-quality programme including shows for children.

45. Lunga

Treshnish Isles
Inner Hebrides
tinyurl.com/mvg654
OS Landranger map 48
Grid reference: NM 277 416
Size: 200 acres
Population: 0

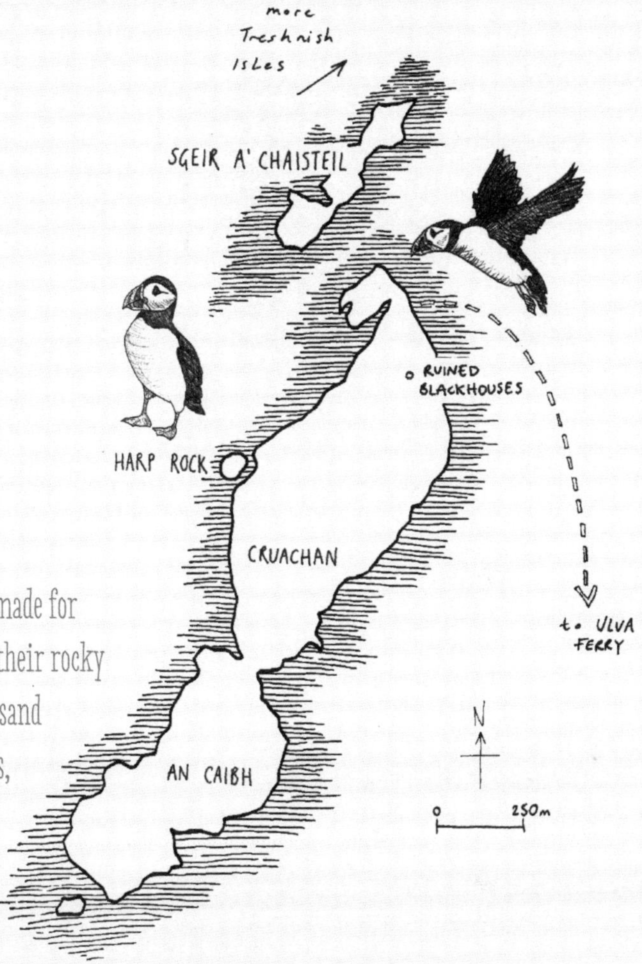

more
Treshnish
Isles

SGEIR A' CHAISTEIL

RUINED
BLACKHOUSES

HARP ROCK

CRUACHAN

to ULVA
FERRY

AN CAIBH

N

0   250m

There are some islands that seem made for war: the waves that boom against their rocky shores recall the thunder of a thousand salvoes from angry cannons. Others, echoing Shelley, can only cry, 'Peace! Peace!' Lunga is very firmly in the latter camp.

By far the largest of the Treshnish Isles, an archipelago of eight small volcanic islands a few miles off the west coast of Mull, Lunga is an island that has cleverly kept its head down over the years. While there's been plenty of history happening around it, the great bulk of it has passed the island by. A few flaps of a fulmar's wings away, the castle that straddles the twin isles of Cairn na Burgh Mòr and Cairn na Burgh Beag saw action in the Scottish Wars of Independence, the War of the Three Kingdoms, both Jacobite Rebellions and various other disputes. On Lunga, meanwhile, the trace of human habitation is a mere line of ruined blackhouses (small, rather spartan stone dwellings with thatched roofs) from the time, a couple of hundred years ago, when around 20 people called the island home. The last family to live here all year round were that of a Donald Campbell. After they left in 1824, a few folk came over each year during the summer months to attend to the shielings but even they stopped coming in 1858 and the island has been quiet ever since.

Once described as 'a green jewel in a peacock sea' – although nobody seems to know who first uttered these less than immortal words – Lunga is not an easy island to get onto. Boats must tie up to a floating pontoon to disgorge their passengers before scurrying away to deeper water, safe from the ministrations of the rocky shelf that girdles the island. Once ashore, visitors are urged to follow a rope that indicates the easiest way across the rocks to the safety of the apparently emerald grass. What the grey seals make of this performance is anyone's guess. It's estimated that around 1,000 pups are born in the Treshnish Isles each year, and every one of them could haul itself out on Lunga with less of a palaver.

The island itself is uncomplicated. Shaped like an elongated number eight, it has one low hill, Cruachan, which takes up most of the northern half; a cave on the western shore that is accessible down some rustic steps; and a flat southern half that will someday be carved up by the sea into a row of miniscule isles. A path, sometimes clear and at other times more of a vague impression on the grass, makes a rough circuit of the island.

What makes Lunga so special is what goes on at Dun Cruit, otherwise known as Harp Rock. A bulbous shard forming its own breakaway republic, there's a 100ft chasm separating it from the rest of Lunga, at the foot of which the sea gushes and frets. During the breeding season it is the fiefdom of some 6,000 birds. Guillemots predominate, along with puffins, razorbills, kittiwakes, shags and any other birds that care to squeeze in. Sit down to watch this spectacle and you will be joined by yet more puffins, who burrow into the earth opposite the rock. They are, as John Donne would have it, 'Before, behind, between, above, below', and make the most excellent fellow spectators. Puffins are truly the dolphins of the avian world. If we all spent an hour a week with puffins, we'd be happier, better adjusted people.

According to renowned Scottish island hopper Hamish Haswell-Smith, in days of yore sailors would bridge the rift over to Dun Cruit with a ship's mast. They would then crawl across to collect eggs and juvenile birds to supplement their diet. 'There is only one record of a man falling to his death,' he notes drily. And that's as close as Lunga gets to being in the news.

How to get there

Take the train to Oban (scotrail.co.uk; 0845 755 0033), followed by the ferry (calmac. co.uk; 0800 066 5000) to Craignure on the Isle of Mull. It's a largely flat 21-mile cycle ride to Ulva Ferry (a place rather than a company), or you can buy the Caledonian MacBrayne/Turus Mara's all-in ticket (01631 562244), which includes transport from Oban and across Mull. Otherwise, it's a case of taking bus 495 (bowmanstours. co.uk; 01631 563221) to Salen and a taxi (mulltaxi.co.uk; 07760 426351) onwards to Ulva Ferry. Turus Mara (turusmara. com; 0800 085 8786) will waft you over to

Clockwise from top left: Over the rocks from the Hoy Lass; Sgeir a' Chaisteil; Lunga's northwestern cliffs

both Lunga (two hours on the island) and Staffa (see p237) from Easter to October. Alternatively, Gordon Grant Marine Boat Tours (staffatours.com; 01681 700338) sail to Lunga from Oban and Kilchoan on the mainland, Fionnphort and Tobermory on Mull, and Iona, also stopping off at Staffa. NB: Don't mistake Lunga for its namesake to the southeast of Mull.

Admission price/landing fee
Free.

View
Other Treshnish Isles, Mull, Gometra, Ulva and Staffa.

Facilities
None.

Accommodation
Lip na Cloiche, a family-run B&B in Ballygown (2 miles from Ulva Ferry; lipnacloiche.co.uk; 01688 500257) has its own show garden (see 'Things to do'). If full, there are a few B&Bs in Salen (10 miles) including **Tigh-an-Achadh** (mull-bed-breakfast.co.uk; 01680 300669), as well as the **Salen Hotel** (salenhotel.co.uk; 01967 431661). Wild camping is discouraged along the lochside east of Ulva Ferry but there is a **camping area at Killiechronan** (6 miles; 01680 300403).

Nearest decent pub/café/tea room
From Ulva Ferry take the eponymous boat to **The Boathouse** (see Staffa p237 for further details). If closed (it's not open on Saturdays – yes, I know – get over it now

and save yourself time later), see Inch Kenneth (p231) for other options.

Nearest shop
In Salen (10 miles) there's a well-stocked **Spar** with sections for toys and local books, and a post office.

Rules
None.

Things to do
Indulge in one of the **four waymarked walking routes** around Ulva (isleofulva.com/walks), from a short circular farm walk to a hike off to Livingstone's Cave.
Lip na Cloiche Garden (2 miles from Ulva Ferry; free; lipnacloiche.co.uk; 01688 500257) is a dainty, densely planted affair that also sells some of its plants, so you can take a little piece of Mull home with you.

A Lunga puffin beguiles

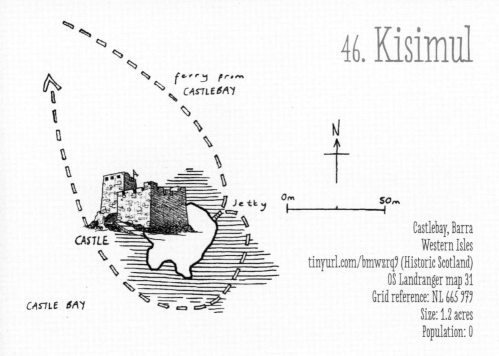

46. Kisimul

ferry from CASTLEBAY

N

CASTLE

Jetty

0m 50m

CASTLE BAY

Castlebay, Barra
Western Isles
tinyurl.com/bmwzrq9 (Historic Scotland)
OS Landranger map 31
Grid reference: NL 665 979
Size: 1.2 acres
Population: 0

Kisimul (let's avoid any embarrassing errors from the start – it's pronounced kish-mul) punches above its weight. While there must be hundreds of islands of similar size around Britain that go unnoticed and unloved, this insignificant rocky outcrop barely breaking the surface of the sea is in possession of not just one discrete phase of history but two.

Indeed, in this respect it rather overshadows the much larger island, Barra, in whose harbour it lurks. Getting out to it on the tiny ferry from Castlebay is not one of the great sea adventures. Hum the *Flower of Scotland* to yourself as you set off and you'll be docking at Kisimul before you've reached the third verse.

The castle covers the vast majority of the island (the remaining rocks are left to otters) and is much restored. Hundred-year-old photographs on display inside show just how sorry it looked back then, largely because the valuable stone had been

looted for building houses on Barra. As you climb up the few steps to the archway and enter the courtyard, there is a sense of the fortress being too new to be true. However, the alternative would be to visit a ruin clutching an artist's impression of what might have been there before, so it would be churlish to complain. And everyone's so friendly here, so you wouldn't want to.

According to remains discovered by archaeologists in 2001, the pre-restoration phase of Kisimul's history began 4,000 years ago. However, although Barra is believed to have been the seat of the

Macneil clan since the 11th century, the earliest structure on Kisimul is the three-storey tower house – one of the least restored parts of the castle and definitely one of its highlights (another, for those who enjoy being appalled, being the pit prison). It was probably built in 1427 by Gilleonan Macneil, when he was granted the island by the Macdonald clan. For good measure, Gilleonan also threw up a house beside it for the crew of his personal galley, which is the kind of thing you can do if you're a clan chief. The building has disappeared, no doubt recycled, but the foundations can still be seen.

The Macneils of Barra claimed to be descended from the Irish high king Niall of the Nine Hostages, who doubled as the great-grandfather of St Columba. They were members of the Council of the Isles which met on the loch island of Eilean Mòr (p221) on Islay; dabbled with piracy (the 35th chief, Ruari the Turbulent, plundered ships from his safe haven on Kisimul); and took part in the 1715 Jacobite Rebellion.

Meanwhile the 40th chief, Roderick the Gentle, belied his name (unless, of course, it was ironic) by fighting in the American War of Independence. However, they were never a very powerful clan and in 1838 they hit an all-time low when Roderick's successor was ignominiously forced to sell Barra in order to pay off creditors. By then, the clan chiefs had long since abandoned Kisimul, preferring the comforts of a more opulent house in Castlebay.

The ferry approaches Kisimul

It fell to the 45th chief, Robert Lister Macneil, to appear over the horizon like the 5th Cavalry (he was, in fact, American) to restore the ancestral seat. He bought Kisimul in 1937 and set about attempting to make the castle inhabitable once more.

However, he was faced with a dilemma. As Historic Scotland's leaflet on the island points out: 'He wanted to make the castle a home, but to do so he introduced features such as bathrooms that had not existed before. He used materials, such as concrete, to try and make his repairs last longer.' The commentary continues rather ruefully: 'Modern conservation practices and reconstruction standards have changed enormously [since then].'

At least the evocative smell of damp stone gives the castle a thoroughly authentic twang. Furthermore, there's now a restored feasting hall, chapel, tanist's (heir's) house and gokman's (watchman's) house to mooch around. In the hall the sight of half a dozen Brown Besses (muskets fitted with long gut-splitting bayonets) and a brace of halberds (short pikes) is all the more impressive when one discovers they were recovered from the battlefield of Culloden that saw the collapse of the second Jacobite Rising. Next door in the chapel, Robert is buried in the left-hand side of a twin vault, the right-hand side remaining unused. You could cut the pathos with a halberd.

The Macneils handed over the island and its castle to Historic Scotland in 2000 on a 1,000-year lease. In return, every year the government agency pays them one pound sterling and a bottle of Talisker whisky (Robert's favourite tipple). 'The family handed the whisky on to me one year,' Donald the ferryman told me as we headed back to Castlebay. 'Did you drink it?' I asked. 'Ach yes,' he replied, his voice betraying not a single hint of regret. 'It's long gone.'

How to get there

Take the train to Oban (scotrail.co.uk; 0845 755 0033), then the ferry (calmac.co.uk; 0800 066 5000) to Castlebay on Barra in the Western Isles. Historic Scotland's ferry over to Kisimul (April to September, 9.30am–5.30pm daily; tinyurl.com/bmwzrq9; 01871 810313) leaves from the

A castle garderobe now sporting ferns

jetty opposite the post office, by the CalMac terminal. The ferry sails on the hour and half hour and takes a little over a minute.

Admission price/landing fee

Adult £5, child £3 (including ferry).

View

From the battlements there's a 360-degree panorama of Castlebay's natural harbour including the bulbous island of Orasaigh and the village of Castlebay, dominated by the awkwardly named Church of Our Lady Star of the Sea.

Facilities

The ticket office in the castle has a diminutive souvenir shop. Curiously, the loo is in a bathroom that doubles as one of the exhibits.

Accommodation

Castlebay has two hotels – the **Castlebay Hotel** (castlebayhotel.com; 01871 810223) and the **Craigard Hotel** (craigardhotel.co.uk; 01871 810200) – as well as the odd B&B and the **Dunard Hostel** (dunardhostel.co.uk; 01871 810443) which has dorms, a family room, several twins and a little cabin for two out back. Some small basic **campsites** (isleofbarra.com) have started to appear in Barra in recent years, but there are still plenty of spots in which to wild camp.

Nearest decent pub/café/tea room

The lovely **Café Kisimul** (cafekisimul.co.uk; 01871 810645) is opposite the Kisimul ferry jetty and specialises in Indian and Italian food (vegetarian and vegan options available) – bookings advisable for evening meals. There are no pubs in Castlebay but the **Craigard** and the **Castlebay hotels** (see 'Accommodation') have public bars, the former with a grandstand view of Kisimul.

Nearest shop

Just a few seconds' walk from the Kisimul jetty is an apparently anonymous grocer's (it's actually called **A & C Maclean**, but it's not the sort of thing that's likely to come up in a pub quiz, so don't bother committing it to memory). It's Barra's newsagent and has a good stock of basic foodstuffs. More exotic purchases can be made in the **Co-op**, about 0.5 miles away.

Rules

None, aside from the usual appeals to upright behaviour.

Things to do

Climb **Sheabhal** (1,257ft), Barra's highest peak, on which you'll come across a statue of the **Madonna and Child** erected in 1954 (which was a Marian year).

Guided sea kayak trips are available at Dunard Hostel (clearwaterpaddling.com; 01871 810443).

Castlebay's harbourside **Herring Walk** explains the industry that once dominated village life and is a must for fans of *Clupea harengus*.

The **Barra Heritage and Cultural Centre** reveals some of the heritage and culture of Barra, Vatersay and Mingulay and has a bright cheery café.

47. Eilean Bàn

Loch Morar, nr Morar
Inverness-shire
OS Landranger map 40
Grid reference: NM 697 922
Size: 18 acres
Population: 0

If you want to know what Scotland would be like if human beings suddenly became extinct, look no further than Loch Morar's Eilean Bàn ('White Island'). Left to its own devices for over 200 years, it has become a thoroughly modern jungle.

The island is simply overwhelmed by huge conifers, vast holly trees, bluebells (a great many of them blind), mosses, bracket fungi and, of course, for this is Scotland, rhododendrons. Past owners have planted exotic species here but most have been smothered to death, though the occasional monkey puzzle battles bravely on, elbowing other trees out of the way to secure a patch of sky.

In one corner of the island the treetops are laden with the nests of grey herons, a bird with such a look of a dinosaur that it seems you've not only been propelled forward to a post-human age but sucked back into prehistory as well. Ordinarily, that wouldn't be a thing to will on yourself, but on Eilean Bàn it somehow seems acceptable.

Civilisation comes at the eastern corner of the island in the form of a single short wooden jetty just long enough to tie up a dinghy or two. From here a promising path dies out all too quickly in a flurry of holly. The rest is bog and sheer outcrops of rock that seemingly veer up from

nowhere to block your path and have to be painstakingly worked around. If you do explore the island, be prepared to lose all sense of direction, have your legs pricked, grazed and scratched, and your footwear waterlogged in the bogs. If you explore during or after rainfall, you will get drenched, for everything here drips.

It's fitting for an island that points to both the future and the past that, in the brief span in which it found a certain notoriety, it became a place of a first and a last. In 1714, Scotland's first Catholic seminary was founded here by Pope Innocent XII's Vicar Apostolic for Scotland, Thomas Nicholson. These were post-Reformation times, when Catholics were out of favour in Britain, and clearly Eilean Bàn was chosen for its qualities as a discreet, one might almost say clandestine, location. However, it is doubtful it could have prepared even a single young man for the priesthood as it survived for no more than a year. The first Jacobite Rebellion came in the summer of 1715 but had fizzled out by November. In the ensuing backlash, Eilean Bàn's seminary was razed to the ground.

Happily, what little is left of the building can be seen today without taking on the island's jungle. Right next to the jetty lurk two walls, barely knee high and slathered in moss, bordering a rare open space crossed by shallow water-filled trenches. It's no Stonehenge.

The only other landmark on Eilean Bàn leads us towards the island's other claim to fame. Apparently, on the far northern tip, there is a grave, and tradition has it that it is the final resting place of one Simon Fraser, 11th Lord Lovat, the last man to be beheaded in England.

Although it's rather unlikely that Lovat's body made its way back up to Loch Morar after his head was stricken from it on Tower Hill, we do know that he was captured while hiding out on Eilean Bàn following his support for the Jacobite Rising of 1745 (he'd opposed the 1715 rebellion). He was reputedly discovered in a hollow tree, which can hardly have been comfortable for a man in his 80th year. However, few people wept for him. Known as 'The Fox' and 'The Most Devious Man in Scotland' for his studied lack of principles, about the only thing that those who had dealings with him could rely on was that he would betray them as soon as it became expedient to do so. Sorrow and suffering engulfed those around him even at his death. A stand erected for the crowds who wanted to watch his execution collapsed and killed some 20 spectators.

You can search for the grave if you like, but after a considerable time spent looking in vain for it, I'm rather inclined to believe that the jungle has at last reclaimed it and the body of whoever lies within.

It takes less than 10 minutes to chug back to the mainland in one of Ewan MacDonald's small open motorboats, so it's worth indulging in a brief cruise around the other tiny islands grouped at this western end of Loch Morar. Eilean nam Breac, An t-Eilean Meadhoin and Eilean a' Phidhir have no particularly thrilling stories of their own, but, like Eilean Bàn, they can boast that they are on the deepest lake in Britain. Loch Morar, an Anglicised version of Mordhobhar ('big water'), is over 1,000ft deep in parts. To put that into context, the Atlantic Ocean west of Scotland doesn't reach that depth until it hits the continental shelf 130 miles away.

It means that Morar is an astonishing 400ft deeper than Loch Ness. It's therefore not to be wondered at that the loch is reputed to have its own monster: Morag, otherwise known as the Great Worm (from the Old English *wyrm* meaning dragon). Given the extra depths in which such a leviathan could swim about undetected, it arguably makes it the more likely of the two lochs to harbour such a creature. However, for the sake of the local Macdonald clan (of whom Ewan, the boat owner, is one), don't spend too long looking for her: every time she is sighted it heralds the death of one of the clan's members.

How to get there

Alight at Morar railway station (scotrail. co.uk; 0845 755 0033). It's a 25-minute amble clockwise around the shore of Loch Morar to the second jetty along, where Ewan MacDonald hires out small open motorboats (£30/morning or afternoon, £50/day; 01687 462520 – ring in advance).

Admission price/landing fee

Free.

View

Various other tiny islands and mountains of North Morar and South Morar.

Facilities

None.

Accommodation

In Morar (1.5 miles) there's the **Morar Hotel** (morarhotel.co.uk; 01687 462346) and one or two smaller places such as the **Harlosh Guest House** (tinyurl.com/c54qyp8; 01687 460251), but there's a much wider choice of accommodation in nearby Mallaig (3 miles), including the **Chlachain Inn** (westscotlandinn.co.uk; 01687 460289).

Nearest decent pub/café/tea room

The **Silver Sands restaurant and bar** at the Morar Hotel (1.5 miles; morarhotel.co.uk; 01687 462346) has some splendid views of the Morar river estuary.

Nearest shop

Head for Mallaig (3 miles) where there's a huddle of little shops including a small **Co-op** and a **Spar**.

Rules

None.

Things to do

This is not an area packed with tourist attractions and some would say it's all the better for it. It's a place where people come to **walk, swim, watch birds** and **play on the beach** (Morar's silver strand was used in the film *Local Hero*).

Inveterate island hoppers will be delighted that CalMac (calmac.co.uk; 0800 066 5000) sails from Mallaig (3 miles) to **Eigg, Rum, Muck, Canna** and **Skye**.

48. Eilean Donan

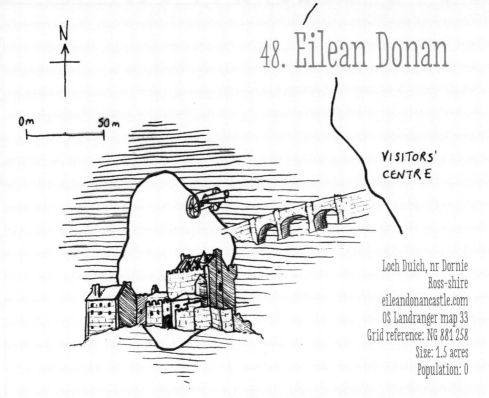

0m   50m

VISITORS'
CENTRE

Loch Duich, nr Dornie
Ross-shire
eileandonancastle.com
OS Landranger map 33
Grid reference: NG 881 258
Size: 1.5 acres
Population: 0

Ah, Eilean Donan, where would the makers of 'A Souvenir of Scotland' tins of shortbread be without you? With its ancient four-square castle on a rocky outcrop at the edge of a dutifully decorous loch, it encapsulates the essence of Scotland in a single scene and imbues the hilariously over-priced biscuits within with a sweet coating of Highlandry.

It's sad to learn, therefore, that to a great extent it's an illusion. Although there has been a fortress on the island since the first one was built around 750 years ago, the last one raised in anger was reduced to rubble nearly 200 years ago. Today's castle is an early 20th-century confection constructed using the surviving ground plan of earlier incarnations. It may work as a symbol of Scotland's trenchant ability to recover from devastating blows and the nation's capacity to reinvent itself along the way, but as a representation of the soul of Scotland it's a beautiful fraud.

It's easy to see why a castle came to be built here. Not only does this little lump of rock guard an entrance to the lands of Kintail, it also controls the meeting point of three sea lochs – Duich, Long and Alsh. Its strategic position would certainly have been the main attraction for the builders of the Iron Age fort, traces of which could still be seen on the island up until the modern reconstruction of the castle. The isle's first named inhabitant, however, was probably an Irish bishop (and later saint) called Donan who is believed to have built a cell or a chapel here towards the end of the 6th century and may even have founded a little community.

The need for something more bellicose than a place of worship arose in the early 13th century to combat Viking raids up the sea lochs. Little is known of the first structure except that it possessed a curtain wall. Indeed, we're not even sure who was the builder – it might have been King Alexander II or III, or the Earl of Ross, Farquar II. Over the following centuries, the castle was variously enlarged or reduced in size (quite drastically on one occasion) and, in the 16th century, hauled into the modern age by the addition of a firing platform on which cannons could be placed. During this period, the habitual clan squabbles saw the island changing hands several times, usually with the spilling of blood – on one notable occasion, 50 men were executed and their heads displayed on the castle walls.

However, it was Eilean Donan's involvement in the first Jacobite Rising that proved to be its undoing. Jacobite forces had taken over the castle in time for the battle of Sheriffmuir in 1715. Four years later, 46 Spanish soldiers – part of a group of 300 who had arrived to support the Jacobites – were positioned in the stronghold protecting a store of 343 barrels of gunpowder (one of history's pleasingly precise numbers) and awaited the arrival of the attendant weapons and canonry from their mother country. This came to the attention of the government in London, which dispatched three armed frigates – the *Enterprise*, the *Flamborough* and the *Worcester* – to deal with the Spaniards. The ships bombarded the castle for three whole days though did less damage than might be imagined, since some of the walls were an astonishing 14ft thick and able to withstand the impact of the huge stone projectiles. Eventually, men from the frigates were sent ashore to wrest the castle from its defenders by hand. When they had subdued the Spaniards, they came across the gunpowder and decided that the best possible use for it was to blow up the castle walls that had stubbornly rebuffed the bombards.

Photographs taken in Victorian times show the island topped by a few sorry stumps that barely hint at the proud castle that once stood there, and it wasn't until 1911 that poor neglected Eilean Donan found a saviour. Lt. Col. John MacRae-Gilstrap, a man of steely determination, bought up the island and, along with his clerk of works, Farquhar MacRae, dedicated the next two decades to reimagining its castle, entrusting Edinburgh architectural firm George Mackie Watson with the design. During this period he also built the arched bridge which, for the first time in its history, afforded the tidal island a permanent connection to the shore. The castle was opened to the public in 1955 by MacRae-Gilstrap's grandson.

The castle blending spectacularly well with the loch's autumnal cloak

What the public has traipsed, mooched and sauntered over delightedly since then is a grass-covered rock with an elegant smattering of small trees that at once beautify the island and create the illusion that the castle is larger than it is. Meanwhile, a brace of World War I field guns flank a memorial dedicated to the MacRae men who fell in that conflict.

With a spectacular Gothic arch for an entrance, the castle's interior reflects the tastes of the MacRae-Gilstrap family for whom Eilean Donan became a home. The highlights include the grand baronial hall, dominated by a vast table evidently made for long hours of feasting; the 1930s kitchen complete with mannequins of cooks and butlers and an unfortunate woman frozen in the agonising moment in which she has knocked over a huge pile of cooking utensils; and, for lovers of the arcane, a left-handed spiral staircase. Spiral staircases in castles are habitually built right handed (i.e. clockwise as you ascend) in order to allow anyone defending the fortress from above to use a sword held in their right hand against an assailant below. The origins of Eilean Donan's all but unique anti-clockwise staircase are obscure and perhaps best left so.

Of course, this is by no means the only British castle that has had to be so exhaustively restored that very little of it can be said to be the genuine article – a similar process, albeit not quite so extreme, has occurred at Kisimul (p245), for example. And we've only ourselves to blame if we've been fooled into thinking that the wonderful castle at Eilean Donan was the work of busy medieval craftsmen because that fine stone bridge should give the game away. After all, what lord of a castle would want to save enemy forces from getting their feet wet?

How to get there
Take the train to Kyle of Lochalsh (scotrail. co.uk; 0845 755 0033) – the last stop on arguably the most spectacular railway line in Britain – then the 61 (macraekintailbuses.com; 01599 511384), or 915, 916 or 917 bus (citylink.co.uk; 0141 332 9644), all of which stop right next to the island.

Admission price/landing fee
Adult £6, child £5, family £15.

View
West and southeast over Loch Alsh, the mountains that rise above it, and the road bridge over Loch Long.

Facilities
None. However, there are toilets at the mainland end of the causeway.

Accommodation
Right opposite the island is the large modern **Donan House** (donanhouse. co.uk; 01599 555304). There are many other **B&Bs in Dornie** (0.25 miles). In Ardelve (0.5 miles), the sloping field of an **unnamed campsite** overlooks Eilean Donan. Or you can stay in **Gavin Maxwell's island cottage** near Kyle of Lochalsh (9 miles; see 'Things to do' for details).

Shortbread never tasted so good

Nearest decent pub/café/tea room

Eilean Donan has its own **coffee shop** at the mainland end of the causeway. In Dornie (0.25 mile), **The Clachan Bar** (theclachan.com; 01599 555366) and the **Dornie Hotel** (dornie-hotel.co.uk; 01599 555205) both serve food, while 200yd further on there's the **Schoolhouse Gallery and Tea Room** (01599 555482).

Nearest shop

Dornie Stores in Dornie (0.25 miles) is a small licensed grocer's-cum-newsagent.

Rules

No photography allowed inside the castle.

Things to do

Fans of *Tarka the Otter* can join a **tour of Eilean Bàn** (not the Eilean Bàn of p249), the island owned in life by author, naturalist and secret agent Gavin Maxwell. The isle helps support the Skye Bridge nowadays, which rather detracts from the magic, but there's still a lighthouse, otter hides and Maxwell's home to be nosed around (eileanban.org; 01599 530040).

Calum Mackenzie's **seal-watching trips** from Plockton (11 miles; daily April to October; calums-sealtrips.com; 01599 544306) come with a promise to refund your money in the unlikely event that you see no seals (even if you spot otters, dolphins and porpoises).

49. Bass Rock

Firth of Forth, off North Berwick
East Lothian
OS Landranger map 67
Grid reference: NT 602 874
Size: 7 acres
Population: 0

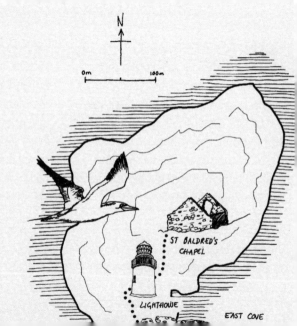

swooping over your boat from behind that the light dawns: the snow is actually thousands upon thousands of northern gannets. At the last count, in 2009, there were 55,482 pairs nesting here, making the Bass Rock the largest single-rock colony of gannets in the known world. It's fitting therefore that their scientific name, given to them by 19th-century ornithologists, is *Sula bassana*, a homage to their extraordinary home.

And the closer you come to the Bass Rock, the more extraordinary that home looks. Nests cover the flat (well, flat-ish) heights, the plunging slopes and, seemingly impossibly, the precipitous cliffs. All the while, restless clouds of gannets hover above the island like midges over a Highland moor. As you approach the seaward side of the island (its gentler lee slope tumbling so alarmingly into the Firth that the ruined prison walls have to cling on for dear life), the cacophony of honks and sharp grating shrieks that assaults your ears causes your sympathy for tinnitus sufferers to blossom exponentially. And every year – as those officials who spend time on the island monitoring the birds will attest – the colony grows.

It wasn't always like this. For centuries, local people used the Bass Rock gannets – or solan geese as they are also known – as a source of meat, oil, eggs (Queen Victoria was a particular fan) and guano (but less a fan of this). The Victorians, bless them, sent men abseiling down the cliffs on ropes to 'harry' the young birds. This wasn't merely to hustle them along, as we might understand the word today, but to harry them in the sense of William the Conqueror's memorable 'Harrying of the North', viz, they bludgeoned them to death with a blow or two to the head. Later they took to shooting them for sport (the future King Edward VII visited in August 1870 so may also conceivably have had a pot-shot), and the birds, who had been nesting there generation after generation for thousands of years, grew low in number. The slaughter became one of the stimuli for the passing of the enlightened Wild Birds Protection Act of 1880, which made particular mention of the gannet and was successful in saving the colony.

Way back in the early 7th century, an evangelist called Baldred founded a monastery at nearby Tyninghame as part of his mission to bring Christianity to the heathen East Lothians. He then chose the Bass Rock as an ideal place for a hermitage where he could see out his final years in peace (so one assumes there were fewer gannets back then). St Baldred's chapel – whose ruins mark the furthest extent to which visitors may intrude on the island – was built over 900 years later on the site of his cell. Around the stones grows Bass mallow, a relatively rare wildflower found on a smattering of islands including Steep Holm (p63) and Ailsa Craig (p208).

Malcolm III, who pops up in Inchcolm's *Scotichronicon* (p277), granted the island to its first known owner, Sir Robert de Lawder, in the 11th century, though even then the church maintained dominion over

Queen Elizabeth made attempts to wrest it from her in 1548 and 1549 without success. In calmer times, 30 years or so later, James VI dropped by and stayed at the castle as a guest, by which time it had presumably been spruced up somewhat. However, the War of the Three Kingdoms (the conflict formerly known as the English Civil War) saw the occupiers in fighting mode again, injudiciously looting and sinking a ship, the *John o' London*, which had Oliver Cromwell's goods and chattels on board. Incensed, the Roundhead leader demanded the capture of the island. It took his troops the best part of two years before the besieged defenders were finally starved out. It's probably just as well Cromwell didn't live to see 1671, for it was in that year that the Bass Rock was bought on behalf of his once defeated rival, Charles II, to be used as a state prison.

And it was as a prison that the Bass Rock entered its darkest days. The Covenanters – Scottish Presbyterians – were severely persecuted by Charles II and about 40 or so of them found themselves imprisoned in the Bass Rock's gaol. Life there was almost intolerable. Prisoners had to rely on friends and family to row across to the island with provisions, or pay the prison governor hugely inflated prices for food to keep body and soul together. Water had to be lapped from puddles and, should any prisoner displease the governor, he was sent down to the lowest cells where sea spray soaked and then froze him. Understandably, those who did not perish in such conditions

the upper part of the island, where Baldred had lived and died. The Lauder family (the spelling shifting slightly) built a castle on the lower lee slopes – the only place that allows access to the island from the sea – in or around 1405 and it fast became King James I of Scotland's favourite place for incarcerating his political enemies. One of these, a Highland chief named Angus Dubh Mackay of Strathnaver, was released in exchange for his 14-year-old son Neil, who was kept hostage in the castle to keep Mackay honest. Neil suffered for nine years until, in 1437 and the murder of James I, he became the first person ever to escape from what has predictably become known as 'The Alcatraz of the North'.

By the early 16th century, the Bass Rock's position at the entrance to the Firth of Forth had made it so strategically important that Mary, Queen of Scots had it garrisoned with 100 soldiers. Her nemesis

Top and right. Bass Rock and its castle/prison are now very much in the clutches of the gannets

emerged with their health so broken that they did not enjoy their freedom for long.

It was left to later Jacobite prisoners to gain some sort of revenge over their gaolers. In 1690, four Jacobites cheekily locked their guards out of the prison while the latter were down at the jetty unloading coal. Smartly reinventing the prison as a castle, they managed to hold out for the next four years with support from fellow Jacobites – some of whom joined them in the prison – and supplies dropped off by the occasional French frigate that evaded the attempted blockade. Eventually the Jacobites, numbering 16 by the end, negotiated a surrender with one Major Robert Reid by which they, and those friends who had been sentenced to death for aiding them, were deported to France.

The prison had long fallen into ruin when a juvenile Robert Louis Stevenson spent several summer holidays at a farm opposite the Bass Rock. Duly inspired, in his novel *Catriona* he had his hero David Balfour imprisoned there. The Stevenson family connection with the island was cemented in 1902 when its lighthouse was built by Robert Louis' cousins Charles and David. The last keepers left in 1988 when it was automated, since when the island has been left to the birds. And to those who count the birds.

How to get there

Take the train to North Berwick (scotrail.co.uk; 0845 755 0033). A trip around the Bass Rock (combined with a visit to the island of Craigleith) is available from the Scottish Seabird Centre from March to October (by boat: adult £15, child £9; by RIB: adult £22, child £17; seabird.org; 01620 890202). Landing trips on the Bass Rock give 5.5 hours on the island but sail less frequently, only run from April to September, and are much more expensive (£98 per person; seabird.org; 01620 890202). The Scottish Seabird Centre has exclusive landing rights, granted by the island's owner. Booking essential.

Admission price/landing fee

£7 landing fee per person.

View

North Berwick, Tantallon Castle, Craigleith, North Berwick Law (a volcanic plug) and the Isle of May.

Facilities

None.

Accommodation

On the outskirts of North Berwick you'll find **Gilsland Caravan Park** (gilslandcaravanpark.co.uk; 01620 892205). As a rule of thumb, places that have the words 'caravan park' in their name are what you might imagine Hell's car park to look like, assuming it has one. Gilsland is an exception – lots of grass, sheltering trees, peace and quiet, rabbits, and friendly owners. They also rent out a couple of pleasingly bonkers outsize Wendy houses (sleep four). B&B-wise, you could try **Seaholm** (seaholm.co.uk; 01620 895150) which has views of the Bass Rock (and the Isle of May if the weather behaves). There's further accommodation listed at seabird.org.

Nearest decent pub/café/tea room

The **Scottish Seabird Centre's café** has fantastic sea views as well as telescopes and binoculars on the Telescope Deck next door.

Nearest shop

North Berwick has a good range of shops.

Rules

Keep to the marked path. No dogs.

Things to do

The **Scottish Seabird Centre's Discovery Centre** (seabird.org; 01620 890202) sports webcams that spy on wildlife on nearby islands, a range of short nature films, a 'Migration Flyway' tunnel and more.

A collection of vintage cars, motorbikes and, for non-petrol-heads, bicycles can be found at Aberlady's **Myreton Motor Museum** (8 miles; myretonmotormuseum.co.uk; 01875 870288).

There's more metal on display at the **National Museum of Flight** (5 miles; nms.ac.uk/flight; 0300 123 6789). Based on East Fortune airfield, the museum has interactive galleries, a whole fleet of aircraft, and a restored World War II parachute store in which you can learn the silky skills required to pack a parachute.

50. Isle of May

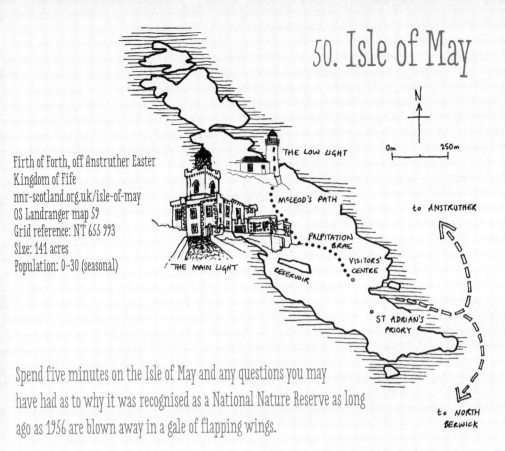

Firth of Forth, off Anstruther Easter
Kingdom of Fife
nnr-scotland.org.uk/isle-of-may
OS Landranger map 59
Grid reference: NT 655 993
Size: 141 acres
Population: 0–30 (seasonal)

Spend five minutes on the Isle of May and any questions you may have had as to why it was recognised as a National Nature Reserve as long ago as 1956 are blown away in a gale of flapping wings.

From the moment Arctic terns greet you with anguished cries and sharp bills as you walk up from the little harbour at Kirkhaven, there's simply no getting away from the natural world. A staggering quarter of a million seabirds breed here every year, of which 90,000-odd are puffins, the very best creature that ever flew over the face of the Earth. (Fans of rabbits will be excited to learn that the loveable souls keep the puffin numbers up by grazing undergrowth that the birds wouldn't be able to penetrate and, on occasion, obligingly allowing the puffins to use some of the upper chambers of their burrows to nest in.)

Of course, that's not to belittle the shags, eiders, kittiwakes, guillemots, razorbills, fulmars and the dive-bombing Arctic terns, whose cousins the Sandwich and common tern also make an appearance. In fact, an astonishing 250 species of birds have been spotted here, including unexpected visitors such as owls, woodpeckers and nightingales. How do we know this? As Maggie, a guide on boats from North Berwick, points out: 'This has to be one of the most thoroughly researched islands anywhere – if it moves on May, it's been studied.' That goes not only for the birds (May is one of only four National Seabird Monitoring Sites in the UK), but also for the

rodents (the island has its own indigenous mouse which, since 1982, has been interbred with mice from the Orkney island of Eday in a genetic experiment that will someday no doubt prove something vital, or end in tears) and the flora (sea campion and thrift abound).

And then there's the marine life. An incoming boat will often have to run a gauntlet of grey seals as it makes its way around the cliffs to the harbour. There are about 200 resident all year round (though this number balloons to nearer 4,000 in autumn when their pups are born), while dolphins and minke whales are frequent summer visitors. All three are drawn to the island by the good foraging to be had in the kelp forests just off shore.

A little up from the harbour stand the scant ruins of a 12th-century monastery dedicated to St Ethernan, as well as traces of earlier remains of religious buildings on the same site. May was almost certainly a place of spiritual significance long before a Christian missionary called Monanus (later St Monanus, naturally) arrived around AD840, probably as one of a group led by St Ethernan all the way from Hungary. However, in 875 he and all the new converts (about 6,000 men, women and children) were slaughtered on the East Neuk mainland by the men of the Danish King Humber, who had been asked by the Picts to wage war against the invading Scots (who, confusingly, were actually Irish). A small band of Christians including

Ethernan escaped to May but the Vikings tracked them down and murdered them on 4 March (St Ethernan's Day). Half of the saint's stone coffin later took it into its head to float miraculously across to the mainland, where it can be seen to this day in Anstruther Wester churchyard. The island's status as a focus for Christian pilgrimage was duly sealed.

It's hardly surprising, therefore, that in 1145 King David I thought it was high time that there was a priory on the island and so handed it over to the Benedictines of Reading. These monks are credited with ensuring that the holy water from the island's well – drunk by local women as a cure for infertility – had a surprisingly high success rate. The priory experienced less amicable relations with its male visitors. During the Scottish Wars of Independence the island was grabbed back by the Scots (who by now were no longer Irish). The English retook it after the battle of Dunbar in 1296, the Scots retaining it for good after Bannockburn in 1314. The monks had long since gone by then though. With both sides intermittently raiding the island and despoiling it during this period, they'd sagely taken their tonsure scissors and left May to the rabbits and the birds. Nowadays the grey stone priory, battered to a skeleton of its former self, stares its unblinking stare over the harbour, secretly consoled that it has found a purpose again: terns breed here now, luxuriating in the all-around shelter the ruins afford from the Forth weather.

In those turbulent days the island was known as Maeyar, similar to the Gaelic *machair* – a low meadow. Given May's grassy covering and lack of peaks, it's tempting to imagine that this was how it came by its name. However, a more likely explanation is that it's from a corruption of the Old Norse *maa* (gull) *øy* (island) or even the Icelandic *maer eyar*, which means the same. If you want to seem less of an outsider when conversing with local people, always refer to the island as May Isle rather than the Isle of May, which is reputed to have been an invention of the Ordnance Survey. And best steer clear too of 'The Jewel of the Forth', its rather hackneyed nickname.

A short climb away to the west of the priory is Fluke Street, May's main drag, where most of today's human inhabitants live. The unappealing utilitarian buildings – including the former engine house for

the last of May's three lighthouses – lead to a man-made freshwater loch. Above is the main lighthouse, up a sharpish incline jokingly nicknamed 'Palpitation Brae' for its ability to get hearts pounding violently when climbed.

The lack of great hills on the island is explained by the unusual way in which May arrived on the scene. Around 1.3 miles long by 0.3 miles (at its widest point), it's a long thin lump of rock called teschenite that oozed up as molten lava through an almighty fissure in the sandstone and limestone bedrock beneath the Firth of Forth. Unlike the nearby Bass Rock (p258), which is the husk of a traditional volcano that exploded up from the Earth, May's subtler entrance has left it relatively flat. The island does have some 150ft cliffs on its southwestern side though, so it's unlikely to disappear beneath the seas anytime soon.

However, May has been all but split into four by the grinding and gnashing of the waves. Indeed, to reach the far northwestern portions of the island – Rona and North Ness – a bridge is necessary (and has collapsed, so that bit of May is off limits until it's repaired).

The first visitors to the island, around 8,000 years ago, would probably have laughed if you'd shown them a bridge (or fallen down and worshipped it perhaps, depending on their cosmology). May would have provided them with a good base for hunting seals and fishing. Flint arrowheads found on the island certainly suggest that it was worth coming here to stock up on victuals.

Fast forward to around AD515, when an unmarried young Christian called Thenaw became pregnant by one Prince Ewan. Accused of being a witch by her father, the pagan King Loth, after she had miraculously survived being thrown down a hill in a chariot as punishment for her condition, she was unceremoniously dumped in the sea near May where she was expected to drown. However, Thenaw exhorted her God to help her and was miraculously washed ashore near the monastery at Culross. She promptly gave birth, ending something of a busy day for her. The child grew up to be St Kentigern, better known nowadays as St Mungo, and was later adopted as the patron saint of Glasgow.

Many seafarers passing the island have come to unluckier ends than Thenaw, as witnessed by the numerous wrecks with which the rocky shallows around May are littered and which have become a draw for recreational divers. One wreck has even made its way inland. Start walking around the flanks of the East Brae and you'll see the rusting ribs of a Danish steamship that ran aground in 1937. Subsequent storms have driven this section of it a frightening distance up onto the isle. The owners had it coming to them really: with remarkable if unfortunate prescience, they had named the ship *Island*.

However, you really can't fault the effort made to try to put a stop to this practice of crashing boats, ships and sundry vessels into the island's rocks. May was home to

Scotland's very first manned 'light beacon' way back in 1636 – a beautiful three-storey square tower with a beacon on top fired by coal lifted by a pulley from a shed below. The fact that the ground floor is still here is thanks to Sir Walter Scott, who, when visiting the island, suggested that the newly obsolete structure should not be pulled down in toto as was planned but 'ruined *à la picturesque'.*

While the beacon doubtless saved many lives in its 180 years, it was also the scene of tragedy. For two nights in January 1791 sailors noticed that there was no light coming from May. When they investigated they discovered seven members of the Anderson family, keepers of the light, dead. They had perished while they slept due

to carbon monoxide and sulphur dioxide blowing in from smouldering ashes. Only an infant survived, though quite how is not known.

From a distance, the Main Light built by Robert Stevenson (Robert Louis' grandfather) in 1816 to replace the light beacon looks very like a church. Its square tower on top of a short spire are fine enough to grace any village in the land. It was apparently meant to resemble a castle and closer inspection does indeed reveal castellated walls, giving it the look of a rather underwhelming fort. Stevenson can probably be forgiven his folly for he'd not long finished building the lighthouse on tiny wave-ravaged Bell Rock – one of the finest engineering achievements of its

Left: Haunted McLeod's Path leading to the Low Light; Right: Compressed air tank for powering foghorns   267

time – and so clearly decided to stretch his wings a bit on May. The last keepers left in 1989 when the light was automated, and their huge sunken walled garden is now sadly overgrown.

Walk down the hill and you'll reach the Low Light, a much more modest lighthouse first used in 1844 to give shipping a second light, which, when aligned with the Main Light, indicates the position of the dangerous North Carr Rock. However, when the rock was given its own lightship in 1887, the Low Light was turned off. It lives on today as a bunkhouse for birdwatchers.

The way down to the Low Light – known as McLeod's Path after one of the keepers – is flanked by a whitewashed stone wall and boasts its own miniature viaduct built to take lighthousemen swiftly over a dip in the landscape. People staying in the Low Light have reported hearing footsteps along this path, and a shadowy figure passing before their windows, only to discover that there is no one outside.

May saw service in both world wars. In the Great War the island played host to a gun battery and a signal station for warning of enemy shipping and Zeppelin airships. It also overlooked one of the most bizarre and shocking naval episodes of the war. The so-called Battle of the Isle of May occurred on the night of 31 January 1918. A large force including battleships, destroyers, cruisers and the new K class submarines set forth from Rosyth. They were ordered to sail without navigation lights and to keep radio silence due to the suspected presence of German U-boats. Unfortunately a malfunction with one of the submarine's rudders near the Isle of May caused an almighty pile-up. In the chaos, two submarines were sunk and a large number of ships and other submarines very badly damaged. At least 105 men were killed. All this without encountering a single German ship, so it's little wonder that for years the Admiralty attempted to cover up the disaster.

In World War II, the island was used as a base for submarine and shipping detectors and a signalling station. On 16 October 1939, naval personnel stationed there witnessed a Junkers Ju88 crashing into the sea just north of the island after being attacked by a Spitfire. It was the first German plane shot down over Britain in the war and the first aerial victory chalked up by the RAF.

Populated for most of the year – the servicemen and women now replaced by researchers and Scottish Natural Heritage rangers – and with summertime visitors arriving daily from Anstruther and North Berwick, May is rarely an entirely peaceful place, especially when you throw those 250,000 seabirds into the mix. However, at least the island's two huge foghorns now lie silent, victims of technological progress. Radar killed the audio star.

How to get there

Either a) take the train to North Berwick (scotrail.co.uk; 0845 755 0033) and then a Seafari RIB from the Scottish Seabird

Centre (March to September; adult £45, child £39; seabird.org; 01620 890202) for about 2.5 hours on the island and a lap around the Bass Rock (p258), or b) take the train to Markinch (scotrail.co.uk; 0845 755 0033), the 43A bus to Leven, then the 95 (both stagecoachbus.co.uk; 01592 642394) to Anstruther to board either the Anstruther Pleasure Cruises' *May Princess* (April to September; adult £22, child £11, family £55; isleofmayferry.com; 01333 311808), or the Osprey of Anstruther's speedier RIB (April to September; adult £25, child £12, family £60; isleofmayboattrips.co.uk; 07966 926254). Both offer two to three hours on the island. The Isle of May is open to the public from April to September.

Admission price/landing fee
Free.

View
The Anstruther coastline, and (in clear weather) the Bass Rock (p258) and North Berwick Law (a volcanic plug on the mainland).

Facilities
Toilets and a small visitor centre.

Accommodation
Avid birders can stay at the island's bird observatory (mid/late March to early November; isleofmaybirdobs.org; 01896 848126) in the former **Low Light lighthouse**. The facilities are very basic but a major refurbishment took place in 2012. In Anstruther, try **The Grange** (thegrangeanstruther.com; 01333 310842),

a fine Edwardian house unusually built in a Canadian style, while just outside the town is **Kilrenny Mill Farmhouse** (accom-kmf. tripod.com; 01333 311272). Both offer B&B. For North Berwick accommodation see p262.

Nearest decent pub/café/tea room
The **Anstruther Fish Bar** (anstrutherfishbar. co.uk; 01333 310518) has won numerous awards including Les Routiers Café of the Year for Scotland. In North Berwick, try the **café at the Seabird Centre** or **North Berwick Fry** in Quality Street.

Nearest shop
Both **North Berwick** and **Anstruther** have a hearty selection of shops.

Rules
Keep to the marked paths – a single step off them could see you plunging through a burrow and crushing a puffin under your elephantine foot. No dogs. No disturbing the seals.

Things to do
The **John Muir Way** (visiteastlothian.org/ activities-walking.asp; 01620 827671), a 45-mile footpath celebrating the Dunbar-born nature writer, passes through North Berwick on its way along the coast from Musselburgh to Dunglass. (For more North Berwick ideas see p262.)

In Anstruther, the major attraction is the harbour-front **Scottish Fisheries Museum** (scotfishmuseum.org; 01333 310628), set in a number of venerable buildings and boasting 19 boats, '66,000 objects' and a tea room.

51. Cramond Island

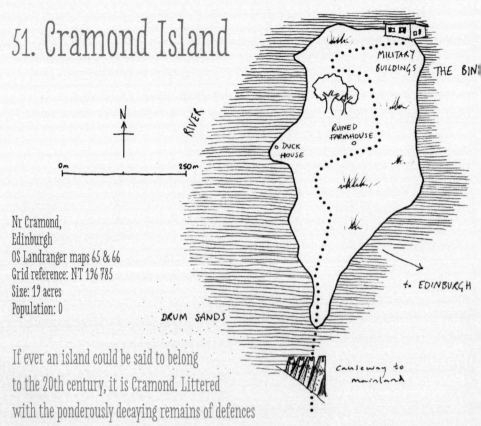

Nr Cramond,
Edinburgh
OS Landranger maps 65 & 66
Grid reference: NT 196 785
Size: 19 acres
Population: 0

If ever an island could be said to belong
to the 20th century, it is Cramond. Littered
with the ponderously decaying remains of defences
from both world wars, it is reached by an arrow-straight causeway that looks like a set from
a Fritz Lang film. Even its information boards hark back to the good old days of the 1970s and
80s, having been thoroughly defaced by football fans.

Arriving at the Firth of Forth as it glides past the village of Cramond, the first thing any visitor notices is not the island itself but that Lang-esque 0.75-mile path across to it. The scores of 15ft-high reinforced concrete teeth that accompany the walkway and give it the look of a crocodile's bottom jaw are in fact an anti-submarine boom built during the last war to dissuade any U-boats, and indeed any other Axis shipping, from sneaking that way up the Forth at high tide.

Both the teeth and the path are crumbling, with the latter exposing the attractive sewage pipe that runs beneath it. At low tide, the mudflats either side of it become a grazing ground for curlews, bar-tailed godwits, redshanks and knots, among other birds.

Part of the Dalmeny Estate, the island's main topographical feature is its one small hill roughly in the centre. Below this a small copse hides the ruins of a farmhouse, as if the island is somehow ashamed of its sheep-rearing past. On the western shore, meanwhile, are the remains of the tiny Duck House, a stone building that appears to have emerged out of a rock and was once a popular holiday let, apparently sleeping four people – though four contortionists is probably nearer the mark.

The War Department requisitioned the northern end of the island during World War I. However, it is its sequel – when the whole island was taken over for defensive purposes – that has provided most of the maundering hulks still in evidence today. Many still peer out along the Firth, searching the skies for enemy aircraft that do not come. The brick-built 75mm gun emplacement that guards the causeway is the most impressive of these, though for sheer persistence the volley of small and preternaturally ugly concrete buildings at the northern tip are perhaps the greater attraction for the keen historian of the 20th century. They're a big hit with graffiti artists too.

Since shelter is plentiful, you're unlikely to die of exposure if you find yourself stranded on the island until the next low tide. Adventurous souls often deliberately maroon themselves here with generous supplies of alcohol (to which piles of bottles and cans are an unsightly testament) to ward off both the cold and any unwelcome rational thoughts that might stray across their minds. Unintentional maroonings appear to be a major problem. According to *The Scotsman* newspaper, the RNLI boat at South Queensferry was called out 70 times in 2009, picking up a total of 118 people. This made it the busiest lifeboat in the whole of Scotland and helped earn its nickname of 'The Cramond Taxi'. Pricelessly, in January 2011, the long-suffering lifeboat crew was also called to the island to rescue a man named Daniel Defoe, who apparently didn't see himself as latter-day *Robinson Crusoe* material.

The island is not entirely a child of modern times though. The Romans almost certainly made use of the place after building a fort on the mainland shore nearby around AD142. Even more out of keeping with the island's character is the revelation that the earliest evidence of human activity anywhere in Scotland was found here: hazelnut shells, apparently thrown away by a group of Mesolithic hunter-gatherers and carbon dated to 8500BC.

While you're on Cramond Island, it's worth drinking in the wonderful views of some of the other islands on the Firth. There's Inchcolm (p274) a little to the north, while closer still lies Inchmickery. Barely more than a large rock, the remains of the fortifications built in the two world wars have left it looking unerringly like a battleship, albeit one whose fate is to be becalmed in the Firth of Forth forever. Further away to the northeast, you can also make out the outline of Inchkeith, the setting for one of history's oddest experiments. Keen to know whether God had installed Hebrew in humans as a default language, King James IV of Scotland is said to have ordered two newborn children to be brought up on the island by a mute nurse. He waited until such time as the children gained the power of speech and reputedly joined his retinue in proclaiming that they 'spak extremely guid Hebrew'. Which just goes to show. Sadly, Inchmickery is firmly out of bounds to visitors, so if you wish to repeat the experiment, you'll have to choose another island.

How to get there

From Edinburgh Waverley station (scotrail. co.uk; 0845 755 0033) take the 41 bus (lothianbuses.com; 0131 555 6363) to Cramond where Cramond Glebe Road runs down to the causeway. A notice board there gives safe crossing times (roughly two hours either side of low tide). These are, as one might expect, somewhat conservative but try not to get yourself marooned.

Admission price/landing fee

Free.

View

Inchcolm (p274), Inchmickery, Inchkeith, the Forth coastline, Port of Leith and (from the higher ground) the Forth bridges.

Facilities

None, but there are public toilets at the mainland end of the causeway.

Accommodation

Cramond is not a large community but does possess the smart, modern **Cramond Guest House** (cramondguesthouse.co.uk; 0131 312 8424).

Nearest decent pub/café/tea room

Cramond Inn (0131 336 2035), a pleasantly rambling Sam Smith's pub (food served), is a stone's throw from the causeway. An ice cream van often lurks near the causeway too.

Nearest shop

There are various small shops ranged along **Whitehouse Road** towards Barnton (1.5 miles).

Rules

The first decaying gun emplacement you come to bristles with signs proclaiming it to be a dangerous building.

Things to do

There are no walls left at **Cramond Roman Fort** (200yd; tinyurl.com/bum3gwf) but it's free if you want a look around.

Walk west along the coast and you'll come to the Tudor Gothic pile that is **Dalmeny House** (1.5 miles; open Sunday to Tuesday, June and July; dalmeny.co.uk; 0131 331 1888) with its 18th-century French furniture and Sèvres porcelain.

Clockwise from top: Cramond at low tide; the battleship-like Inchmickery; the anti-submarine boom alongside the rather less aesthetically pleasing sewage outfall pipe

52. Inchcolm

Firth of Forth
Kingdom of Fife
tinyurl.com/7hxay8m (Historic Scotland)
OS Landranger maps 65 & 66
Grid reference: NT 189 826
Size: 22 acres
Population: 2 (seasonal)

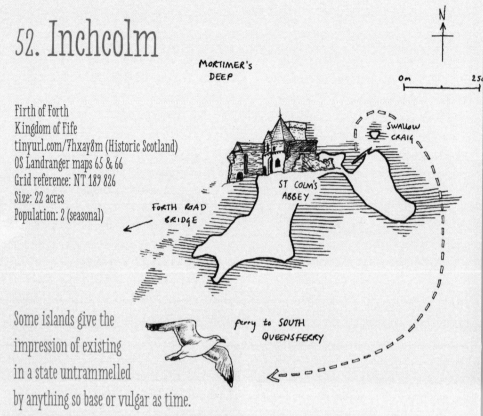

Some islands give the impression of existing in a state untrammelled by anything so base or vulgar as time. From their shores you just know that your view is exactly the same as that seen for aeons past. Inchcolm, for all its ancient abbey, is not such an island.

The Firth of Forth has been a restless place ever since humans began to take up residence beside its banks, and one suspects that Inchcolm's first known residents – hermits who successively inhabited the island from before Norman times – may have done so in the knowledge that there would always be a steady supply of human company to see them through their otherwise solitary existence.

It's fitting, therefore, that today the boat trip to the island starts practically underneath another symbol of human restlessness, the Forth Bridge. Opened in 1890 to take the railway from Edinburgh over to Fife, it's become Scotland's most recognisable landmark. It's also the subject of one of its greatest urban myths – painting the Forth Bridge is not, it turns out, a Sisyphean task. It was last completed in 2011 and probably won't need doing again for at least a couple of decades. This is doubtless a great consolation to the 63 men who died building it in the first place.

The ferry ride to Inchcolm moves the traveller forward in time from this late Victorian monolith to the World War I and II gun emplacements on Inchgarvie and then the modern oil tanker berths off Hound Point. Even Inchcolm itself seems stripped of all things ancient. The view from the southwest reveals merely a couple of low green hills capped by a smattering of suspiciously squared-off concrete extrusions. It is only when the boat slides along the island's southern shore to the dip between its hills that Inchcolm Abbey materialises to the accompaniment of a score of 'Ooh, look!'s and an ecstasy of fumbling for cameras.

However, the abbey was not the first building constructed on Inchcolm. The hermits who guarded its holy places (the means by which they came by such sanctity is, alas, somewhat obscure) would have had their own makeshift cells. Indeed, the presence of one of them is said to have led directly to the founding of the abbey. In 1123, King Alexander I of Scotland was in a ship that got caught by a strong gale. Forced to seek shelter on Inchcolm, he and his retinue were welcomed by a hermit who took them into his cell. For three days the unknown recluse shared his food with his august guests while the storm raged outside. When Alexander did at last reach Fife, he was so thankful to have survived the episode that he vowed to found a monastery on Inchcolm. Unfortunately, he wasn't able to keep this promise, carelessly dying the following year. However, his younger brother David, who succeeded him to the throne, took it upon himself to establish a priory some years later, inviting some Augustinian canons to make the island their home. Tradition has it that Inchcolm's impressive hermit's cell – about the size of a decent garden shed but made entirely of stone – is the one in which Alexander sheltered. And there's no reason why the fact that it was probably built at least 300 years after his death should shake our faith in that assertion.

The name Inchcolm means 'Colm's island', inch being a corruption of the Gaelic *innis*. Colm is a reference to a saint, but which St Colm remains in doubt. In the Middle Ages it was believed to be a shortening of Columba, the 6th-century abbot who founded the community on Iona in the Inner Hebrides. This gave rise to the island's nickname: 'The Iona of the East'. However, since Columba has no known links with eastern Scotland, Inchcolm's Colm is more likely to have been a saint whose sole surviving mark on this world is his name – his virtuous deeds and faith-inspiring miracles having been swept away by the rush and roar of passing centuries. Weep ye not, though, for it is a fate better than the one afforded to most of us.

Indeed, by association with the island, Colm also manages to sneak into Shakespeare's canon, in no less a play than *Macbeth*:

Sweno, the Norways' king,
craves composition;
Nor would we deign him burial of
his men,
Till he disbursed, at Saint Colme's Inch,
Ten thousand dollars to our general use.

This is testament to Inchcolm's status as a holy island. After the battle of Kinghorn in Fife, which took place around 1040, the defeated Scandinavians (probably Danes rather than Norwegians) are reputed to have paid the victorious King Macbeth a considerable sum in gold to have their slain soldiers buried on Inchcolm.

Many years later, according to Inchcolm Abbey's register, the local Lord of Aberdour, Alan Mortimer, gave half his lands 'to the monks of St Colme's Isle' in order to be interred there himself and thus assure himself a place closer to the throne of Heaven. The Augustinians agreed to this, despite the fact that they had fallen out with him. Under cover of night, when they were ferrying his body over to the island for burial in the church, they avenged themselves on him by casually tossing him overboard into the Forth. The narrow sound to the north of Inchcolm is still known as Mortimer's Deep.

Inchcolm's influence grew and, in 1235, permission was obtained from Pope Gregory IX to upgrade the priory to an abbey. However, the Wars of Scottish Independence, which sparked into life in 1296, all but finished off the island's monastic community. English raiders pillaged the abbey in 1335, carrying off a venerated statue of its patron saint, only to return their loot when they interpreted a sudden storm as a sign of God's displeasure.

Fifty years and many raids later, a band of 140 English soldiers found themselves prone to similar fears. After they had gone about their customary plundering, they set fire to an outhouse. The church roof subsequently caught fire, but, before any substantial damage could be done, the wind suddenly changed direction, blowing the flames back onto the infidels. Fearing the wrath of the Almighty was upon them, they fled across the Forth to South Queensferry, where they were duly captured by a band of Scottish knights, so they were probably right.

One of the few items of value not to have fallen into English hands was the *Inchcolm Antiphoner*, a book of plainchants written around 1300. Some of these chants are recorded nowhere else and the antiphoner – the hymn book of its day – thus gives us a unique insight into what was being sung in Celtic churches of the time.

The other great document that first saw light on the island was written by its most famous resident (not counting King Alexander's three-day stay), one Walter Bower. He was abbot of Inchcolm from 1418 to his death in 1449 and was the author of the beautifully monikered *Scotichronicon*. Based on earlier annals written by John of Fordun, the book charted the history of Scotland from King Malcolm III's rule (1058–93) right up to the beginning of James II's reign, during which Bower died.

A little more than 100 years later, religious life on the island all but came to an end. In 1547, Inchcolm was not merely raided by the English but occupied by a garrison for a whole year. The canons returned after the soldiers had left but the Protestant Reformation of 1560 finally dissolved all Scotland's Catholic monastic communities, including the one at Inchcolm. Generously, the canons were allowed to stay on, as long as they no longer practised Catholic forms of worship. However, the last evidence of their presence comes in the form of a charter signed in 1578 by Dominus Johne Brounhill and Dominus Andro Anguss. After that, all is silence.

Over the remaining centuries, the island's fall from the spiritual heights to the worldly depths reads like a history book of the home front. After being used for some time as a quarantine station for ships carrying the plague, it became a hospital serving the Russian fleet just prior to the Napoleonic Wars, then a base for gun batteries in anticipation of both a French invasion (ah, those were the days) and German intrusions (in both world wars). The Territorial Army tore down most of the 20th-century defences but there are still plenty to be mooched around, particularly on the east hill, where the most impressive remnant is a long brick-lined tunnel dug during World War I to take gunners safely from their sleeping quarters to the batteries.

It's the east hill that also affords the best views of the abbey complex. This includes the remains of a 12th-century church, an octagonal chapter house with a warming house above it (where the abbots were afforded the luxury of thawing out in winter), the abbot's residence and, most impressively of all, a structure proudly proclaimed to be 'the best preserved mediæval cloister in Scotland'.

The island is also populated again, at least for seven months of the year. Two amiable Historic Scotland wardens – at time of writing, Hayley and Jackie – live from April to October in the Colonel's Cottage, a hangover from the 20th century, and look after Inchcolm and its visitors. They share the island with a selection of seabirds, including various gulls and terns, fulmars, puffins, cormorants, guillemots and skuas. Grey seals, meanwhile, haul themselves out on nearby Haystack rock to gaze unblinking at day trippers and their unfathomable ways.

How to get there

From Dalmeny railway station (scotrail.co.uk; 0845 755 0033), the Hawes pier at South Queensferry, in the shadow of the Forth Bridge, is just a 0.5-mile walk. There are two options for getting to Inchcolm: Forth Tours (adult £11, child £4, family £28; forthtours.com; 0870 118 1866); and Maid of the Forth (adult £16, child £7, family £44; maidoftheforth.co.uk; 0131 331 5000). Both offer 1.5 hours on Inchcolm, with almost daily sailings from April to October. Forth Tours also provides a direct bus from Edinburgh Waverley railway station.

Admission price/landing fee

Historic Scotland landing fee: adult £5, child £3 (pay on board boat). Historic Scotland members land for free.

View

Cramond Island (p270), various other tiny islands, including Inchmickery and Inchkeith, the Forth bridges, Dalgety Bay and Edinburgh.

Facilities

Toilets and a visitor centre/small souvenir shop (the island's former NAAFI).

Accommodation

The **Innkeeper's Lodge** (innkeeperslodge.com; 0845 112 6001) at the Hawes Inn has 14 bedrooms and is right opposite the ferry terminal in South Queensferry. Robert Louis Stevenson is said to have stayed there and written part of his novel *Kidnapped* in one of the rooms.

Nearest decent pub/café/tea room

The 17th-century **Hawes Inn** (innkeeperslodge.com; 0845 112 6001) is right by the ferry terminal and was name-checked in Sir Walter Scott's *The Antiquary*. Close by there's also **The Two Bridges** (a posh pub) and, 100yd west of the pier, **The Railbridge Bistro**.

Nearest shop

The attractively cobblestoned main street of **South Queensferry** has a range of small independent shops.

Rules

Not a rule as such, but in the breeding season (roughly May to July) the gulls take over the two extremes of the island so you may want to avoid them for your own good.

Things to do

Two miles west along the Firth of Forth stands **Hopetoun House** (open Easter to September; hopetoun.co.uk; 0131 331 2451), which makes a grand claim to be 'Scotland's finest stately home' and rejoices in 150 acres of gardens.

Two miles the other way is the rival **Dalmeny House** (open Sunday to Tuesday, June and July; dalmeny.co.uk; 0131 331 1888) containing 18th-century French furniture and Sèvres porcelain inside its Tudor Gothic walls.

South Queensferry is on Sustrans' 134-mile **Round the Forth cycle route**, more prosaically known as National Cycle Route 76 (tinyurl.com/86nwndo; 0117 926 8893).

53. Lochleven Castle Island

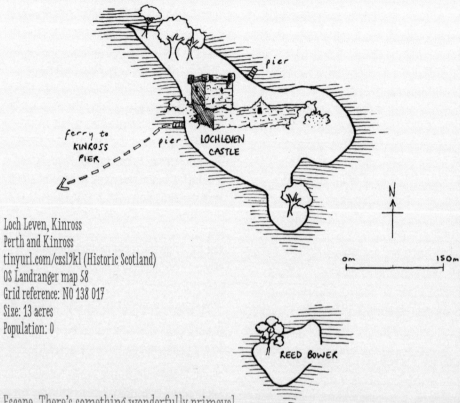

Loch Leven, Kinross
Perth and Kinross
tinyurl.com/czsl9kl (Historic Scotland)
OS Landranger map 58
Grid reference: NO 138 017
Size: 13 acres
Population: 0

Escape. There's something wonderfully primeval about that word. How many of us do not feel a vicarious thrill when we hear of someone who has escaped from somewhere – for a person who has escaped has tasted life, adventure, excitement, or at the very least a revitalised appreciation for freedom.

And that gives any visit to Lochleven Castle Island an extra lustre, for it was from here, in 1568, that the 25-year-old Mary, Queen of Scots made a clean getaway. The seven-minute ferry ride across Loch Leven with Charlie, a friendly bearded Historic Scotland skipper, is undertaken in a small boat not dissimilar in size to the one in which Mary escaped. Flanked by geese, gadwall, tufted ducks and teal (tens of thousands of migrating birds spend time on the loch), the ferry sallies past the 17th-century Kinross House and a clutch of minute islands with intriguing names such as Roy's Folly and Alice's Bower. Castle Island (the full 'Lochleven' name only tends to be used to differentiate it from all the other Castle Islands around the world) is very much the alpha male among these unweaned whelps. However, look across to the far side of the loch and you'll see St Serf's Inch, an island that dwarfs Mary's former prison. There was once a priory there but the island's a bird sanctuary now and off limits to humans.

Satisfyingly, this approach to Castle Island is a full-frontal assault on the fortress. Advance on it from any other direction and you wouldn't know it was there at all, for the trees that dominate the island almost encircle the castle and would devour it in a trice if not held back. And given that the castle has not been occupied for over 400 years and is one of the oldest built of stone in Scotland, it's in astonishingly good shape. A mighty curtain wall greets visitors today, or rather attempts to ward them off. A square five-floor tower house built in the 1300s stands immovably behind it, daring intrusion. It was here, on the third floor, that Mary spent most of her imprisonment. At least that's when she wasn't wandering around the island (which was a lot smaller in those days, the level of the loch being higher) chatting with castle owner Sir William Douglas who doubled as her unwilling gaoler.

Mary would already have known the island well, having visited as a guest on three occasions. By the time she escaped, having spent almost a year under lock and key, she had not only lost twins in a miscarriage, she had also been stripped of her crown.

But Mary was not the only sovereign to grace Castle Island with the royal presence. Well before her deed of derring do, King Robert I (aka the Bruce) enjoyed a sojourn in the castle in 1313, no doubt on good form having just recaptured Perth from the English. Indeed, it's very possible that the castle itself was built by the Sassenach foe, for when Edward I invaded in 1296 he would have come this way, Loch Leven being strategically placed between the royal burghs of Edinburgh and Perth. Sir William Wallace is said to have captured the castle at some point before 1305 so it's not unreasonable to assume that he took it from English hands.

Robert the Bruce was the first of a line of monarchs who were alive to the possibilities of the castle as a place for detaining their enemies. He promptly instituted it as a state prison, banging up the pro-English John MacDougall of Lorn in 1316. Bruce's successor, David II, went one better and had his own nephew locked up in the castle for a winter for upsetting the queen. The king had stayed there himself in 1361–62, in a sort of self-imposed imprisonment in order to escape the Black Death which was then ravaging the Lowlands. His flight was recorded by Walter Bower of Inchcolm (p274) in his *Scotichronicon*.

However, when the childless David died (not of the plague), his nephew Robert succeeded to the throne (founding the House of Stewart) and did a Mary in reverse by being a prisoner first and then a visitor to the castle, by which time he also owned it.

Mary, Queen of Scots' fina[l]
Castle Island began on 17 Ju[ne]
having surrendered to rebelli[ous]
lords after the so-called Battl[e]
Hill. A first escape attempt, a[ided by]
the love-struck George Dougl[as]
of the castle's owner and a m[inor]
age – was a simple affair. She [swapped]
clothes with a servant woma[n sent]
up to her room, put a muffle[r over her]
face, and walked out of the c[astle to]
a ferry boat.

You can trace her route too[. The]
wooden steps that led up to t[he]
tower house entrance have r[otted away]
and been replaced by a smar[t modern]
set. Unfortunately for Mary, t[he boatman]
smelled a rat, uncovered the [escape]
route and swiftly rowed her b[ack.]

This, as can be imagined, g[ave rise to]
increased vigilance over the p[risoner. To]
no avail however, for she suc[ceeded in]
flew the nest on the night of 2[...]
again following a plan hatche[d by George.]
His adopted brother William [managed to]
spirit away a set of keys from [the table]
at which he was eating dinne[r with his]
parents. He let Mary and one [of her maids,]
Jane Kennedy, out of the towe[r, before]
unlocking a window that was [usually]
used as a postern gate. The pa[ir made]
to a boat that George had bro[ught to the]
island under cover of darknes[s.]
William then rowed for all the [was]
worth, with Jane and apparen[tly]
Mary helping out. At the south [shore,]
confederates were waiting for [them]

View
The Loch Leven shoreline, various scattered islands.

Facilities
Toilets and an emergency radio for use should you strand yourself by missing the last boat home.

Accommodation
A fraction east of the M90, **Kelson Lodge** (1 mile; kinrossbandb.co.uk; 01577 863245) is a B&B glorying in a fantastic view of Loch Leven and Castle Island.

Nearest decent pub/café/tea room
The large **Boathouse Bistro** is on the lochside, right next to the quay from where the ferry leaves.

Nearest shop
The small town of **Kinross** (0.5 miles) is home to a healthy variety of shops.

Rules
None.

Things to do
The **Loch Leven Heritage Trail** (lochlevenheritagetrail.co.uk; 01738 475349) is an 8-mile signed path for walkers and cyclists around the north side of Loch Leven from **Kinross Pier** to the **RSPB visitor centre** at Vane Farm.
Kinross House (01577 862900) is privately owned but its magnificent gardens laid out in the 17th century are open to the public from April to September.

The tower house of Lochleven Castle from which Mary escaped

54. Moncreiffe Island

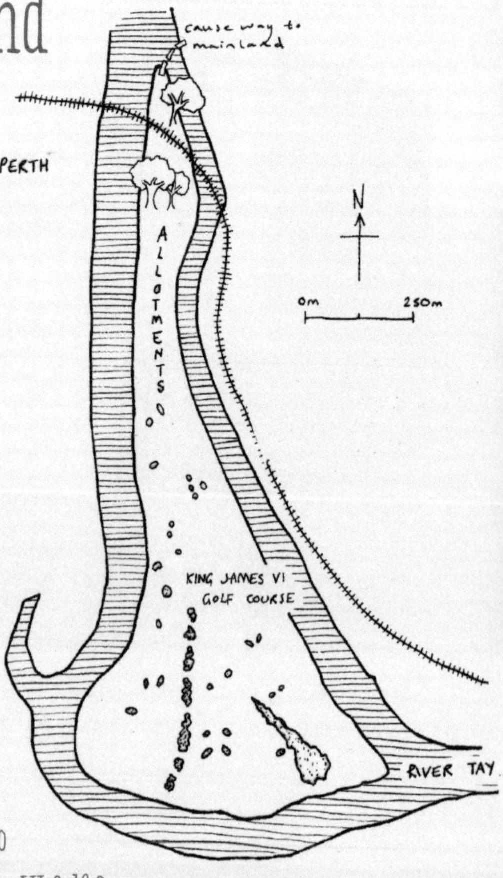

Perth
Perth and Kinross
kingjamesvi.co.uk
OS Landranger map 58
Grid reference: NO 122 221
Size: c. 120 acres
Population: 0

Let's be honest, first impressions of Moncreiffe Island are not promising. A set of steps up from Tay Street in Perth rise to a pedestrian walkway awkwardly tacked onto a bridge carrying a railway line. Even the sign at the foot of the steps makes no mention of Moncreiffe, but merely King James VI Golf Course.

Roughly halfway across, an unprepossessing metal staircase (built in 1895 for a princely £67) winds down to terra firma. The bulk of the island lies to the south, but wander north and the scrubby trees shield not only the blackened detritus of illicit bonfires but also an enigmatic stone sculpture topped with a blue metal pyramid bearing the legend 'Fortune'. At the tip of the island, where grass gives way to stones, lie the beginnings of a concrete track across the Willowgate, the name given to the narrower of the two

streams into which the Tay divides to pass around the island. Kinnoul Ford, as this shallow crossing is called, is only completely dry in times of drought.

Heading south from the bridge, you must first pass the Perth Working Men's Garden Association, a throwback to different times and whose allotments must rank as some of the tidiest in the land. The well-tended sheds speak of men who spend less time at home than they might. The association's request to the town council in 1890 to lease the land for allotments is the reason why the golf course doesn't cover the whole island. Judging from the official history of the club, written by one of its members, this still rankles slightly today.

The course itself opened in June 1897, nine years after the council had purchased the land from the Moncreiffe family, the local line of baronets who had owned the island for centuries and had habitually rented it out to tenant farmers. The King James VI club already existed, playing on an open area of Perth called the North Inch, and its removal to the island was apparently a cause of some celebration to locals fed up with dodging their shanked or sliced drives. The island was duly lain down to grass, an 18-hole course devised (by four-time Open winner Tom Morris), and the clubhouse built (to which ladies were admitted from the start). The annual rent was fixed at £210 for 30 years, with the provisos that 'golf caddies should not... stand for hire near the stair leading to the bridge [and] the club be obliged to admit non-golfers the privilege of walking the island at a reduced rate of subscription'. Sunday play was prohibited (a clause rescinded in 1940).

Today a walk around the edge of the island involves a polite request for permission at the clubhouse and an ear kept on the *qui vive* for shouts of 'fore'. Aside from the various wedges of evergreens that separate one hole from another, and the copse that fills the southeastern corner of the island, there's nothing to see as such. Most of the joy of exploration comes from reaching the southern end, where a view across the Tay to Moncreiffe Hill can be enjoyed.

Only three events have occurred to trouble the island golfers of Perth. The first was in 1943 when half the course was temporarily ploughed up to help Britain dig for victory. The second came on the night of 4 March 1955 when the wooden clubhouse was completely destroyed in a fire, killing one canary. The third was the terrible flood of 1993.

Perth has been home to Picts and Romans (who named the town Victoria) and the scene of a regicide (James I of Scotland, whose flight from his murderers was ended in a blocked-off sewer). It's been the scene of so many Anglo-Scottish and inter-clan struggles – as befits a former capital – you'd think all that spilt blood would the multitudinous soils incarnadine, making the brown one red (to paraphrase Lady Macbeth).

While the town of Perth has kept many reminders of its torrid past, Moncreiffe shows the world a clean slate. There's no mystery to this – it's simply been washed clean every 20 or so years by the flooding of the Tay. The 1993 devastation occurred when the entire island was submerged but for the clubhouse, which had sagely been built on a plinth of stone dredged from the riverbed. It was the worst flood for 179 years and prompted the building of higher defences. To no avail – the course has been partially inundated twice since then and it's unlikely that the Tay will ever be entirely tamed.

Perth railway station (scotrail.
45 755 0033). Access to the
from Tay Street (0.5 miles) via a
e attached to the railway bridge.
le it is also possible to walk across
rth tip of the island from the east
he Tay.

price/landing fee

s of the Tay, St Matthew's church,
ay line that crosses the river,
er bridges to the north, and the
fe and Kirkton hills to the south.

toilets in the golf course
e bar but you'll need a member
ou in first.

lation

plentiful supply of places to
s head in Perth, and two good
esthouses within easy walking
of Moncreiffe Island are **Rosebank**
<guesthouseperth.co.uk; 01738
and **Ardfern** (ardfernguesthouse.
738 637031).

cent pub/café/tea room

eat in the **King James VI**
se bar** on the island but only if a
signs you in. They're an affable
u might get lucky if you cosy up
therwise try **Willows**, a popular

Fortune, here seen favouring the brave

coffee shop and restaurant in St John's Place (0.3 miles; willowscoffeeshop.co.uk; 01738 441175).

Nearest shop

Perth is a city with a glut, possibly even a surfeit, of retail outlets.

Rules

Take care to keep to the very edge of the golf course and don't put the golfers off their stroke.

Things to do

The **Fergusson Gallery** (open Monday to Saturday; tinyurl.com/cfoseqq; 01738 783425) is right opposite the Tay Street steps that lead to the island and houses the collections of artist J D Fergusson and modern dance choreographer Margaret Morris.

Don't be put off by the less-than-snappy title of the **Royal Scottish Geographical Society's Visitor and Information Centre in the Fair Maid's House**. The house is Perth's oldest secular building and is filled with fascinating exhibits revealing the character of our home planet (open April to October, Monday to Friday; free but donations appreciated; rsgs.org; 01738 455050). Three miles north of Perth stands **Scone Palace** (open April to October, daily; scone-palace.co.uk; 01738 552300), where Robert the Bruce was crowned in 1306 and where lies the mysterious Stone of Destiny. Of rather more recent origin is **Stanley Mills** (8 miles; open April to October, daily; tinyurl.com/d8hpnxr; 01738 828268), an exceptionally well-preserved cotton mill built during the Industrial Revolution.

Moncreiffe from on high, with Perth spread out beyond

55. Inchcailloch

Nr Balmaha, Loch Lomond
Stirlingshire
lochlomond-trossachs.org
OS Landranger map 56
Grid reference: NS 409 903
Size: 128 acres
Population: 0

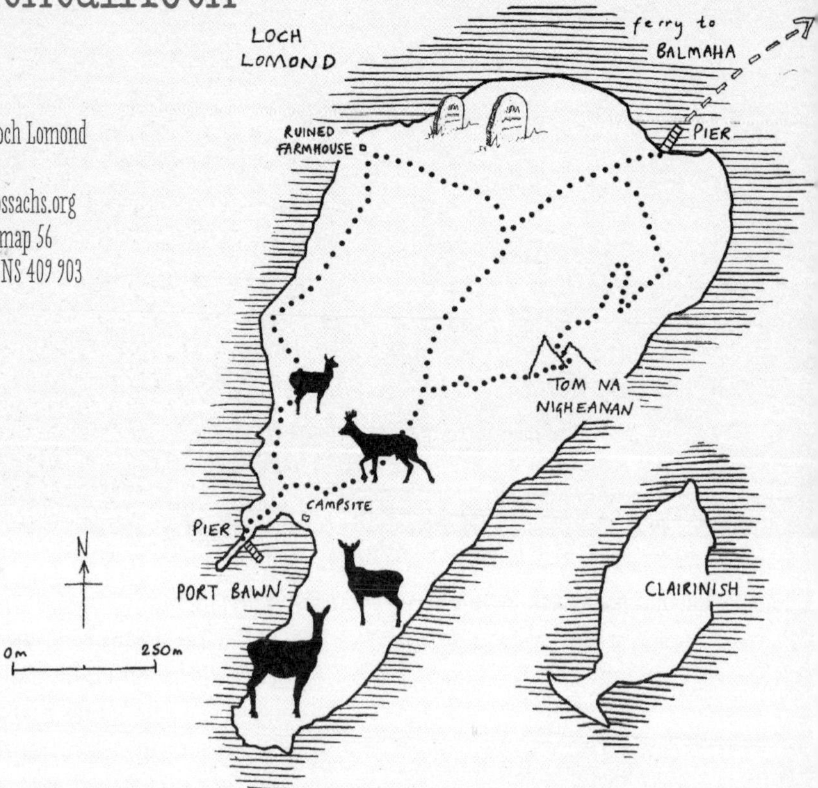

Ah, Loch Lomond, where the banks are famously not just 'bonnie' but 'bonnie bonnie'. Stretching 23 miles from Balloch to Ardlui, it contains 23 tiny islands, the vast majority scattered around the southern end. And of all the 23, the most interesting is Inchcailloch, for it tells the story of the making of Britain.

Once you step off the ferry onto Inchcailloch's north jetty you enter the world of the MacGregors. Or rather the world of MacGregors who have passed to hunting grounds anew, for this thrillingly lawless clan (many of whom were murdered at Glencoe) used the island as their burial ground for several centuries.

Visit the cemetery and aside from seeing the grave of Gregor MacGregor (Rob Roy's uncle), you'll also come across a good many MacFarlanes. This latter clan found such notoriety on account of their nocturnal raids on other people's cattle that their long-suffering neighbours referred to the moon as 'MacFarlane's Lantern'.

Both clans are, however, comparatively modern interlopers. Meaning 'island of the old women' in English, Inchcailloch is said to have been the site of a nunnery, albeit that there's no physical evidence of it. There was definitely a church here though. St Kentigerna's was built in the 12th or 13th century and used until 1670, when parishioners, presumably tired of rowing over for Sunday services, built a new place of worship on the mainland. The scant ruins of the church remain today, next to the burial ground. It was named after a princess – the daughter of a King of Leinster – who arrived on Inchcailloch in AD717 as a Christian missionary to Scotland. She died on the island in 733 or 734, possibly having founded or inspired the founding of a nunnery, or possibly not. Her son, called Fillan, became the patron saint of the mentally ill.

The remnants of the last permanent habitation on the island are close by on its northwestern tip. The farm's final lease expired in 1770 and the farmhouse was abandoned. What's left of its stone walls can be made out beneath oak trees that were planted sometime after the demise of the farm. Pyroligneous acid was distilled from Inchcailloch's oaks, while the bark was employed in the leather tanning industry. When technological advances made these products redundant, the oaks were themselves abandoned. This has rather suited them for they've thrived and now cover the greater part of the island.

A carefully maintained nature trail comprises a central path running about 1,000yd from the north jetty to Port Bawn with two large loops off it. The low circuit takes in the church, burial ground and farm, while the high loop climbs Inchcailloch's hill, Tom na Nigheanan ('Hill of the Young Women' – presumably a reference to the alleged nunnery). From the top, amid Scots pines that have resisted the invasion of the oaks, there's an almighty view over the islands of the loch and across to Ben Lomond and Ben Vorlich. A Spitfire came a cropper here during World War II, crashing into the trees at the summit. However, St Kentigerna was evidently looking out for the pilot, who emerged from his machine with nothing more serious than a broken leg to show for his misadventure.

The path snakes down the hill to Port Bawn, a natural harbour where a small clearing with some picnic tables, a compost loo and a warden's hut serves as a commendably unfussy campsite. Those fortunate enough to spend the night here get to share the island with redstarts, woodpeckers, treecreepers and wood warblers, among other birds. There are also fallow deer about, circumspect and elusive descendants of those brought to the area by Robert the Bruce, though it's a patient stalker indeed who spots one.

But perhaps the most enchanting thing about Inchcailloch is something that could not be guessed at, even by visiting it: beneath the island, running right along its length, is the Highland Boundary Fault. To the north is the Highlands, to the south the Lowlands, making Inchcailloch part of a sort of *cordon sanitaire*. The fault is a deep fracture in the Earth's crust fashioned when the continents of Laurentia and Avalonia collided about 450 million years ago. The crash caused some Laurentian islands to fuse together over the course of the next 40 million years, so creating what we now know as the Scottish Highlands. These crumpled up against an Avalonian island, consisting of (in today's terms) England, Wales and the Scottish Lowlands, and mainland Britain was born.

So, as we can see, the Scottish Lowlands are really part of England and Wales and have nothing whatsoever to do with the Scottish Highlands. It's probably best not to mention this to a Scot, however.

Instead, brush up on your Sir Walter Scott. In *The Lady of the Lake*, the novelist, playwright and poet mentions Inchcailloch describing the journey of the fiery cross sent to call Clan MacGregor to battle:

The shafts and limbs were rods of yew
Whose fellows in Inch Cailliach wave
Their shadows o'er Clan Alpin's grave,
And, answering Lomond's breezes deep,
Soothe many a chieftain's endless sleep.

Most of the other islands on Loch Lomond have stories to tell. Inchfad has its own canal and was once home to a flourishing (if illegal) whisky distillery. A number of castles have been built on Inchgalbraith, which is not a natural island at all but a crannog (see p168). Inchmurrin, Britain's largest inland island, once boasted the only hotel out on the loch. You can still stay there today in one of its four self-catering lodges (inchmurrin-lochlomond.com). Inchconnachan,

were introduced there in 1975 by Lady Arran Colquhoun. There is still a small colony on the island, though there are occasional murmurings by the powers that be that in order to let native species flourish they should be wiped out. You'd need a heart of stone to agree with them though.

How to get there
From Balloch Central railway station (scotrail.co.uk; 0845 755 0033) take the 309 bus (mccolls.org.uk; 01389 754321) to Balmaha. At MacFarlane's Boatyard (balmahaboatyard.co.uk; 01360 870214) a ferry runs on demand to Inchcailloch. Boats are also available for hire at the boatyard (see 'Things to do'). Please note that most of the other islands on Loch Lomond are privately owned. Day-tripping picnickers are tolerated on most but not all of the islands, and private piers and jetties should not be used at any time.

Admission price/landing fee
Free.

View
Sundry islands (notably neighbours Inchfad, Clairinsh and Torrinch), the shores of Loch Lomond and the mountains beyond, including Ben Lomond.

Facilities
A compost loo and half a dozen picnic tables at Port Bawn.

Accommodation
You can camp on the island in the gorgeous tiny campsite (tinyurl.com/d3y98d2;

01389 722600) in **Port Bawn**, though for a maximum two-night stay and you have to take all your own drinking water. In Balmaha, there's **The Oak Tree Inn** (oak-tree-inn.co.uk; 01360 870357) and the **Balmaha House Bunkhouse and Canoe Hire** (balmahahouse.co.uk; 01360 870218), which offers B&B and bunkhouse accommodation (and canoe hire).

Nearest decent pub/café/tea room
The **Oak Tree Inn** (see 'Accommodation') in Balmaha was Gastropub of the Year 2008 and prides itself on its malt whiskies and locally brewed ales.

Nearest shop
The **Village Shop** (01360 870270) in Balmaha stocks basics, gifts and a few curiously exotic items.

Rules
No bicycles allowed (if you arrive on one you may be able to leave it in the shed at MacFarlane's Boatyard if you smile nicely).

Things to do
Hire a rowing boat or a motorboat from MacFarlane's Boatyard (balmahaboatyard.co.uk; 01360 870214) and explore the loch. Various cruises are also available from the boatyard.

The **Loch Lomond and The Trossachs National Park** (lochlomond-trossachs.org; 01389 722600) is 720 square miles of mountains, woods and water that you can walk, cycle, horseride, watch wildlife, sail, water ski or just stand around in.

56. Inchmahome

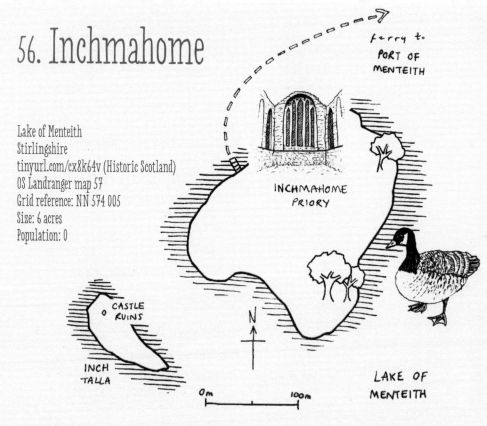

Lake of Menteith
Stirlingshire
tinyurl.com/cx8k64v (Historic Scotland)
OS Landranger map 57
Grid reference: NN 574 005
Size: 6 acres
Population: 0

FERRY to PORT OF MENTEITH

INCHMAHOME PRIORY

CASTLE RUINS

INCH TALLA

N

LAKE OF MENTEITH

0m   100m

Lake Menteith is not an imposing body of water. Tucked beneath the Menteith Hills, just inside the southeastern border of the Loch Lomond and The Trossachs National Park, it looks like the sort of lake that might have been created in the grounds of an imposing stately home to give the fifth duke something to look at while he gorged on his poached quail eggs of a morning.

Despite this, the journey in the little open boat from Port Menteith to Inchmahome is pleasingly long (a full seven minutes), so one can only conclude that the lake is larger than it looks (or the boat slower than it seems).

What impressed the canons who came here in 1238 – at the behest of Walter Comyn, Earl of Menteith – was not the lake's beauty or size so much as the fact that the island on which they had been

invited to establish a monastery would give them all the tranquillity and seclusion from the world they desired (give or take the fact that the earl lived in a castle on the next-door island of Inch Talla).

Jumping off the boat at the discreet wooden jetty, visitors are drawn through an arch of trees into a complex of grey stone buildings, most of which show the marks of the four and a half centuries of abandonment since the priory fell victim to the Protestant Reformation. In its day, the church must have been a fine sight with its large east window and exquisite processional doorway, the latter apparently modelled on the one at Dunblane Cathedral. The nave sports a mighty bell tower but it's the little three-seat sedilia built into the wall that most catches the eye. This is where the priests sat during Mass and it's easy to imagine them there in their finery, with a wisp of incense smoke curling up around their tonsured heads.

The cloister buildings have fared less well, with the exception of the chapter house, which was converted in the 17th century into a mausoleum. It contains a set of rare medieval memorials, the most endearing of which bears the effigies of Walter Stewart (died 1295) and his countess, Mary, clearly about to have a good old smooch. It's a refreshing change from the usual pious poses.

Once you've had a swift peek at the drains of the reredorter, if only for the opportunity to use the word (so much nicer than 'latrine block'), the walk around the rest of the island throws up further unexpected felicities, even if you don't manage to spot the otters and ospreys that often hunt here.

Queen Mary's Bower – a small enclosure of boxwood trees – was reputedly planted by the four-year-old Mary, Queen of Scots during her brief stay in 1547 following her nation's disastrous defeat at the Battle of Pinkie to an army led by the Duke of Somerset. As H V Morton puts it in *In Scotland Again*: 'On Inchmahome she was hidden when the English were hammering at the gates of Stirling, and from Inchmahome she passed out into the world, a little child with a crown upon her head, a child of storm and destiny.'

Robert the Bruce visited Inchmahome three times between 1306 and 1310 and carelessly never once thought to plant a small enclosure of boxwood trees, so his connection with the island is rather less trumpeted. His interest in Inchmahome is likely to have been piqued by the first abbot being a sworn ally of Edward I, the English king.

Meanwhile, at the island's southern end is the little hillock known as Nun's Hill. Here it was, if tradition is to be believed, that a nun was buried in an upright position as punishment for having enjoyed carnal relations with the son of an earl of Menteith. If it were so, it seems a curious form of chastisement, but perhaps one that should be brought back into fashion. I'm sure, if given the choice, most of us would prefer retribution for our wrongdoing to be meted out after death rather than before.

Back at the church, having been careful to evade the attentions of the inordinately protective Canada geese that nest on the island, there's a gravestone marking a much more recent burial, that of Robert Bontine Cunninghame Graham, who died in 1936. Adventurer, author, friend of Buffalo Bill and Oscar Wilde, founder of both the Scottish Labour Party and the Scottish National Party, Cunninghame

Graham is perhaps best known as being the first MP ever to have suffered suspension from the House of Commons for swearing.

The ruins of the abbey that surround him became a popular draw in Victorian times, particularly among English tourists. It was on account of these unholy Sassenachs that the loch became better known as a 'lake'. It has borne this effetely English name ever since, part of a tiny coterie of Scottish lakes. Should independence ever come about, expect changes.

How to get there

Take a train to Stirling railway station (scotrail.co.uk; 0845 755 0033) then the C11 bus (virgintrains.co. uk; 01709 849200) to Port of Menteith, from where a Historic Scotland boat will convey you to the island (open April to September, 10am–5pm; October 10am–4pm – the last ferry over leaves 30 minutes before closing time; tinyurl.com/cx8k64v; 01877 385294).

Admission price/landing fee

Adult £5, child £3.

View

The lake's two other islands – Inch Talla and Dog Isle – and the Menteith Hills.

Facilities

Toilets and a very small Historic Scotland souvenir shop.

Accommodation

A 19th-century manse, the **Lake of Menteith Hotel** (tinyurl.com/cs33hyh; 01877 385258) is right on the shore near the Historic Scotland jetty and commands views of the island. **Inchie Farm** (1 mile; inchiefarm. co.uk; 01877 385233) is also on the lakeside and offers B&B in a rural setting.

Nearest decent pub/café/tea room

The Inchmahome-facing **Waterfront Restaurant** at Lake of Menteith Hotel (see 'Accommodation') is open to non-residents. Alternatively, there's **The Forth Inn** (4.5 miles; forthinn.com; 01877 382372) at Aberfoyle, where, awaiting your well-tutored palette, are 50 malt whiskies, three real ales and as much locally grown organic produce as a man can look upon and still live.

Nearest shop

You'd be best to high-tail it to Aberfoyle where you'll find the **Aberfoyle Delicatessen** (4.5 miles; 01877 382242) ready with your picnic ingredients.

Rules

Don't mess with the Canada geese during the breeding season or they'll have your hand off

Things to do

The 77-mile **Rob Roy Way** (robroyway. com) passes close to the Lake of Menteith on its journey from Drymen to Pitlochry in Perthshire, apparently following paths used by the great man himself.

The 14th-century **Doune Castle** (11 miles; open all year; tinyurl.com/cya7nk8; 01786 841742) – or 'The Castle in *Monty Python and the Holy Grail*' as it's better known – is well worth a visit, especially since the audio tour is narrated by Terry Jones.

Top: The abbey church; Bottom: Walter, Mary and gooseberry

57. Inchbuie

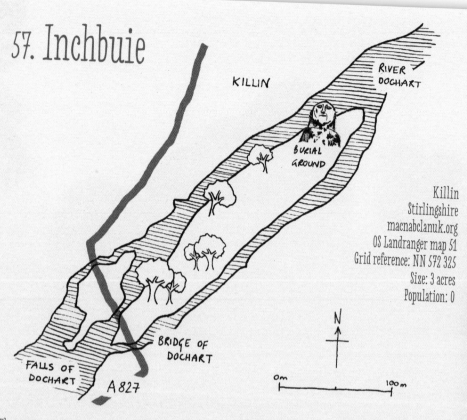

KILLIN

RIVER DOCHART

BURIAL GROUND

BRIDGE OF DOCHART

FALLS OF DOCHART

A 827

N

0m   100 m

Killin
Stirlingshire
macnabclanuk.org
OS Landranger map 51
Grid reference: NN 572 325
Size: 3 acres
Population: 0

There are many uses to which you can put a river island. Monkey Island (p72) on the Thames is home to a glorious hotel. In Perth they've turned Moncreiffe Island (p284) into a golf course with some allotments on the side. At Inchbuie, meanwhile, the Macnabs have chosen to bury each other.

Joined to both riverbanks by the Bridge of Dochart, the western end of Inchbuie (pronounced Inch-boo-ee) hardly feels insular at all. Access to the island – which belongs to the Macnab Memorial Trust – is via an unprepossessing green metal gate set in a wall on the bridge, whose five unequal black arches span the plunging River Dochart. Meanwhile, the far western tip of the island pokes cheekily out beneath the bridge as if desperate to sneak into the

background of the myriad tourist snaps of the Falls of Dochart, a feature that attracts thousands of sightseers every year.

The forbidding stone archway beneath the gate is grand in an understated, rustic way and bears a sign saying, rather prosaically, 'Clan Macnab Burial Ground – Keys available from the Tourist Information Office'. Underneath, a more recent board bears the timeless legend 'Access at own risk'. Unhappily, Killin's Tourist Information

Office and the Breadalbane Folklore Centre, whose ground floor it used to inhabit, both closed in 2011. It's unclear now from whom a key can be garnered. When I enquired in various establishments in the village, I was darkly advised, 'Ye'll not find the wall's very high...'

Guarding the entrance are two august pillars topped with disproportionately small stone spheres, as if the designer sought to demonstrate what a mustard seed might look like if you put it on a golf tee. Behind them, beyond the archway, a straight path leads enticingly beneath the conifers. Inchbuie is a thin and not particularly long island so the graveyard enclosure, although towards the far end, is soon reached. It's a curious thing: an oblong of high stone wall with a gothic-style hole for a door and two paneless windows. There are 15 graves inside, nine of which belong to Macnab clan chiefs, with the oldest gravestone dated 1574. The enclosure is kept locked but you can still peer in. And do look upwards too, for on top of the wall at either end are two impassive busts of women that seem to ape the stylings of ancient Assyria.

Outside the enclosure are the graves of the not-so-worthy Macnabs and plaques commemorating the more recently departed. Who knew that the 21st chief, Lt. Col. James Alexander Macnab (1901–90), won a gold medal for rowing at the 1924 Olympic Games in Paris? Or that Colin Duncan Macnab (1902–70) played football for Scotland?

Also known as Innes Bhuidhe ('Yellow Island'), possibly on account of the amber-coloured moss that grows there, the erstwhile Macnabs are by no means its first inhabitants. The centre of the island is the site of two Iron Age forts, though you'd have to know what you're looking for to discern their traces now.

Inchbuie is also reputedly haunted, but for an island with an ancient graveyard hidden in dark woods, not to gain such a reputation would be slack work indeed. It's certainly an atmospheric place and one which, unusually, is probably best visited in the rain or snow when its bleak beauty can best be appreciated. And while you're maundering about beneath the towering trees you can ponder on this. In 1680 the Lady of Lawers prophesied that when a Scots pine branch on Inchbuie fell on another Scots pine and grafted itself onto it, the Macnabs would be stripped of their lands. In 1820, a storm caused this to happen and three years later Archibald, the 17th Macnab chief, fled to Canada to escape his creditors and the Macnab lands were lost. In 1949, the 22nd chief, Archibald Corrie Macnab, bought back the island and 7,000 acres of his clan's former domain. Within two years the grafted branch was dead.

How to get there

For an out-of-the-way place, getting to Inchbuie by public transport is remarkably easy. Just take the train to Crianlarich (scotrail.co.uk; 0845 755 0033) then the

978 coach (citylink.co.uk; 0141 332 9644) that runs from outside the police station.

Admission price/landing fee

Free.

View

Limited due to the trees but Killin can be glimpsed between them.

Facilities

None.

Accommodation

The **Riverview Bed and Breakfast at The Old Smiddy** (theoldsmiddykillin.co.uk; 01567 820619) provides modern yet homely lodgings in a former blacksmith's with views of Inchbuie thrown in. Overlooking the island from the other side is the **Falls of Dochart Inn** (falls-of-dochart-inn.co.uk; 01567 820270) with their very-much-better-than-your-usual pub rooms. There's more accommodation listed at the Killin village website (killin.co.uk/stay).

Nearest decent pub/café/tea room

The Old Smiddy, aside from being a B&B (see above), is also a swish café and bistro. Meanwhile, to your left as you emerge from Inchbuie is the **Falls of Dochart Inn** (see above again), which has a tea room as well as a bar and serves food.

Nearest shop

The village of Killin has a small **Co-op** (0.3 miles) as well as a smattering of other small shops including a bakery and, perhaps more surprisingly, a haberdashery.

Rules

None.

Things to do

Explore the area by **canoe, kayak or bicycle**, all of which can be hired at The Killin Outdoor Centre and Mountain Shop (0.3 miles; 01567 820652).

Take your bike for a spin on **Cycleway 7** (tinyurl.com/cjdtmp9) which runs 23 miles from Killin to Callander partly along a disused railway line and almost entirely off-road.

Kenmore's **Scottish Crannog Centre** (16 miles; crannog.co.uk; 01887 830583) at the far east end of Loch Tay offers insights into the ultimate in tiny island living from 3000BC to the 17th century.

Left: The River Dochart sweeps round the island;
Right: A slab marks a Macnab's last stand

58. Ness Islands

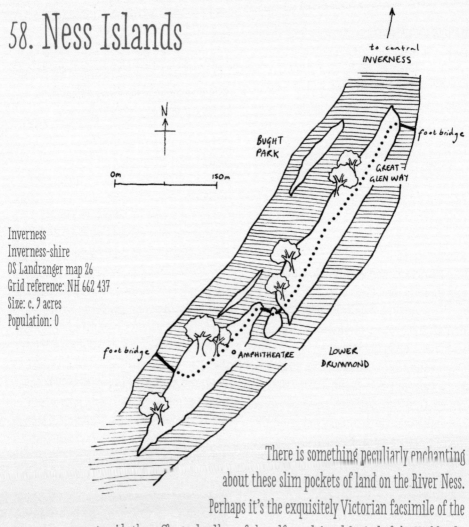

to central
INVERNESS

N

0m   150m

BUGHT
PARK

foot bridge

GREAT
GLEN WAY

foot bridge

AMPHITHEATRE

LOWER
DRUMMOND

Inverness
Inverness-shire
OS Landranger map 26
Grid reference: NH 662 437
Size: c. 9 acres
Population: 0

There is something peculiarly enchanting
about these slim pockets of land on the River Ness.
Perhaps it's the exquisitely Victorian facsimile of the
countryside they offer to dwellers of the self-proclaimed Capital of the Highlands.
Or maybe it's the way they tease their urban visitors with a sense of wild isolation while at the
same time remaining resolutely genteel, like a lumberjack who insists on working
dressed in his Sunday best and bowler hat.

In the 19th century, the Highland Council
bought the islands for use as a public
park, and the two footbridges that join
them to both banks of the Ness represent
the third go the local burghers have

had at making them accessible. The
first bridges were built in 1829 after a
successful fundraising appeal by local civil
engineer Joseph Mitchell. Unfortunately,
he didn't think to raise money for their

maintenance and they fell into disrepair before being washed away completely in the Great Flood of 1849. (They shouldn't feel too bad – one of the central arches of Inverness's railway bridge managed to get itself washed away as recently as 1989.) The next set, also suspension bridges, were constructed around four years later and fared rather better, surviving until 1987 when the current, rather elegant bridges were installed. The span connecting the islands with the city's Bught Park is named after the nearby General's Well, whose water, once crossed with silver, was widely believed to cure rickets. Meanwhile, the two major islands – if that is not too flattering a description of them – are connected by a couple of short bridges that leapfrog the much smaller isle that lies between them. The many other tiny pockets of land that make up the Ness Islands have no bridges linking them to civilisation. They are wild places where dragons live. And if not dragons, then at least pipistrelle bats and the occasional adventurous deer.

However, Eileanan Abhainn Nis, as the islands are known in Gaelic, were a place of recreation long before the bridges came. Robert Carruthers, in his 1843 collection of anecdotes *The Highland Notebook*, records the recollections of a certain Mr Angus B Reach: 'On the grand occasions of the judges' visits, and when the entertainments were on the most extensive scale, the "Isle" was the scene of the revelry. With the embowering branches of the oak and the birch weaving a living canopy over them,

and the pleasant sound of the running stream in their ears, the "lords" doffed their robes and cares of office together and, attended by their busy entertainers, held sylvan court, like the banished monarch in the Forest of Ardennes...The only wonder is, how the river was crossed after the hogshead was empty.'

It couldn't happen today – for one thing, the consumption of alcohol on the islands has been banned. However, it is at least still sylvan. Alders, whitebeams, Douglas firs, beeches and huge Wellingtonia are some of the trees that form today's living canopy. On the ground beneath, a playful snake has been created out of a fallen treetrunk, while modern sculptures formed of curved and bendy wood find service as benches.

The islands also boast their own ruins, albeit of no great antiquity: a few low banks of curved stone seating are all that remain of the open-air theatre created in 1950–51. Entertainments and dances were held here under a pavilion, with fairy lights strung up in the trees, while a special floor was laid to allow rollerskating. This was also the scene of the most exciting event in the life of the Ness Islands: the six days in September 1951 when the Pageant of Inverness was held here.

In 1822, long before such extravagancies were imagined, local man R Jamieson proclaimed: 'The greatest ornament we have in all the adjacent Country is about a quarter of a mile from the town, but not to be seen from it, by reason of the Castle Hill. It is an island about 600 yards long,

surrounded by two branches of the River Ness, well planted with trees of different kinds, and may not unaptly be compared with the island in St James Park.' He would no doubt approve of the mannerly character the islands retain to this day – a little bit of the country, only paved, and with nothing to frighten the horses.

How to get there

From Inverness railway station (scotrail. co.uk; 0845 755 0033) the islands are a pleasant 15-minute walk away. Access is from either bank of the Ness via footbridges.

Admission price/landing fee

Free.

View

From some points you can gaze downriver towards the centre of Inverness. Such is the lavishness with which trees have been planted along this stretch of the river that, viewing it from the islands, you might imagine the city to be composed entirely of woods, churches and parks.

Facilities

None.

Accommodation

Along the eastern bank of the River Ness, there's a clutch of B&Bs (invernessbedandbreakfast.co.uk) and hotels, the closest to the islands being neighbours **Talisker Guest House** (absoluteescapes.com/Talisker.html; 07901

978750) and **Macrae House** (scotland-inverness.co.uk/macrae; 01463 243658). The **campsite** in nearby **Bught Park** (Easter to October; invernesscaravanpark.com; 01463 236920) is no one's idea of a rural idyll but is at least convenient.

Nearest decent pub/café/tea room

Bibliophiles should head for **Leakey's Secondhand Bookshop** (1 mile; Mon–Sat; 01463 239947), a former church now the biggest shop of its kind in the known universe and home to a very pleasing café.

Nearest shop

Inverness is crammed with retail concerns – they're mainly chains, sadly, but there's the odd independent store thrown in.

Rules

No drinking of alcohol, the devil's accomplice.

Things to do

St Andrew's Cathedral, on the west bank of the Ness, can be seen from the islands and is worth a mooch around, if only for the joy of being reminded of your own mortality.

For a provincial establishment, the **Eden Court Theatre** (eden-court.co.uk; 01463 234234), with its top-flight drama, comedy nights and art house cinema, punches some way above its cultural weight.

The 79-mile **Great Glen Way** (greatglenway. com), a trail for cyclists and walkers weaving from Fort William to Inverness, runs the length of the Ness Islands.

Top: Arty bench at the tip of the islands; Bottom: Information board aiding tree identification

59. Brough of Birsay

Off Point of Buckquoy
Orkney Mainland
tinyurl.com/7556hur (Historic Scotland)
OS Landranger map 6
Grid reference: HY 237 285
Size: 52 acres
Population: 0

Pay a visit to the remnants of almost any ancient settlement in Britain and it's difficult not to have the thought, 'Bloomin' heck, I bet these people got cold.' It is something of a surprise, therefore, to come up to the Brough of Birsay – which at 59°N is as far north as Oslo – and a settlement that looks, if anything, rather snug.

Tucked in at the foot of the island's hill and protected from all but the most resourceful of winds, it's tempting to imagine that existence here might have been quite pleasurable, give or take the ill-advised medical practices prevalent and the miserly life expectancy.

It was a place of relative safety for the island's Pictish inhabitants and their Viking successors. Both brough (pronounced 'broch' to rhyme with 'loch' but with an even softer 'ch' sound, if that were possible) and birsay are derived from the Old Norse word for 'fort'. The former refers to the island's advantages as a defendable domain while the latter (from byrgisey) denotes an island reachable only across a narrow slip of land.

It's an irony then that today the Brough of Birsay is an extraordinarily easy island to get onto, at least when the tide is out. Between the mainland and the island lies a short curving concrete causeway that slides over an amalgam of low, dark-grey rocks flecked with ochre seaweed to connect the two small sandy beaches on either side. In two minutes you're across.

Little is known of the first settlers here though it's believed they may have arrived in the 5th century. However, the people who lived here between the late 7th and 13th centuries certainly made sure that they would be remembered. The Picts left a well and a symbol stone (replaced today by a modern cast of same). On the stone are three armed men with four common Pictish tropes above them: a mirror case, a crescent and V-rod, an eagle, and a swimming elephant. Presumably, some of Scotland's ancient indigenous people must have seen these beasts on their travels, but where? And why were the elephants swimming?

Norwegian Vikings arrived in the early part of the 9th century and it is their remarkable array of ruins, including saunas, a smithy and, perhaps most impressively, a complex drainage system, that can be wandered around today. However, the highlight of the settlement is undoubtedly the church.

The Orkneyinga Saga claims that the Norse Earl Thorfinn returned from a pilgrimage to Rome around 1050 and built 'a fine minster at Birsay' which led to widespread speculation that this was it. But most historians now believe that he built

it on the mainland and that this church, though clearly designed in the Romanesque style, was merely part of the short-lived monastery founded here around 1100. Its low sandstone walls and the minimalist block that serves as an altar are things of great beauty nonetheless.

Pass on from the village over the springy thrift-speckled grass and you are greeted with a choice of four paths, three of which climb immediately uphill. The path second from the right leads to the lighthouse (a rather squat and unprepossessing affair built by David Stevenson in 1925 and just 37ft high, albeit another 135ft above sea level), while the path on the extreme right splinters into smaller pathlets (let's imagine this word exists and move on). However, since this island is a simple bare hill, there's no chance of getting lost even in the densest fog, whichever path you take. The worst that could happen is that you fall over the clifftop and have your body dashed on the rocks below.

The cliffs on the far side of the island are truly spectacular, best seen from the outcrop to the right of the lighthouse. Taking the full brunt of whatever the Atlantic chooses to throw at them, their strata appear like a thousand slates piled on top of each other, all arrowing down into the sea. Fulmars and guillemots breed here among the herring gulls and greater black-backed gulls. Even the occasional crow makes an appearance – possibly to investigate rumours of swimming elephants – before returning, downcast, to the mainland.

How to get there

Take the train to Aberdeen (scotrail.co.uk; 0845 755 0033), the ferry to Kirkwall (northlinkferries.co.uk; 0845 600 0449), then the (twice daily) 6 bus (stagecoachbus.com; 01463 233371) to the small village of Birsay, from where it's a 0.5-mile walk to the causeway. Access to the island is possible for two hours either side of low tide. The Birsay Bay Tea Room (see below) has tide timetables.

Admission price/landing fee

Free, but £4 adult, £2.40 child if you want to visit the Norse settlement (open mid-June to September, 9.30am to 5.30pm).

View

It's claimed that on very clear days you can see as far as the island of Westray. On less clear days, you'll have to make do with the Orkney mainland.

Facilities

There's a visitor centre attached to the Norse settlement (but there's no loo even there – the nearest one is in Birsay).

Accommodation

Birsay Outdoor Centre (tinyurl.com/8x3eh2l; 01856 873535 ext. 2417) is a smart modern hostel with a sheltered campsite and is the place to be for sunset views of the Brough.

Nearest decent pub/café/tea room

The **Birsay Bay Tea Room** (0.75 miles; birsaybaytearoom.co.uk; 01856 721399) is open from April to October and offers a wide range of drinks and light meals, binoculars with which to view the Brough, and tide timetables, albeit in a canteen-style setting.

Nearest shop

Palace Stores in Birsay (0.5 mile) stocks basic groceries as well as camping gas canisters and other useful things.

Rules

None.

Things to do

If you leave the island shortly before it has been cut off by the tide, it's strangely satisfying to look back and watch the causeway slowly disappear and the channel fill with bobbing seabirds. In summer there's often a (classier than normal) snack van in the car park behind you.

The remains of the late 16th-century **Earl's Palace** in Birsay (0.5 miles; tinyurl.com/72zclv6) are free to look around and open all the time. The palace was built by Robert Stewart, 1st Earl of Orkney, illegitimate son of Euphemia Elphinstone and James V of Scotland.

Barony Mills, Birsay (1 mile), a beautifully kept working watermill, grinds the locally grown bere grain. Open daily from May to September, 10am to 5pm (closed for lunch 1–2pm), free.

The sun setting behind the lighthouse on the Brough

60. Holm of Papay

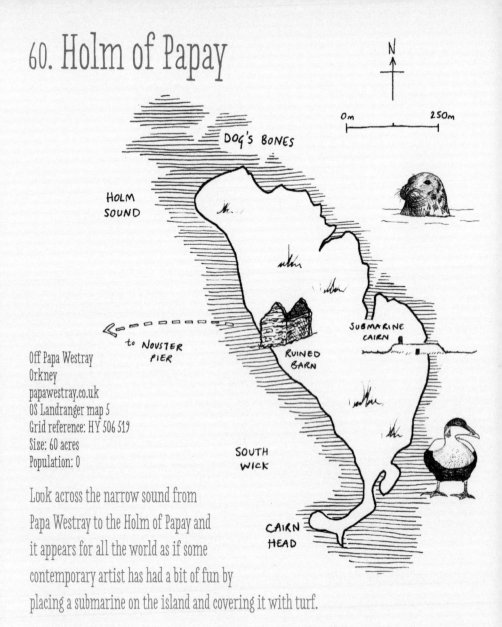

DOG'S BONES

HOLM SOUND

to NOUSTER PIER

SUBMARINE CAIRN

RUINED BARN

SOUTH WICK

CAIRN HEAD

N

0m   250m

Off Papa Westray
Orkney
papawestray.co.uk
OS Landranger map 5
Grid reference: HY 506 519
Size: 60 acres
Population: 0

Look across the narrow sound from Papa Westray to the Holm of Papay and it appears for all the world as if some contemporary artist has had a bit of fun by placing a submarine on the island and covering it with turf.

It makes the discovery that the 'submarine' is in fact one of the oldest existing structures in Northern Europe all the more of a shock.

Around 5,000 years ago, the community living at the Knap of Howar on Papa Westray crossed over to the Holm of Papay to build a burial cairn in which to lay their loved ones to rest. A visit to the fruit of their labours is not something you are likely to forget in a hurry.

While Neolithic Skara Brae and Maeshowe on mainland Orkney hoover up the publicity, this astonishingly well-preserved burial chamber is all but unknown. This means, of course, that there's every chance you'll have the place to yourself. Indeed, if you don't have the whole island to yourself (not counting the birds and the flock of sheep that grazes there) you're entitled to feel rather unlucky, for there's no ferry service to the Holm of Papay. The easiest way to get there is to ask local fisherman Douglas Hourston if he can take you over from Papa Westray (just ask anyone on the island and they'll tell you where to find him).

With no jetty on the Holm of Papay (also known as the Holm of Papa Westray but habitually referred to simply as Papay – the name denoting that an early missionary once settled here – and pronounced 'pappy') it's a case of clambering out of the boat onto rocks and slithering across seaweed to the shore close to the island's one overground building of any note – a ruined dry-stone barn, its gables pluckily defying the elements.

This simple tranquil isle is not quite as it seems, however. Anyone walking over the myriad tussocks to the cairn between late spring and early summer will find themselves crossing a minefield. Every few yards, hidden from sight until almost stepped upon, are the nests of eider ducks, each one topped by a mother eyeing interlopers with profound misgivings. Until you begin to recognise the nooks and crannies into which such nests tuck themselves, the first indication of their

existence will be a detonation of squawking and brown feathers as an eider breaks cover. In other parts of the island, the nests belong to greylag geese and are made of feathers, but the explosion is more or less the same. The sound of a bird crying with what can only be described as resigned terror is distressing and not something that sits easily with one's conscience. The best thing to do to assuage it is to cover each disturbed nest with grass (thus hiding the eggs from the predatory great black-backed gulls) and withdraw swiftly from the scene.

Keeping to the shore will disturb as few nesting birds as possible and you'll still not want for company. For a start, there are shags and various gulls on the low eastern cliffs. Furthermore, the seals in these parts don't get to see a lot of humans and so when one turns up on the island it's a red-letter day. Swimming around the shore, they bottle way out of the water to have a good gawp at what the large bipeds are doing.

Inevitably, the large bipeds are making their way to the burial cairn. In summer they do so to the accompaniment of the kee-aaaaa of Arctic terns, their tail fins as graceful as any swallow's, and that odd rubber-band sound made by the whiffling of greylag geese as they come in to land.

Satisfyingly, the way into the cairn reinforces the idea that this really is a submarine out of water. Halfway along the top a metal hatch opens to reveal a ladder beneath, which drops down to a darkened passageway (there's no lighting but

torches are provided inside). This narrow chamber is separated into sections by stone partitions under which it is possible to crawl. Off to the sides are 10 single and two double-sided burial chambers. When the tomb was first excavated in 1849 no human remains were found, though there were some animal bones. However, above the far southeastern cell there are some curious engravings, now quite hard to see, that appear to depict eyebrows.

A tiny 5,000-year-old stone-carved figurine discovered during excavations on nearby Westray has similar markings on it that are clearly intended to be eyebrows with dots beneath for eyes. It would be nice to think that some Stone Age artist popped down into the Papay cairn with a rudimentary hammer and chisel, and said to his model, 'Right, hold this flaming torch up to your face: today I'm going to do eyebrows. Wish me luck,' and started tapping away. Or perhaps the artist was a woman and the model was a man – the eyebrows are, after all, rather bushy.

For the full Holm of Papay experience, ask to be put on the island when Douglas leaves for the fishing in the morning (which means a very early start indeed) and picked up eight to ten hours later when he returns. It might seem a tall order for an island that consists of one burial cairn you can enter, two burial cairns you can't, and a few ruined barns to provide a full day's entertainment, but if you take off your watch and allow yourself to slow down to the rhythm of the sea lapping the shore,

you'll find Douglas's boat coming back for you long before you're ready to leave.

How to get there
Deep breath. First you need to get to Kirkwall, on mainland Orkney. Either take a train to Aberdeen (scotrail.co.uk; 0845 755 0033), then the ferry (northlinkferries.co.uk; 0845 600 0449); or the train to Thurso (ScotRail), then a ferry to Scrabster (NorthLink), and the X1 bus (stagecoachbus.com; 01856 878014). From Kirkwall, you can either take the ferry direct to Papa Westray (orkneyferries.co.uk; 01856 872044), which typically sails twice a week, or board the more frequent (up to thrice daily) ferry to Rapness on Westray (Orkney Ferries). A minibus timed to coincide with the ferry will transport you to Pierowall, from where a boat called *Golden Mariana* (Orkney Ferries again) will bear you over to Papa Westray. Call in at the island's shop at Beltane and ask after Douglas Hourston, a fisherman with whom you should be able to arrange a crossing from Nouster pier to the Holm of Papay (and back again). The world's shortest scheduled flight (it takes about 90 seconds) connects Westray with Papa Westray but the more leisurely ferry is far more in keeping with small-isle Orcadian life.

Admission price/landing fee
Douglas doesn't charge anything for taking people over to the Holm of Papay but any donations for his services will be passed on to the RNLI, so be nice and dig deep.

Clockwise from top: The distinctive cairn; the main subterranean passage; the cairn's submarine hatch entrance

View

Papa Westray, Westray, Eday, Sanday and, on a good day, far North Ronaldsay.

Facilities

None. However, there is a public toilet next to the school on Papa Westray, a few hundred yards from Nouster pier.

Accommodation

Papa Westray has no hotels or B&Bs but does have the excellent **Beltane House Hostel** (01857 644321) with several (very cheap) twin rooms if you're not a dormitory kind of person. The island also has **two holiday cottages** for rent (papawestray.co.uk/self-catering.html). Ask locals for the best places for **wild camping** on Papa Westray (away from the nature reserve, obviously).

Nearest decent pub/café/tea room

Papa Westray's hostel (see 'Accommodation') is the hub of social life (with Saturday the big night of the week), so pop in and ask if they've got an evening event taking place.

Nearest shop

There are just two shops on Papa Westray: a surprisingly well stocked community-run affair at **Beltane House** (opening hours are complex: Monday to Thursday and Saturday 10am–noon, Monday and Wednesday to Friday 3pm–5pm, Saturday 6–7pm, closed Sunday) and a **tiny post office** that also sells Papa-made crafts (open most of the time – just ring the bell).

Rules

Be very careful not to disturb the numerous nesting birds, the majority of which are cleverly hidden in the machair.

Things to do

For a small island, Papa Westray offers a lot of interesting diversions. At 5,000 years old, the **Knap of Howar**'s little dwellings are as venerable as they are impressive (free; always open; historic-scotland.gov.uk).

An **RSPB hide** kitted out with binoculars looks out over the North Hill nature reserve, home to Arctic skuas.

The small **Holland Farm Bothy Museum** (free; open all year) recreates the living quarters of a farm worker in the not-so-distant past.

Islands by type

River islands

10 Sashes Island
11 Monkey Island
12 Tagg's Island
13 Eel Pie Island
14 Northey Island
15 Havergate Island
31 Ynys Gifftan
37 Threave Island
54 Moncreiffe Island
57 Inchbuie
58 Ness Islands

Loch, lake and harbour islands

7 Round Island
8 Burrow Island
16 Islands of Thorpeness Meare
18 Swan Island
21 Peel Island
22 Islands of Windermere
23 Derwent Isle
30 Llangors Crannog
32 Cei Balast
41 Eilean Mòr
47 Eilean Bàn
53 Lochleven Castle Island
55 Inchcailloch
56 Inchmahome

Tidal islands

1 Gugh
4 St Michael's Mount
6 Burgh Island

8 Burrow Island
14 Northey Island
17 Hilbre Island
19 Piel Island
20 Chapel Island
24 St Mary's Island
27 Gateholm
28 Worm's Head
31 Ynys Gifftan
32 Cei Balast
33 Ynys Llanddwyn
34 Cribinau
36 Hestan Island
39 Davaar Island
51 Cramond Island
59 Brough of Birsay

Islands on which you can spend the night

5 Looe Island
6 Burgh Island
7 Round Island
10 Sashes Island
11 Monkey Island
12 Tagg's Island
14 Northey Island
15 Havergate Island
19 Piel Island
26 Skokholm
29 Flat Holm
39 Davaar Island
42 Easdale
50 Isle of May
55 Inchcailloch

Clockwise from top left: Latter-day Shelley gravely reads the stones on Inchcailloch (p288);
a ferry enters the harbour at Inchcolm (p274); the man-made lagoons of Easdale (p226)

Select bibliography

A History of Part of the Parish of Llandysilio, David Senogles, Parish of Llandysilio (2001)

Concerning Thorpeness, ed. Graeme Kemp, self-published (1925)

Defending Scilly, Allan Brodie & Mark Bowden, English Heritage (2011)

Easdale, Belnahua, Luing & Seil: The Islands that Roofed the World, Mary Withall, Luath Press Limited (2001)

Eyots and Aits: Islands of the River Thames, Miranda Vickers, The History Press (2012)

Far and Sure from Inch to Island, R Bert Laing, self-published (2008)

Farne Islands, M Scott Weightman, Claughton Photography Publications (2001)

Flatholm: An Account of its History and Ecology, D H Worrall & P R Surtees, South Glamorgan County Council (1989)

General Guide to the Isle of May, James Allan, Tervor Publishing (2007)

In Scotland Again, H V Morton, Methuen (1933)

Isles of the Island, S P B Mais, Putnam (1934)

Life on God's Island: Stories from the Inner Hebridean Island of Gigha, Freddy Gillies, Famedram (1999)

Llangorse Crannog (essay),
Mike Davies (1995)

No Boat Required, Peter Caton,
Matador (2011)

*One Man's Dream: The Story Behind G Stuart
Ogilvie and the Creation of Thorpeness*, Ailsa
Ogilvie de Mille, Nostalgia Publications
(1996)

Portraits of Islands, ed. Eileen Molony,
Dennis Dobson (1951)

Scilly's Archaeological Heritage, Historical
Environment Service, Cornwall County
Council, Twelveheads Press (2003)

Secret Nature of the Isles of Scilly, Andrew
Cooper, Green Books (2006)

Some Lovely Islands, Leslie Thomas,
Pan (1971)

Swallows and Amazons, Arthur Ransome,
Red Fox (2001)

The Curse of Samson, Glynis Cooper,
Historic Occasions (2003)

The English Lakes: A History, Ian Thompson,
Bloomsbury (2010)

*The Fortunate Islands: The Story of the Isles
of Scilly*, R L Bowley, Bowley Publications
(2004)

The Great White Palace, Tony Porter,
Deerhill Books (2005)

The Island of Samson, The Isles of Scilly
Wildlife Trust (no date)

The Islands of Loch Lomond, Clair Calder &
Lynn Lindsay, Famedram (2002)

*The Isles of Scilly Museum: Inside the
Archipelago*, Amanda Martin et al, Isles of
Scilly Museum Publication (2011)

The Story of Hestan Island, Mark White,
Auchencairn History Society (2004)

The Story of Samson, Zélide Teague Cowan,
Englang Publishing (1991)

I'd also like to mention *The Scottish Islands*
by Hamish Haswell-Smith (Canongate,
2008), an astonishing labour of love which,
although it's mainly about islands too large
for this book, was inspirational nonetheless.

*Left: An abandoned house on Samson (p24) is reclaimed
by the island's flora; Top: The Isle of May (p263), one of
the many alluring tiny islands on the Firth of Forth*

Author's acknowledgements

Every book is, to a greater or lesser extent, a collective effort. In this case, I can safely say that I couldn't have produced *Tiny Islands* without the help of the following people. May the sun shine on all your backs.

Alex MacKay (Eilean Donan)
Alison Rayner (Staffa)
Amanda Martin at the Isles of Scilly Museum (Gugh, St Helen's, Samson)
Bo and Penny (Northey Island)
Bob Robinson and Anne Driver (Ynys Gifftan)
Bryn Fôn Jones (Cribinau)
Carey and Dave Watson (Northey Island)
Carla Rinaldi at ScotRail
Carol and Wayne (Inch Kenneth)
Carolyn Watson and Lindsay Marsden at Northern Rail
Cheryl Kelday at NorthLink Ferries
Clive Wills
Colin and David (Round Island)
Daniel Start
David Fairhurst (Havergate Island)
David Malpas (Worm's Head)
David Sawkins at Orkney Ferries
Douglas Hourston (Holm of Papay)
Ellen Rossiter and Peter Meades at Greater Anglia
Emma Knight at South West Trains
Erin Clark (Eel Pie Island, Tagg's Island)
Ernie Curtis (Looe Island)
Esther Addley

Fiona Gimson and Sophia Davison (Thorpeness Meare)
Gary McGuire (Burgh Island)
Geoff and Hazel Wills
Hayley and Jackie (Inchcolm)
Heather McCardle at CalMac Ferries
Hilary Lacroix (Ness Islands)
Hugh (Burgh Island)
Isles of Scilly Steamship Company
Jack Thurston
James Davis at First Great Western
Jennifer Foley (Holm of Papay)
John and Pauline Clark (Cei Balast, Ynys Gifftan)
John Gelson and Paul Williams at East Coast
Keith (Cara)
Keith, Bridget and John Fortowsky (Inchcailloch)
Kim and Nick Hoare (Thorpeness Meare, Havergate)
Lara Frances and Lewis 'Ricky Martin' Kinneir
Lewis Brencher at Arriva Trains Wales
Linda Burnell (Flat Holm)
Lis Mahoney (Cei Balast)
(Rev) Madalaine Brady (Cribinau)
Margaret Johnson and Katharine Street (Cara)
Martin Gregory (Looe Island)
May Mcgillivray (Easdale)
Michael James Houston and Carl Palmer, the jolly farmer (Peel, Derwent Isle, Windermere)

Mike Brown at King James VI Golf Club (Moncreiffe Island)

Monika Koch (Havergate)

Paul Spence and Fran Caine at Historic Scotland

Sam and Paul Mallon (Gugh, St Helen's, Samson)

Sarah West (Holm of Papay)

Seamus McSporran (Cara)

Sineag at Castlebay TIC (Kisimul)

Sophie Dawson

Sophie Hughes (Samson, Gugh, St Helen's) – with particular thanks for her considerable help and ready smile

Steve Dimmick (Cei Balast) – special thanks for his Welsh/English translation skills

The Boys (including the Shelf Boys)

Tim the Vaughan

Tommy Rendall (Holm of Papay)

Tracy Clifton at Virgin Trains

Twm Elias (Cei Balast, Ynys Gifftan)

With special thanks to Claire Robertson for sharing her in-depth knowledge of Castle Douglas, and to Marigold Atkey of the Dylan Thomas estate for permission to use an extract from the short story *Who Do You Wish Was With Us?* from *The Collected Stories* (Orion, 1992), and to Marion Wasdell for permission to use a quotation from the work of H V Morton.

I'd especially like to thank my agent Ben Mason, the best dressed man in the West End. My immense gratitude goes to Harriet Yeomans for drawing fantastic maps and for not once killing me during our marathon meetings. I'd also like to express my appreciation for Donna Wood and her painstaking copy-editing skills and to Judith Forshaw for her assiduous proofreading. And last, but by no means least, I'd like to thank my editor Helen Brocklehurst for her constant enthusiasm, fantastic haircuts, and general all round cheeriness. It's been fun.

Barbie – all washed up on Inch Kenneth (p231)

Picture credits

The Automobile Association wishes to thank the following photographers and organisations for their assistance in the preparation of this book.

Abbreviations for the picture credits are as follows – (t) top; (b) bottom; (l) left; (r) right; (c) centre

15 Robert Harding Picture Library Ltd/Alamy; 19 David Chapman/Alamy; 20t David Chapman/Alamy; 26 Hemis/Alamy; 39 SuperStock/Alamy; 40tr Erin Moncur/Alamy; 44 David Chapman/Alamy; 47 David Chapman/Alamy; 50tl BANANA PANCAKE/Alamy; 50b Mark Mercer/Alamy; 56t Natural Visions/Alamy; 56b Getty Images; 64 Steve Taylor ARPS/Alamy; 67 REBimages/Alamy; 78 Londonstills.com/Alamy; 93 Remo Savisaar/Alamy; 112 Robert Harding World Imagery/Alamy; 115 Nigel Ollis/Alamy; 128 VisitBritain/Martin Brent; 131 Henn Photography/cultura/Corbis; 134 Peter Sumner/Alamy; 136 David Hatfield/Alamy; 153tl PCJones/Alamy; 153tr Andy Myatt/Alamy; 153b PCJones/Alamy; 156 James Osmond/Alamy; 164t Neil Setchfield/Alamy; 164b Ken Edwards/Alamy; 171t Garnet Davies Lakeside Caravan Park; 171bl Garnet Davies Lakeside Caravan Park; 171br Garnet Davies Lakeside Caravan Park; 210 Andrew Scott-Martin/Alamy; 214tr Ian Cowe/Alamy; 223t Plinthpics/Alamy; 223b Pete Favelle/Alamy; 250b South West Images Scotland/Alamy; 255 colinspics/Alamy; 257 Derek Croucher/Alamy; 287 Guthrie Aerial Photography; 290 David Robertson/Alamy; 298 John Peter Photography/Alamy.

All other photographs were taken by Dixe Wills.

Every effort has been made to trace the copyright holders, and we apologise in advance for any unintentional omissions or errors. We would be pleased to apply any corrections in a following edition of this publication.